Welcome to GoodCo

Dedicated to Ken Spencer
Who showed me that good could be done through the process of business

I promise to use what brains I have to meet problems with intelligence and courage. I promise that I will be candid about what I know. I promise to all of you who have the right to know, the whole truth so far as I can speak it. If I have been wrong, you may tell me so, for I really have no pride in judgment. I know all judgment is relative. It may be right today and wrong tomorrow. The only thing that makes it truly right is the desire to have it constantly moving in the right direction.

Frances Perkins, early speech as New York State
Industrial Commissioner, 1929, later
US Secretary for Labor, 1933–45

Welcome to GoodCo

Using the Tools of Business to Create Public Good

TOM LEVITT

GOWER

Published by
Gower Publishing Limited
Wey Court East
Union Road
Farnham
Surrey, GU9 7PT
England

Gower Publishing Company
110 Cherry Street
Suite 3-1
Burlington, VT 05401-3818
USA

www.gowerpublishing.com

British Library Cataloguing in Publication Data
A catalogue record for this book is available from the British Library.

Library of Congress Cataloging-in-Publication Data
Levitt, Tom.
  Welcome to GoodCo : using the tools of business to create public good / by Tom Levitt.
     pages cm
  Includes bibliographical references and index.
  ISBN 978-1-4724-0931-7 (hardback) – ISBN 978-1-4724-0933-1 (ebook)
 1. Social responsibility of business – Great Britain. 2. Public–private sector cooperation – Great Britain 3. Common good. I. Title.

  HD60.5.G7L48 2014
  658.4'08–dc23

                                                                                    2014000093

ISBN: 9781472409317 (hbk)
ISBN: 9781472409324 (ebk – ePDF)
ISBN: 9781472409331 (ebk – ePUB)

Printed in the United Kingdom by Henry Ling Limited, at the Dorset Press, Dorchester, DT1 1HD

Contents

List of Figures

List of Tables

About the Author

Tom Levitt is a writer and consultant on mission-driven cross-sector partnerships, trading as Sector 4 Focus.[1] As the Member of Parliament for High Peak, 1997–2010, he specialised in charities and volunteering in the UK and developing countries, which led to an interest in corporate social responsibility.

Today he is a non-executive director of Digital Outreach Ltd and the business consultancy Good Measures, an adviser to the social enterprise Good People and a trustee of four charities, including Concern Worldwide UK (Chair) and The Work Foundation.

In Parliament he was political aide to the Secretary of State for International Development (2003–7), Deputy Regional Minister for the East Midlands (2008–10) and a member of the Department for Work and Pensions Select Committee (2008–10). He chaired the Community Development Foundation (2004–10) and was a member of the Commission on the Future of Volunteering (2008–9).

He writes occasionally for *The Guardian* and Progress websites and elsewhere. He has an honorary doctorate from the University of Derby.

---

1   http://www.sector4focus.co.uk.

Acknowledgements

Many people and many conversations contributed to this book; some will not have known they were doing so at the time. Some who went out of their way to be helpful include: Lord Victor Adebowale (Turning Point), Aishlyn Angill-Williams, Richard Alderson and team (Journeys for Change), Kay Allen, Laura Barnard (Working Chance), Andrew Barnett (Calouste Gulbenkian Foundation), David Connor (Coethica), Dan Corry (New Philanthropy Capital), Lisa Cunningham (Business in the Community), Gordon d'Silva (Good Business Alliance), Chad Dickerson (Etsy), Michael Durkin (United Way of Massachusetts Bay), Melanie Dutfield (Serco), Anna Easton (BT Group), Richard Ellis (Alliance Boots), James Featherby (Church of England Ethical Investment Advisory Council), the late Chris Frost (Merton Voluntary Services Council), Bana Gora (Joseph Rowntree Foundation), Mark Goyder (Tomorrow's Company), Paul Hackett (Smith Institute), Fiona Halton (Pilotlight), Karen Hamilton (Redwood Advisors, Boston), Ariel Hauptman (Greyston Bakery, NY), Charlotte Hill (UK Youth), Catherine Howarth (ShareAction), Sophie Hulm (City of London Corporation), Ray Kinsella (Merton Connected), Mark Leyland (Marriott Hotel, York), Thomas Lingard (Unilever), Stephen Lloyd (Bates, Wells and Braithwaite), Tony Manwaring and team (Tomorrow's Company), Colin Melvin (Hermes), Rob Michalak (Ben & Jerry's USA), Wendy Mitchell and Emma McKay (Charity Retail Association), Jenny North (Impetus Trust), Lucy Parker, David Pitt-Watson (London Business School), Jill Poet (Organisation for Responsible Businesses), Fran Pollard (Catch 22), Andrew Robinson (CCLA), Terry Ryall (v-Inspired), Eithne Rynne (London Voluntary Services Council), Ed Shepherd (Ben & Jerry's, Europe), Lord David Sainsbury, Alison Seabrooke (Community Development Foundation), Esther Shoustra-Hofstede (Beursvloer, Holland), Sonia Sodha, Jeremy Stafford (formerly of Serco), Diana Sterck (Merton Chamber of Commerce), Henry Tam, John Tizard, Brian Tjugum and Deepa Mirchandani (Weber Shandwick), Richard Tyrie (Good People), Julia Unwin (Joseph Rowntree Foundation), John Varney, Cat Walker (DSC), Pam Webb (Zurich Community Trust), Rob Wilson (Ashoka) and Charles Wookey (A Blueprint for a Better Business).

My thanks for permission to use graphics to Colin Melvin (Hermes/ United Nations Principles for Responsible Investment), Matthew Gitsham

(Ashridge Business School) and Jake Hayman (The Social Investment Consultancy). Specific permission to use quotes at the start of each chapter was obtained where necessary: from Ben Cohen, Random House publishers (in respect of Charles Handy) and Lush Cosmetics.

Chapter 1

Business: A Community Resource

For my part I think that capitalism, wisely managed, can probably be made more efficient for attaining economic ends than any alternative system yet in sight, but that in itself is in many ways extremely objectionable.

John Maynard Keynes[1]

There is one opinion that unites the whole world, all strands of opinion and all shades of attitude in every nation. It is this:

Things aren't working as well as they should be.

This is an endless source of frustration, especially to those who provide services for the community, or who receive such services, or whose money is spent on them, or who would like to enjoy them but somehow cannot – in other words, all of us. There are debates, of course, as to how to make things better: get in new providers, strip out the dead wood, provide more money – get someone else to pay for it. Some even advocate wholesale change, but isn't it clear, they are asked, that no alternative to the capitalist economic model is feasible? After all, look what happened to Russia – and what about human rights in China? Terrible. But then look at the USA: Ben Bernanke of the US Federal Reserve told us in 2011 that at the time of the 'crash', in September 2008, 12 of America's top 13 banks (all except J.P. Morgan) were within hours of failure – of disappearing.

Advocates of change agree that the forces of conservatism and reaction in Western economies are so powerful, so ingrained, that real change is very, very difficult indeed to achieve. So how do we make the best of what we have?

In recent years a consensus about the nature of the problem has at least started to develop: that the economic status quo is no longer either sustainable or defensible. Climate change has focused the minds of the powerful on our use of energy and shows the environment to be more fragile than industrial man had

---

1   J.M. Keynes, *The End of Laissez-faire: The Economic Consequences of the Peace*, Macmillan, 1926.

ever previously conceived it to be. Competition for our planet's resources – not just energy, but the oil that makes our plastics, the rare earths that drive our IT industry and even the wholesome water that many of our fellow humans can't drink in sufficient quality or quantity – will lead to friction, strife, waste and even wars in decades to come. And there's a growing realisation, fermented by ubiquitous 24-hour news media dedicated to stories and not solutions, that our trade relations, industrial practices and economic models are making the situation worse rather than better. Is that the fault of the practices or the practitioners? Does the prevailing economic system – capitalism – have to be so profligate? Must it inevitably sow, as Marx predicted, the seeds of its own destruction?

Society, along with many in the business community, has moved on from the ideas of a generation ago which held that the business of business is only business, that shareholder value is king and to hell with the hindmost. But if the ideas have moved on, have the practices? A national economy gives democratic government the wherewithal, through taxation, to provide for those who need to be defended from poverty, squalor and indignity, and to do so where, by consensus, the market is not the best provider. Does the way we run the economy achieve those aims as well as it could?

No – another universal truth agreed.

This book isn't really about economics. It's certainly not about party politics. And it won't go into detail on service delivery. It looks at relationships, roles and responsibilities of bodies corporate within society; between the state as a paternal figure, business as the engine of the economy and the community of individual citizens. It isn't written by an economist, but by a former science teacher, a former politician, a friend of civil society.

The purpose of this book is to explore, celebrate and stimulate how the tools of business – the tools of capitalism – can be and are being used to create public good:

- investment generating socially responsible outcomes as well as profit;

- the market being used to boost fair and ethical trade;

- social enterprise aping the basics of capitalism to deliver a social purpose;

- regulation utilised to curb excesses and maintain discipline;

- corporate citizenship benefiting capitalism's footsoldiers, small and medium-sized enterprises (SMEs);

- companies adopting the strong (but too often silent) business case for community engagement;

- reporting practices emulating the disinfectant power of sunlight.

By the late 2000s it became so clear that some fundamentals of the system that generates collective and individual wealth weren't working in a sustainable way that no one could gainsay it. In the words of Al Gore, the high priest of sustainability:

> *The ideological condominium formed in the alliance between capitalism and representative democracy that has been so fruitful in expanding the potential for freedom, peace and prosperity has been split asunder by the encroachment of concentrated wealth from the market sphere into the democracy sphere.*
>
> *(Gore, 2013)*

For two hundred years capitalism worked alongside democracy, through shared adolescence and maturity. Then this eloquent history was put at risk by some reckless capitalists who grew too big for their boots. When most of the world's top 100 economies are companies and not countries; when some companies have become not only too big to tax properly but too big to fail; when bonuses awarded for fortunate ineptitude run into millions of dollars for the lucky few while the base of the pyramid tries to live on a dollar a day; while all this is happening, Gore's 'split asunder' is plain to see:

> *Capitalism – if reformed and made sustainable – can serve the world better than any other economic system in making the difficult but necessary changes to the relationship between the human enterprise and the ecological and biological systems of the earth.*
>
> *(Gore, 2013)*

Reform is urgent: peering into the abyss should not be the only way to call the vanguards of capitalism to order. Capitalism must be brought to heel, to mend that rift Gore has identified and have it again complement democracy so that the economy serves the needs of the people of the world, and not the other way round.

It was peering into the abyss alone that narrowly avoided that catastrophic global meltdown of the financial systems, so we are led to believe, after mortgages had been sold on properties with no value to people who couldn't afford them, and then bundled up and sold as assets which came to be described as toxic.[2] Bankers had put at disproportionate risk everything except their own extravagant bonuses, while the rape of the planet's resources continued almost unabated. Scandal then followed scandal: some multinational corporates developed an optional (if generally legal) approach to paying their share of tax – even though paying tax is as much a hallmark of the corporate citizen as of the individual one; banks were rigging the LIBOR interest rates to suit themselves, and even in 2014 those million-pound bankers' bonuses were continuing to reward performance which could only be described as abject failure. The financial system had become self-propagating and divorced from the reality of the streets around our financial centres. The very existence of the currency of Europe was in crisis, calling Continental stability into question; divided American politicians were wrestling on the edge of a fiscal cliff like Holmes and Moriarty at the Reichenbach Falls. In Britain, in the name of austerity and deficit reduction, huge swathes of public spending on the services upon which so many rely, especially those meeting local need, were being axed by a government committed to the values of a 'Big Society'.

Businesses start small, and growth is a traditional measure of their success – arguably not the only one, as Charles Handy argues in his copious works, including *The Hungry Spirit* (Handy, 1998). Handy, an Irish business guru turned philosopher, served ten years as a marketing executive with Shell, a period as an economist in the City of London and 28 years at London Business School. His many astute observations include: 'It is because the corporate citizen can be an agent for change *where other agents can't* that the concept of corporate citizenship is so important' (my emphasis).

There is almost universal agreement that society should limit – regulate – the market, but that restrictions should be kept at a minimum (say business) or an optimum (say politicians) rather than a maximum (as in the former Soviet Union). Limitations on the market define boundaries to corporate behaviour and, on the basis that one volunteer is worth ten conscripts, other market constraints should be voluntary – when that works. There are too many examples of voluntary self-regulation failing when corporates hunt in packs to

---

2   As of October 2013 the bank J.P. Morgan alone faced costs of $9 billion in fines, $4 billion in compensation and legal costs of up to $23 billion as a result of its part in the crisis: http://www.bbc.co.uk/news/business-24599345.

exploit regulatory weakness; the self-discipline shown by those companies that are committed to being a force for good is commendable.

Friends of the private sector believe that the public are less tolerant of imperfection in private business than elsewhere; perhaps this is because they have been told to expect the highest standards from them:

> They [the public] grudgingly accept that capitalism works, but they continue to treat the profit motive with suspicion, as morally inferior to other forms of social organisation such as state ownership or mutuals. Capitalism may deliver prosperity but it isn't loved .... The public seems hard-wired to favour altruistic behaviour, however unrealistic.

So says Allister Heath, editor of London's *City AM* newspaper.[3] He claims that the public regard errors in the public sector with indulgence or resigned indifference. He asks why the fixing of the LIBOR rate by a few bankers was seen as more heinous than the high levels of unnecessary death and suffering exposed in some NHS hospitals. Surely nurses do not neglect patients out of self-interest? LIBOR proved sufficient for Barclays' new boss, Antony Jenkins, to tell employees in a famous 'leaked' memo of January 2013 that anyone who didn't accept the bank's code of ethical conduct could leave, while in Mid-Staffordshire there was considerable fury about the way the local hospital had been run. People simply didn't want to believe that the service upon which their loved ones' lives depended was unreliable, but when the doubt set in, the release of focused emotion was huge.

The public sector, Heath went on, gets away with sloppy decision-making in a way that the private sector never could. He argued, with a neat sense of irony: 'A scandal caused by greed is deemed worse than any other; and greed, in this nonsensical world view, only exists in the private sector.'

The reason why many private companies have had their fingers burned with government outsourcing is precisely that which Heath identifies: we tolerate low aspirations and poorly drawn up procurement contracts in government with which the conscientious in the private sector would not normally associate themselves.

Things are certainly not working as well as they should be.

---

3   *City AM* editorial, 17 July 2013.

And yet …

The resources to put things right do exist – utilising, as ever, wealth which is almost wholly generated, unquestionably, by the private sector. Methods of reducing, reusing and recycling energy and resources work within the dedicated green economy, one of the most successful new battalions in an economic landscape which, in places, is a metaphorical Somme. And some fundamental capitalist practices are under serious challenge, as giants like Unilever eschew the 'normal' short-term approach to profit and a small but booming social enterprise sector enjoys counter-cyclical growth without the need to make a conventional net profit at all.

This book will explore practical options for how triple bottom line sustainability can serve society and how those options are being tested and trialled by those with the power to use them: the private sector.

Solutions are there for the taking.

What Do We Mean by 'Capitalism'?

Capitalism makes profits. That's what it's intended to do. From profit comes investment in future economic sustainability and reward for those who take the risks of investing, leading, managing, producing, distributing and otherwise contributing to the process.

Capitalism creates jobs. Jobs give workers purpose and their families security, as well as income to spend on the essentials for human dignity, comfort and happiness.

Capitalism generates taxation revenue in huge quantities from individuals and corporates, which governments employ to promote and defend public good and provide those services which it is deemed inappropriate to source from elsewhere.

Capitalism produces goods and services that people need – or, to be precise, for which they are willing to pay.

Capitalism has spare capacity. It needs to have spare capacity to do some of the things listed above, but some of that surplus capacity could to be put better use.

Capitalism relies on innovation. Without new ideas, insights, ways of doing things, new markets would not be found and changing social, economic, cultural and environmental circumstances could cause the market to fail – with no back-up.

Capitalism thus unlocks human potential and – at its best – fosters attitudes of economic responsibility, stewardship and long-term sustainability. Certainly there is no reason why socially positive values shouldn't drive players within the capitalist system, and this often happens, through corporate citizenship and philanthropy, at one level or another.

As Adam Smith and every other economist have taught us, capitalism relies on the operation of markets. They, in turn, work best when supply and demand are in approximate balance and when economic inequalities are sufficient to drive the market – but no more powerful than the level which the market requires to work effectively.

There is no serious alternative system to capitalism as the predominant political and economic force for the twenty-first century. Yet the freedoms capitalism releases can be and are being abused, not in a systematic, underhand, insidious way, but throughout its commanding heights.

Capitalism is using up the world's non-renewable resources, hydrocarbons and minerals in a way that's irresponsible and will lead to shortages. These will cause price rises which will be universally unaffordable.

Capitalism is using up the world's renewable resources, too – clean water, timber and flora – faster than it replaces them. In particular it's contributing to climate change to the tune of 94 million tonnes of excess carbon being produced every day without generating sufficient mitigation, let alone creating the now essential global reduction in carbon emissions.

Capitalism is generating inequalities which the market can't bear: 93 per cent of all new wealth created in the USA since the 2008 crash has gone to the richest 1 per cent of the population.[4]

Capitalism is working to a timescale within which the responsibilities of ownership are impossible to discharge, with the average time an equity stake

---

4   Several statistics in this section are from a speech made by former US Vice President Al Gore at the launch of ShareAction at London Guildhall on 18 March 2013.

in a company is held having reduced from eight years a generation ago to just six months now; indeed, through modern technology some assets are traded in seconds.

Capitalism appears to have abandoned many of the positive values it was credited with in times gone by, making them all subservient to the production of profit.

Capitalism is today built on a distorted concept of 'market' in which over six million people in Britain can't fully participate. They are at work, but nevertheless live in poverty (compared to five million ten years earlier). In Britain today there are more children living in poverty who have a working parent than children who live in workless households,[5] and 800,000 more adults are living in poverty than was the case fifteen years ago.[6] That a centre-left government in Britain with a working majority and years of feast presided over these trends for thirteen years is not to condemn it (or 'us', for I was a very junior member) for lack of principle, courage or policy, but to further recognise the disconnect between capitalism and democracy that Gore has identified: over three centuries capitalism and democracy together created and shared wealth, prompted technological revolutions and rebuilt Europe after a devastating war.

Internationally the problem is worse, reports Secretary General Ban Ki-Moon in the United Nations 2013 Millennium Development Goals report:

> *One in eight people worldwide remain hungry. Too many women die in childbirth when we have the means to save them. More than 2.5 billion people lack improved sanitation facilities, of which one billion continue to practice open defecation, a major health and environmental hazard. Our resource base is in serious decline, with continuing losses of forests, species and fish stocks, in a world already experiencing the impacts of climate change.[7]*

On a positive note, they report that 38 countries have already met their 2015 hunger reduction targets to halve the number of hungry people. Just 870 million people are now classed as 'hungry', with millions more malnourished, while

---

5   http://www.guardian.co.uk/society/2012/nov/26/working-people-in-poverty-report.
6   http://webarchive.nationalarchives.gov.uk/+/http:/www.cabinetoffice.gov.uk/media/410872/
    web-poverty-report.pdf.
7   http://www.un.org/millenniumgoals/pdf/report-2013/mdg-report-2013-english.pdf.

elsewhere in the world 1.4 billion children are classed as overweight and 500 million 'obese'.[8]

Capitalism on a grand scale is measured by growth: Gross Domestic Product (GDP) is a poorly defined concept in which numbers relating to certain selected criteria grow larger over time. 'Growth' is a driver of capitalism, and is necessary in moderation. But GDP excludes 'externalities', which includes both negative costs – of pollution, climate change, threats to the supply of natural resources, disease and poverty – and also the benefits that can be brought to society by investment in science, culture and the arts. It's particularly convenient to assume that those negative externalities are someone else's responsibility, as otherwise the costs would be … frightening. To fail to take negative externalities into account is to give a highly unrealistic view of the world in which each country wedded to GDP lives – and it's a denial of the 'polluter pays' principle. Positive externalities are ignored because it's just too difficult to measure the cash benefit of investing in music or wildlife conservation.[9]

And capitalism is generating levels of risk which are not only wholly unsustainable, but are becoming mainstream. New financial products are being designed not to mitigate or reduce risk, but to hide it – a process illustrated by nothing better than those 7.5 million American sub-prime mortgages which were sold with no meaningful credit checks and the debts re-bundled, re-sliced and re-sold time and again as assets on the financial markets of the world, in possibly the largest single contribution to the process that brought us within hours of that total meltdown of the global financial system in 2008:

> *A wide range of financial institutions (including banks and shadow banks and many other market participants) engage in [speculative and claims-based trading], and it mostly produces short term results. Up to half of any profits may go to the individuals who are running the institution and conducting the trades. The losses tend to be borne by the shareholders in the institution, unless of course the losses are so large that the institution becomes insolvent in which case the losses are borne by the institutions that are its creditors. This seems a poor*

---

8 http://www.un.org/apps/news/story.asp?NewsID=45153&Cr=mdg&Cr1=#.UfVXyBYRbzJ.
9 Gore told his Guildhall audience that when he became US Vice President in 1992 he established a unit to calculate the cost, in GDP terms, of the positive and negative externalities to growth. When, two years later, the Republican Party took control of the country's purse strings, the unit was scrapped.

deal from the perspective of the individual savers who are the ultimate
end-owners of all financial institutions.

(Featherby, 2012)[10]

In the twenty-first century we can surely do better than this.

Responsible capitalism needs rules. When Adam Smith published *The Theory of Moral Sentiments* in 1759 and *The Wealth of Nations* in 1776, he argued that the merchant who provided a service to a community did so because it was in his own self-interest; the butcher plied his trade in his market niche in order to put food on his own family's plates, not on those of others:

> *It is not from the benevolence of the butcher, the brewer, or the baker,*
> *that we expect our dinner, but from their regard to their own interest.*
> *We address ourselves not to their humanity but to their self-love, and*
> *never talk to them of our own necessities but of their advantages.*
>
> *(Smith, 1776)*

He went further, claiming that he never saw much good coming from those whose principal purpose was to do good rather than to trade. But while he believed that the net effect of every individual working to serve their own self-interest was to benefit the nation, he pleaded that excesses had to be curbed; he was calling for fair, if light-touch, rules for trade. Indeed, Smith railed against letting business and commerce become too opulent, 'fix' market prices and have too strong a hold on government, about which he was cynical:

> *Civil government, so far as it is instituted for the security of property,*
> *is in reality instituted for the defence of the rich against the poor, or of*
> *those who have some property against those who have none at all.*
>
> *(Quoted in Phillipson, 2010)*

The man held up to be the messiah of the free market had identified in his seminal work a huge contradiction: for a free market to work effectively, it had to obey rules. The rules should be fair, reasonable, proportionate and inclusive, but they should be enforceable and set by civil society, not by the market itself. A market with a purpose, he was saying, has to have a direction; he was calling for the marriage of democracy and capitalism, whose divorce Al Gore was lamenting 300 years later.

---

10 James Featherby chairs the Church of England Ethical Investment Advisory Group.

Smith pointed out that the 'stock' of the labouring poor was only enough to provide for immediate consumption, and therefore that the progress of opulence (which he saw as positive, in moderation) could not include them if they had no surplus capital to circulate; economic progress towards a fairer society depended on the surplus stock of those engaged in trade, manufacture and agriculture. He talked of both 'fixed and circulating capitals' in a 'relatively' free market; he would not have approved of the fact that since 2008 almost all the new wealth created in the USA was accrued by the richest 1 per cent – money that was, to a large extent, being taken out of circulation.

This highlights a major contradiction in UK government policy when it comes to austerity: at times of stress and hardship, if you give poorer people money, they spend it, they keep it in circulation, they benefit the local economy in a way Smith (and later Keynes) would have understood. If you take money away from poor people through, say, reducing Housing Benefit for those with more than the absolute minimum number of necessary bedrooms, you reduce the money in circulation in poorer communities and the local economy worsens. If, on the other hand, you give more money to rich people, say by reducing the top rate of tax by 5 per cent, there is no guarantee that the money 'released' by the measure will be spent at all, or spent in Britain, let alone spent in the local economy; the benefit it will bring to the wider economy will be minimal.

But if this sounds like a left-wing interpretation of Smith's cause, he was also dismissive of government, which he regarded, even before the days of the NHS and the welfare state, as spendthrift and profligate: 'Let [the government] look well after their own expense, and they may safely trust private people with theirs. If their own extravagance does not ruin the state, that of their subjects never will.'

So, for the purposes of this book, let's take the government out of the equation except where there's no alternative but to comment or include it. Let's also not speak of charities, the voluntary sector or civil society except where they are the agents of change through corporate partnerships or where useful comparisons can be drawn. Let's concentrate simply on how the individual corporate citizen – albeit with values, a conscience and an eye for the longer term – does, might and should behave in a modern capitalist economy.

There are lessons to be learned in Britain and elsewhere; certainly I will draw on firsthand experiences of the USA, Holland and India and merge them with the objective experiences of others from elsewhere.

First: how might a Good Company appear? What might its prospectus look like?

Welcome to GoodCo!

Here at GoodCo we do things right. We are for-profit and profitable, making a variety of things that people want, delivering services that people need. When sourcing our supplies, we consider our supply chain and our customers – with whom we engage sensibly and regularly – as all part of our family. We don't waste resources or exploit vulnerable communities, and we do conform to or exceed international standards of corporate behaviour. We are good to the environment, and our investments in waste reduction, energy saving, recycling and lowering carbon emissions have paid off; we invest, as it were, to save – both money and the planet.

Although we were set up by a visionary entrepreneur, our workforce has a stake in the long-term success of our company through a partial share ownership model. Employees are meaningfully represented on the board and, in particular, on the remuneration committee: not even our CEO can earn more than 20 times the salary of the lowest-paid;[11] bonuses are moderate but available to all who contribute, when applicable, according to clear and agreed rules. We enjoy a good relationship with our trade union partners who represent our people, and in return they work hard to keep jobs secure through a common commitment to success.[12]

We consider GoodCo to be a good corporate citizen. We engage in the communities where our people live and work by supporting them in volunteering their skills and passions for local good causes. Our people make a difference, whether as trustees of local charities, mentors to struggling young people or advisers to a social enterprise. We don't have a Charity of the Year as such, but we do match the first £200 any of our employees raises or donates

---

11 In some American companies a ratio of 400 to 1 can be found. Some economists say that a ratio of as low as 17 or 19 to 1 will combine incentives, career structures and equity, equivalent to a ratio of £15,000 to £270,000. In 2013, in a nationwide referendum, Switzerland rejected a legally binding 12 to 1 ratio of highest to lowest pay within an institution. This was undoubtedly an over-ambitious proposal whose rejection set the cause of pay equality back instead of taking it forwards.

12 In *Everybody's Business* (Miller and Parker, 2013) the authors look in depth at specific examples of corporate community engagement. While they do not highlight the point, good relations between employers and unions appear to be a hallmark of those companies with the best engagement practices. In the USA the world's largest charitable body, United Way, had its origins in the Detroit trade union movement over a hundred years ago.

to charity annually – we encourage them to support voluntary groups in the local community (and the annual Children in Need appeal, of course). We work on impact-driven projects with local voluntary organisations, and we support them to grow capacity in various ways – mentoring, skills exchange – and pro bono donations like auditing are very much appreciated. We work closely with local secondary schools to help improve young people's transition from education to employment, and (although we don't shout about it) we are proud of the small contribution our managers make to help rehabilitate, even employ, ex-offenders from a local institution. But we don't reinvent the wheel, preferring to support existing opportunities and networks rather than making up our own and branding them as such.

We consider ourselves to be diversity-friendly, so we are positive about all our staff and customers from whatever background or lifestyle. You would be surprised how much we benefit from employee skills and experiences this way. We work hard to engage with our staff – loyal, enthusiastic, productive and valuable team members – so we can afford to give them better than average terms and conditions at work.

From some of our surplus profits we make fixed rate low-interest loans to local social enterprises; this is community investment, not donation. We receive a lower return than we would on the capital markets, but at least the Social Return On Investment (SROI) ratio is positive and we know that our intervention does good.

A lot of the rest of our profits are reinvested in the company to make production smoother, customers and employees happier, and to cut costs. As I said, we invest to save.

For us, the laws on reporting do not go far enough. We are listed on the stock exchange, and our reporting practice exceeds the standard required, with clear, annual, objective reporting on our financial, environmental and social impacts. We have abandoned quarterly financial reporting in favour of annual as it distracted attention from the longer-term vision of our company's future – and our shareholders agree. We take on apprentices every year, even in hard times, and help them acquire the skills they, we and companies like us will need for the future.

All the tea, coffee and sugar we use is fair trade, and any wooden furniture we buy is FSC certified. It's not much, but it's a start – we encourage our suppliers to do likewise.

You will not find us mis-selling products or bribing foreign officials, or being part of a cartel to fix prices or interest rates, or cutting corners on health and safety issues or, heaven forbid, registering our brand offshore with the sole aim of reducing our tax liability. We are proud of paying our taxes: it reflects the wealth we bring to our nation. If we make more profits, we must pay more tax – that's fair! When we open a new factory, we are likely to develop a brownfield site in a relatively deprived part of the country where the jobs we bring will be appreciated.

We are proud of our brand, and rightly so. We are held in high esteem by our customers, the market and our investors. Reputation sells, they say, and the position we have adopted in the market does give us a competitive advantage.

GoodCo works.

With one rather important caveat: GoodCo does not exist.

But thank you for listening anyway.

Fortunately, everything we would do (if we did exist) is already being done by someone, somewhere. A few companies engage in much of what we would regard as good practice, some do very little, too many do none at all. Our ethos is applicable to both large corporates and to SMEs, and we recommend it.

Try it.

One person who has tried it is Craig Dearden-Phillips. In a fascinating article,[13] he describes a move in the opposite direction to that which enlightened business people are traditionally reputed to take after some Damascene conversion. After fourteen years as a charity chief executive at Speaking Up, he left the job (remaining as chair of the newly merged charity, now called VoiceAbility) to establish a private company, Stepping Out. Stepping Out advises and works with the public sector to develop and support social enterprises.

Having made the switch and raised several eyebrows among former charity colleagues, what explains his new-found passion for private enterprise? He describes himself as having been a 'slightly careworn' charity executive,

---

13 http://www.thirdsector.co.uk/news/1187239/craig-dearden-phillips-i-done-good-running-business-i-running-charity/.

and contrasts this with fellow business owners' 'energy, drive and generosity of spirit'. His new company has created seven new jobs in three years, including two for recent graduates. The business gives the Treasury enough money to fund a school classroom for a whole year, as well as £15,000 each year to its own foundation which supports social enterprises. And his staff take 30 days' paid leave each year between them to sit as charity trustees.

He sees SMEs as the driving force for economic recovery and the principal source of new employment, celebrating the fact that 400,000 new ones were registered in 2012. Without economic recovery, he implies, the questions we ask about the viability of our public services, the sustainability of our communities and the funding of our charities are of merely academic interest.

He's not wrong.

Chapter 2
Responsible Business

Doing good business and business doing good are not alternatives.
Ian Livingston, CEO of BT Group[1]

Since 'the crash' there has been much discussion about what constitutes 'responsible' capitalism. Indeed, on 19 January 2012 UK Prime Minister David Cameron dedicated a whole speech to it in which he concluded:

> *I want these difficult economic times to achieve more than just paying down the deficit and encouraging growth. I want them to lead to a socially responsible and genuinely popular capitalism, one in which the power of the market and the obligations of responsibility come together.*[2]

By 'socially responsible', he meant: 'a vision of social responsibility which recognises that people are not just atomised individuals *and that companies have obligations too*' (my emphasis).

But he didn't spell out what those responsibilities were, other than implying that they shouldn't be reckless and that business should support social reform. The examples he gave of the latter were the repeal of the Corn Laws in favour of free trade in 1846 (where there was possibly a degree of self-interest) and opposition to slavery (where the evidence is weak), rather than the campaigning zeal for the legalisation of same-sex marriage exhibited by the ice cream company Ben & Jerry's.

He continued: 'But social responsibility – watching over business, correcting market failure, recognising obligations … that's been the Conservative mission from the start.'

---

1   Ian Livingston (now Lord Livingston), then CEO of BT Group, speaking at the launch of BT's 'Net Positive' initiative at the RSA, London, on 18 June 2013.
2   Full transcript: http://www.newstatesman.com/uk-politics/2012/01/economy-capitalism-market.

So what are those obligations that business has? Cameron concluded: 'Soon after I was elected leader I said that we should not just stand up for business … but also stand up to big business when it was in the national interest.'

Again, examples were in short supply. In short, whatever the responsibilities and obligations were that fell on the shoulders of business, they should be achieved with the minimum of regulation – preferably less than exists at present. He derided 'turbo-capitalism', which, he claimed, had caused the financial sector to overheat under Labour and teeter on the verge of self-destruction. In terms of redefining the purpose of business, he was silent, other than implying that a share-owning democracy was one in which people exercised proper restraint and more positive influences over business activity through their votes at corporate AGMs as well as and at the same time as through the ballot box.

We have heard 'share-owning democracy' before: it was the purpose, we were told, of Margaret Thatcher's sale of the previously nationalised utilities, epitomised by the 'Tell Sid' campaign to sell British Gas shares in 1986, reappearing with the privatisation of the Post Office late in 2013.

The evidence that individual shareholders are inherently more responsible when organised in larger numbers hardly holds water: traditionally, shareholders' interests have been and still are defined principally by the company share price, and business has been organised to that end. Such was the restraint exercised at British Gas that in 1990 those newly democratised shareholders granted the company chairman a 66 per cent pay rise, to £370,000. Even in the naughty noughties that sort of rise might have been regarded as reckless. A category of major corporate shareholders, the pension funds, may in fact be more effective at ensuring corporate responsibility than are 'atomised' individual shareholders – witness the way in which one of the world's largest pension funds, that of the Norwegian government, disinvested from Walmart in 2006 in protest at its poor supply chain standards.[3]

Back in the 1980s, that attempt to create a shareholding democracy didn't last long. There was a rush by the newly empowered individual shareholders to cash in their assets by selling to corporate investors such as French water and energy companies. Many cynics suspected that privatisation had been designed to benefit major corporates, irrespective of their country of origin.

---

3   http://www.guardian.co.uk/business/2006/jun/07/supermarkets.asda. Despite acknowledging improvements a major Dutch pension fund followed suit in 2012, though no US pension fund has done likewise as yet: http://www.huffingtonpost.com/2012/01/05/walmart-blacklist-abp-pension-fund_n_1186384.html.

This was the era of globalisation, a natural consequence of capitalism in its third century, a force which would plough the oceans with supertankers containing consumer goods, oil, plastic for recycling and almost any raw material the rich North could extort from the poor South; a force which ultimately would grant multinational corporations the option of where (and consequently at what rate) to pay their taxes.

The official Labour Party view of responsible capitalism, developed following Ed Miliband's second speech as Leader to its Party Conference in 2011, is slightly more specific, but still framed by the view that the role of responsible business is to do business better rather than working towards a new and wider definition of what constitutes a 'corporate citizen'.

What upset Miliband, as described both in that speech and in another for the Social Market Foundation,[4] was the operation of cartels (in fixing consumer prices such as energy), extravagance and what can only be described as 'dislocation'. In short, the Labour view of responsible capitalism doesn't change what capitalism does nor where its responsibilities lie, but urges that the private sector conduct itself in a more restrained, aware and economically responsible, rather than necessarily socially positive, longer-term manner. Its outputs would still be measured by traditional Labour economic measures of wealth, productivity and jobs: 'our argument for a new, more responsible, productive capitalism is hard-headed – not soft-hearted. It's based on how we pay our way in the world, build long-term wealth and deliver rising living standards for the majority of people.'

Miliband cites six fields of economic reform, which I paraphrase as:

1.　　the finance sector to be better geared to the needs of business rather than driven by self-interest;

2.　　measures to promote investment for the longer term;

3.　　developing the skills base of the workforce (both economically sound and fulfilling for individual workers);

4.　　responsibility and accountability in the boardroom and among shareholders, shop floor representation on board remuneration committees;

4　http://www.newstatesman.com/economy/2011/11/term-business-government.

5.   an end to large concentrations of banking power, separating investment banking from retail banking;

6.   business and society working together to make Britain better by paying tax on secure profits and employing more taxpayers.

Other than disagreeing on how to take these measures forward – with Labour less reticent to use regulation or legislation than its Coalition counterparts, who favour cheering from the sidelines – there's little in these proposals that divides Britain's main parties. Miliband cited this somewhat traditional view of what constitutes a 'good company' again in a contribution to the IPPR thinktank in May 2012:[5]

> Britain has some world-class businesses. Firms such as Rolls Royce and GlaxoSmithKline create high-quality jobs, train, develop and engage their workforces, invest in their communities and take a long-term view of their role in our society. Our country is also fortunate to have inspiring and dynamic small enterprises. They often emerge directly out of the communities in which they are located. They serve people, create new products and make an invaluable contribution to the dynamism of our national life.

So Labour is thinking about these issues. Mike Buckley, writing on the blog site Labour List in March 2012, implies that a more robust approach is desirable, but is sceptical that progress is being made:

> [Responsible capitalism] suggests a capitalism which treats the Earth's resources as valuable and finite and which rightly regards inequality as iniquitous and poverty as an evil which diminishes us all. Responsible capitalism even has the pleasing implication of recognising and even tacitly apologising for previous irresponsibility, whether this be the behaviour of bankers or political elites which turned a blind eye to bad practice or enabled it through rampant deregulation or their toleration of the 'filthy rich' and growing inequality.[6]

So far, so good. He goes on:

> Sadly responsible capitalism doesn't really mean any of these things, at least not yet. At worst it is an empty phrase designed to distract attention

---

5   http://www.ippr.org/juncture/171/9200/building-a-responsible-capitalism.
6   http://labourlist.org/2012/03/responsible-capitalism-a-christian-socialist-perspective/.

from the fact that very little has changed in how we run our economies; at best we are witnessing the beginnings of a set of ideas which may lead to real change. Responsible capitalism – or language similar to it – is currently in vogue for the very good reason that capitalism as practiced has clearly got us into a fix, those responsible are rightly unpopular, and there is the strong sense that something must be done. Responsible capitalism is a vacuous enough phrase that I can, as above, attach to it my own shopping list, my own hopes for how the world can be. It is not however a clearly thought through policy portfolio on either side of the house, and nor is it yet a vision for a better future.

Much innovative Labour thinking in recent years has come from local authorities where government cuts have forced politicians to 'think the unthinkable'. One of the best, broadest and most sustainable initiatives – based on sound principles of employee, service user and stakeholder engagement through co-operative and mutual models traditional and otherwise, a genuine commitment to partnership working – has been the Co-operative Councils.[7] The model was pioneered by the London Borough of Lambeth and adopted in a variety of practices by more than twenty others. In January 2013 they published a 100-page collection of essays, a landmark in the development of the Co-op Council concept, which consolidated progress and proposed attractive, practical and sustainable options for the future (Reed and Ussher, 2013).

Yet you have to reach page 93 before you find a serious assessment of where corporate citizens might play a part in service delivery other than as mere contractors or providers of employment for the masses. In that final chapter former Labour Business Minister Kitty Ussher says:

But there is a third avenue that needs a serious exploration, to fully complete the picture, and that is how to involve the private sector in the public policy debate. The risk is that by remaining located firmly in the intellectual space inhabited by local government councillors or officers, we ignore the potential contribution to be made by existing private sector organisations.

Is this a recognition that the corporate citizens of the private sector have a legitimate role alongside the public and the voluntary in both community leadership and service delivery? No: but she does urge that stakeholder status be bestowed on the sector:

---

7   http://www.councils.coop.

> *The good news is that the general co-operative approach to council service delivery ... is just as applicable to the relationship with business. All you have to do is add in the business voice to the other stakeholders, whilst being fully aware that they are free to walk away at any stage.*

To some in the Labour Party, the capitalist leopard may be forever unable to change its spots – and nor should it, according to those establishment figures whom Will Hutton calls the 'uber-capitalists'. In a fascinating essay, Hutton distinguishes between 'Good' and 'Bad' capitalism roughly along these lines (Hutton, 2011):

Good capitalism believes that:

- Productive entrepreneurs should be permitted to earn their due rewards.

- Firms are social creations, entrepreneurism is something positive from which you make profits; a shared sense of purpose inspires people to invent, innovate and deliver to their markets.

- Governments must keep markets open and intervene to keep them working and innovative whilst encouraging investment in common physical, knowledge and social assets.

- Capitalism espouses the values of fairness, proportionality and mutual respect.

- Risk is essential because it prompts innovation in an unpredictable world which is constantly renewing itself.

Bad capitalism:

- Is represented by bloated incumbents, politically fixed markets, too little public investment.

- Is over-influenced by self interest with a disjoint between achievement and reward.

- Believes that capitalism has to be inherently 'unfair', with winners and losers, and the rich simply deserve to be rich; that risk is essential for the reasons given above (but then does what it can to remove risk from future planning).

- Is comfortable with falling philanthropic giving, rising tax avoidance and exponentially rising executive pay in some sectors (despite evidence that societies with lesser financial inequalities are happier, fairer and more productive than others).

Hutton argues that the left in Europe and America, which opposes bad capitalism but fails to champion good capitalism, is ceding political ground not just to the conventional right, but to those who would prey on the sense of injustice that bad capitalism creates among the working classes: the far, nationalist right. He says that those who blame 'capitalism' for all the world's ills are as blind as those who claim only 'socialism' can cure them; he worries that although America is the home of 'good capitalism', it's in danger of lurching in the direction of 'bad', while 'bad' generally already has the upper hand in Europe.

According to Business Secretary Vince Cable, it's also 'the government's aim for a market economy based on responsible capitalism', but Cable's definition appears even more timid than that of the Prime Minister:[8]

> The crucial factor is ensuring investors have the information they need to make long-term decisions, on pay and a range of other issues. John Kay[9] was scathing about the effect of quarterly reporting on long-term investment. I agree with his analysis, and the government will work with our European counterparts to change the law so it is no longer required.

I hope he consulted Unilever, which has topped the Dow Jones Sustainability Index for 14 years and is committed to a broad 'sustainable living plan'.[10] In 2013 Oxfam's *Behind the Brands* report ranked Unilever as the world's second most responsible food-producing company.[11] It has already abandoned quarterly reporting for precisely this reason, demonstrating that legislation isn't required to achieve the outcome the Business Secretary seeks. Cable went on: '… there is a challenge here too for asset owners, including pension funds, who need to look beyond quarterly performance to judge their managers'.

---

8   https://www.gov.uk/government/speeches/responsible-capitalism.
9   John Kay produced a report for the government on reform of the financial sector (Kay, 2012).
10 http://www.unilever.com/sustainable-living/ourapproach/reportingourprogress/.
11 http://www.guardian.co.uk/sustainable-business/oxfam-multinational-companies-failing-csr?INTCMP=SRCH.

Indeed there is. We shall return to the world of investors in later chapters, though it's an investor who gets the closest so far to the heart of responsible capitalism. Stephen Beer, senior fund manager and strategist at the investment arm of the Methodist Church, calls for its definition to be wider than the raw economics. It's not about 'taking sides', he told the *Financial Times*; it's about using available resources properly:[12]

> *Within the investment management sector is a relatively small group of responsible investment funds. Labelled ethical, socially responsible, or environment, social and governance (ESG) funds, they have promoted the notion of responsibility in the relationship between shareholder and manager, at the heart of capitalism. The debate about responsible capitalism would do well to take heed of these funds and recent changes in their approach.*
>
> *Integrating ESG concerns with long-term growth strategies is at the basis of a responsible capitalism or what former US vice-president Al Gore calls 'sustainable capitalism'. However, from an investor point of view, this requires more than ticking the ESG and growth outlook boxes. It requires a deeper level of engagement with companies and an understanding that change takes time. Fund manager scepticism and the desire for rigour extends to NGOs and campaign groups when they allege companies have been acting irresponsibly. Responsible investors are interested in solutions and we are prepared to act as catalysts to help companies, governments and campaigners find better ways to work together. Should this approach become more mainstream, we will be on our way to a more responsible capitalism.*

This is what responsible capitalism should be about! We shall return to 'Sustainable Capitalism' later.

Many argue that the responsible capitalism agenda should include transparency, accountability and an over-riding sense of stewardship: the environment, the planet's resources and societal values should be conserved, protected and where possible enhanced by the prevailing economic system for the next generation to enjoy, and responsibility for that should rest with individual companies as well as broader society. Historically this approach was perhaps best seen in the era of the family company, where fathers had a demonstrable duty to hand over the mill as an asset to their descendants,

---

12 http://www.ft.com/cms/s/0/1970e904-37b8-11e2-8edf-00144feabdc0.html?siteedition=uk#axzz 2iGygh4rm.

operating in a social and economic environment which would have been familiar to D.H. Lawrence. In a report which draws upon the experience of family companies, Tomorrow's Company and the Institute for Family Business (2011) lay down the arguments for the attitude of mind they call stewardship and the rationale behind it. They define stewardship as 'the active and responsible management of entrusted resources now and in the longer term, so as to hand them on in better condition', and they say it has four interacting, inter-related elements: family capital, people capital, financial capital and social capital. The latter isn't exclusive to the company, but it can influence it. Social capital is that of the community, the supply chain and the customer.

Such corporate behaviour is known to generate employee engagement – a valuable commodity for any company seeking loyalty, longer-term commitment and productivity (Bowles and Cooper, 2009).

The age-old dilemma facing campaigners for change is whether to be guided by the head or the heart, to build on what's there or to tear it all down and start again. Where it's a case of supporting vulnerable people, of deciding how the resources of the state should best be deployed, it's Hobson's choice: no period of anarchy, generated either by rebellion from below or the austerity slashers above, can be allowed to disrupt the flow of support and make life even worse for those least capable of looking after themselves. This is certainly the view of the charitable sector, which, like nurses, has a reputation of tolerating much if not every iniquity in order to 'keep the show on the road'.

Evolution, not revolution, is the order of the day.

But why is there such a dichotomy, even a chasm, between 'doing good' and making a profit? Why do we seem to regard the two as incompatible?

A fascinating talk by the American social entrepreneur Dan Pallotta was viewed more than 250,000 times in its first year as a TED talk from the spring of 2013.[13] In a passage which I will quote at length he argues that the idea that it's wrong to make money out of 'doing good' has its roots in the early days of colonialism in the United States:

> *Like most fanatical dogma in America these ideas come from old puritan beliefs. The puritans came here for religious reasons, or so they said, but they also came because they wanted to make a lot of money.*

---

13 http://www.youtube.com/watch?v=bfAzi6D5FpM&feature=youtu.be.

They were pious people but they were also really aggressive capitalists and they were accused of extreme forms of profit-making tendencies compared to the other colonists.

At the same time the puritans were Calvinists, so they were taught literally to hate themselves. They were taught that self-interest was a raging sea that was a sure path to eternal damnation. This created a real problem for these people right here. They've come all the way across the Atlantic to make all this money and making all this money will get you sent directly to hell. What were they to do about this?

Well, charity became their answer. It became this economic sanctuary where they could do penance for their profit-making tendencies, at five cents on the dollar. So, of course, how could you make money in charity if charity was your penance for making money?

Financial incentive was exiled from the realm of helping others so that it could thrive in the area of making money for yourself and in 400 years nothing has intervened to say that's counterproductive and that's unfair.

Pallotta pleads for a more business-like approach to doing good, more investment in good causes rather than philanthropic giving; he's scathing about the widespread belief that any charity that spends more than a single-digit percentage of its turnover on 'overheads' is necessarily profligate, inefficient or downright criminal. He argues implicitly that the very same procedures that produce profit for personal gain can and should be used to generate social benefit and community dividends.

While his analysis is devastatingly simple and sensible, he doesn't claim that a revolution is required to redirect these tools of private capital towards public purpose as long as open minds allow them to be so used. Others over recent decades have sought to redesign the established economic system in order to reach similar goals.

Perhaps the most radical and forthright of the evolutionaries for responsible capitalism is John Elkington, a leading thinker in this field for over twenty years. The father of the 'triple bottom line' – that triumvirate of financial, social and environmental responsibility which influenced Britain's 2006 Companies Act – he coined the phrase 'Breakthrough Capitalism'.

He sees this as the third in a sequence of stages in which the market, the state and the citizen coexist:[14]

> **Breakdown** – the inexorable consequences of the old economic order, resistance to change, a blinkered approach to global crises, the diminution of natural resources through waste and over-use, leading to 'bringing the planetary roof down on our heads';

> **Change-as-usual** – the elders of society (business and political leaders and the investment community) acknowledge both the nature of some of the critical scenarios and possible solutions, but progress is 'dangerously relaxed and incremental', with the tough challenge of system change being largely ignored;

> **Breakthrough** – society and the economy are focused on and actively engaged in addressing key global issues such as climate change, poverty, pandemic and population growth.

It doesn't take a genius to recognise that the economic community which dominates our planet is very much in 'Breakdown' mode, although a growing minority of influential people within it, companies and other leaders, are well established in 'Change-as-usual'. 'Breakthrough' can only be achieved by qualitative changes in approach and a quantum leap in dynamism by sector leaders working together – and political leaders also need to be involved. Elkington identifies partnership, especially cross-sectoral, as essential to generating this momentum.

It's an interesting analysis with much merit. It recognises the problems faced by minority and fringe views in becoming mainstream and creating culture change, and it recognises the need for short-term incentives to 'get the ball rolling'. This will be a major difficulty. As we saw in the passage through the UK Parliament of the Public Services (Social Value) Act 2012, the spirit of government may be willing, but the flesh is weak. This Act requires public bodies procuring goods and services to consider the relative impact of the organisations bidding in delivering a broadly defined 'social value' over and above the benefit inherent in the contract itself. Having considered this, the law doesn't require procurers then to act upon it, such as by awarding the contract to the provider which offers the greatest 'social value', though it allows them to

---

14 Report of the Breakthrough Capitalism Forum hosted by Volans, London, May 2012: http://www.breakthroughcapitalism.com/files/Breakthrough_Capitalism_Progress_Report.pdf.

do so. 'Social value' may reflect how the bidder treats its low-paid employees, how much it recycles, whether it encourages employees to volunteer in the community, how equitably it manages its supply chain and so on. It's a law which will be observed, hopefully, to the letter by all, although in the spirit adherence is likely only to be seen in those public agencies which are already well disposed towards responsibility and engagement, as we shall see in Chapter 3.[15]

By any definition, 'social business' must be key to responsible capitalism. It's all very well having a theory, a movement, an idea; the social business will put it into practice. Mohammed Yunus, awarded the Nobel Peace Prize for his work establishing the inclusive (pro-poor) Grameen Bank, favours a much tighter definition. He describes a social business as exhibiting seven principles (Yunus, 2009):

- Its objective is to overcome a problem which threatens people and society (such as poverty, disease, hunger, education, access to technology) rather than to maximise profit.

- It has financial and economic sustainability.

- It relies on investors who can get their money back, but do not receive a dividend.

- Any profit made on the investment stays with the company to assist it to improve or expand.

- It is environmentally conscious.

- Its workforce receives a market wage and good working conditions.

- It operates with joy.

He envisages such businesses working alongside conventional for-profit models, but supported by their own appropriate institutions such as a 'social stock market' in which impact rather than profit is the driving force (Yunus, 2009 and 2011). He stresses that 'corporate social responsibility' (CSR) doesn't mean

---

15 The Government has published a review of the first year of activity under the Act which suggests that some local authorities are generating considerable social value in this way: https://www.gov.uk/government/publications/public-services-social-value-act-2012-1-year-on.

the same thing as 'social business', as CSR rarely accounts for more than a tiny fraction of the turnover of a for-profit company and may be aimed at image rather than substance; a social business is wholly focused on being an active and positive (corporate) citizen working for change and social good.

The Good Business Alliance, the brainchild of social entrepreneur Gordon da Silva, exists to take the values of social business and inculcate them into the mainstream; it argues that a 'good company' should enjoy success both in economic terms and in creating a positive social impact. It's especially keen to see responsible and engaged business practice taught in business schools through its Good Business Charter.[16] 'A Blueprint for a Better Business' is an initiative involving business leaders, designed to engage business with social policy in line with Catholic social teaching, launched in 2012.[17]

A Social Stock Exchange was established in Britain in 2013[18] to 'connect Social Impact Businesses with investors looking to generate social or environmental change as well as financial return from their investment', while they define Social Impact Businesses as those with 'social and environmental aims at the core of their activities'. One thing the Social Stock Exchange is not is a Stock Exchange; there's no trading of shares or derivatives here. Yet the concept is well established internationally: the first Social Stock Exchange was created in Brazil in 2004, and since 2006 SASIX, the South African Social Investment Exchange, has been selling shares in itself for as cheaply as 50 rand for people to engage in what would today be called 'crowdsourcing' of social enterprises.[19]

The Australian Business School at the University of New South Wales offers an undergraduate course on 'Creating Social Change: From Innovation to Impact', designed to support an increasing number of students who regard social value as a high priority in their future working life in the private sector.[20]

I pay homage to Mohammed Yunus's vision and insight, but I would use the phrase 'social business' in a much more generic way than he would. I use it to explore, encourage and praise those private sector institutions and individual players which undertake activity designed principally to achieve a social good using the tools of the for-profit sector – putting to one side the fact that in the private sector such practices rarely, if ever, dominate a large

16 http://www.goodbusinessalliance.com/index.php.
17 http://www.blueprintforbusiness.org.
18 http://www.socialstockexchange.com.
19 http://www.sasix.co.za/about_us/about_sasix/about_us/.
20 http://www.handbook.unsw.edu.au/undergraduate/courses/2014/COMM2000.html.

company's purpose. The emphasis should be on the activity, and not on the corporate body. My justification for this is that Yunus's label would be impossible to apply to an existing for-profit body, even one in an advanced state of transition to becoming what he would recognise as a social business. Every leopard (or capitalist hyena) must be allowed to change its spots. Achieving *a process* of change is the best we can hope and aspire for, with no certainty that the total transformation of the economy will ever happen if led by carrots alone, nor that sufficient power will ever be gained to create such change through the use of sticks. In any case, sticks generate resistance, reticence and reluctance, which damage the quality of the 'good' so generated; sticks tend to lead to compliance limitations, while carrots are more likely to lead to over-performance.

No, I want to celebrate those private sector bodies which, even though they are designed to make a profit, do some of the following:

- monitor and report their social impact in a way which is critical, responsible and long-term, with the purpose of increasing the social benefit generated;[21]

- adopt triple bottom line accounting and awareness;

- engage with the wider stakeholder community in key business decisions (employees, customers, neighbours, elected representatives and so on);

- co-ordinate their social impact activity with others, including public sector bodies, to maximise local impacts;

- use investment to create a social return (even if not exclusively);

- strategically deploy surplus resources (staff time, skills, cash, product, surplus, services and so on) to create positive social impact;

- engage in partnerships to enhance the social return (qualitative or quantitative) of a not-for-profit social purpose-orientated partner.

---

21 In September 2013 Fujitsu became the first major corporate to publish a full social value analysis of the 772 companies in its supply chain using a new British tool: http://www.tradingforgood. co.uk and http://www.fujitsu.com/uk/about/local/corporate-responsibility/csr-report/supply-chain/.

Such bodies can be seen as somewhere along the road of transition from the Friedmanite for-profit, red in tooth and claw, archetypal private sector monster to the Yunusian model; in reality, the best we can hope for is that they remain in transition, as short of rebuilding the West following a nuclear holocaust, there's no way that evolutionary transition will be complete in my daughter's lifetime.

For society to reject capitalism and start over isn't an attractive proposition.

There's an argument that Gandhi's attitude to capitalism in the 1930s helped bolster the poverty and deprivation that dominates India today.[22] He persuaded a nation to strive for the status quo and stagnation, to eschew 'progress', by burning the imported cloth Indians needed to clothe themselves, banning imports that India needed to trade, opposing all but the most humble industrial machinery, rejecting technology and substituting less efficient methods of production. 'Production by the masses' was his byword, rather than mass production, while advocating a modest diet wholly inadequate for a manual labourer or nursing mother. Perhaps this wasn't surprising as he considered pregnancy, whether in wedlock or outside, to be evidence of moral lapse.

Charlie Chaplin, on the other hand, was born in London in 1889, the son of an alcoholic father, who abandoned him at two years old, and a mother with severe mental illness. He spent two periods in a workhouse in his youth. Fame allowed him access to the rich and famous, and by 1931, visiting Britain to promote his film *City Lights*, he had already discussed politics with Bernard Shaw, Ramsay MacDonald, H.G. Wells and Winston Churchill. He wanted to add Gandhi, in London to discuss Indian independence, to his list.

A private meeting took place at a community centre in Newham, East London. It's likely that there was much agreement, as Chaplin had previously said that capitalism, specifically machinery in the workplace, would create unemployment. The conversation may even have inspired his ground-breaking 1934 film *Modern Times*. Over the years, however, Chaplin changed his view, arguing that machinery and the pursuit of profit could, after all, help and benefit mankind – as long as it was kept under control. 'Something is wrong,' he told an interviewer, 'Things have been badly managed when five million men are out of work in the richest country in the world.' He went on to be a strong supporter of Roosevelt's New Deal and was accused of being a Communist.

---

22 http://www.forbes.com/sites/kylesmith/2011/07/28/what-were-gandhis-views-on-capitalism/.

In 2011 I visited Gandhi's ashram in Mumbai as a member of a group studying innovative ways of delivering services through social enterprise.[23] The associated toilet museum was fascinating: toilets promote not just hygiene and sanitation, but gender equality, as modesty obliges women with no access to toilets to wait until dark to defecate out in the fields in much of the subcontinent, rendering them significantly vulnerable to attack. In the museum we saw over 60 types of clay and porcelain toilets, bowls, urinals, footrests, with modesty screens and without, with two common qualities: none were flushable, and none required a sewer. We met students studying bodily health through a Gandhian lens and discussed the issue with a giant barefoot cotton-clad American university drop-out who could have been cast for the role of gentle Gandhi acolyte. What annoyed some of our group wasn't the lack of ambition of the project (its 170-year programme to put a toilet in every home was, we were told, on track), but the attitude. 'If I give a man bread, I make him happy; if I make one person happy each day, I have done what I exist to do,' the American told us, his eyes glazed in ecstatic bliss. Never have I heard a firmer denial of the philosophy of 'teach me to fish and I shall eat for a lifetime' – complacent, unconvincing and wholly inappropriate for India's situation, which cries out for robust, imaginative and ambitious business planning.

Back to the real world.

John Mackey, CEO of Whole Foods, runs a very successful US company. His salary is 19 times that of his average employee. This may sound a lot: it's actually modest. The multiple is consistent with the principle that the CEO is a team member and owes it to his employees not to be extravagant. In 2005 the average American CEO received no less than $411 for every $1 the average employee earned. Mackey's business philosophy, he claims, is consistent with a re-reading of Adam Smith. 'Conscientious Capitalism', he says, 'does not deny or decry the profit motive':

> *One common objection to philanthropy is where to draw the line? If donating five percent of profits is good (as Whole Foods does), wouldn't 10 per cent be even better? Why not donate 100 per cent of our profits to the betterment of society? But the fact that a business has responsibilities as a citizen in the various communities it exists in doesn't mean that it doesn't have any responsibilities to investors or other stakeholders. It's a question of finding the appropriate*

---

23 http://www.journeysforchange.org.

balance and trying to create value for all of the stakeholders simultaneously.[24]

This position describes the transitionary company missing from the Yunus model, and it could also describe the shared value ethos of Michael Porter.

Shared Value

Michael Porter of Harvard Business School is one of the world's most influential business academics. Writing in a definitive blog in 2011,[25] he notes that despite adopting so-called corporate responsibility policies over many years, business is nevertheless blamed for everything that goes wrong – the economy, global poverty, bonuses, the crash, resource depletion – and for prospering at the expense of the broader community. Perhaps people have construed the word 'responsible' in both its meanings at the same time ('a responsible approach'/'responsible for crime'), and maybe they have been right to do so. Identifying the same 'brand' problems that business has in public perception and the power of private business to influence change, especially in global challenges to the triple bottom line, Porter says:

> *The solution lies in the principle of shared value, which involves creating economic value in a way that also creates value for society by addressing its needs and challenges. Businesses must reconnect company success with social progress. Shared value is not social responsibility, philanthropy, or even sustainability, but a new way to achieve economic success. It is not on the margin of what companies do but at the center. We believe that it can give rise to the next major transformation of business thinking.*[26]

Companies, he says, must take the lead in bringing business and society back together – not politicians, institutions or some amorphous global movement:

> *Capitalism is an unparalleled vehicle for meeting human needs, improving efficiency, creating jobs and building wealth. But a narrow conception of capitalism has prevented business from harnessing its full potential to meet society's broader challenges. The opportunities*

---

24 http://www.wholefoodsmarket.com/blog/john-mackeys-blog/conscious-capitalism-creating-new-paradigm-for%C2%A0business.

25 http://hbr.org/2011/01/the-big-idea-creating-shared-value.

26 Ibid.

have been there all along but have been overlooked. Businesses acting as businesses, not as charitable donors, are the most powerful force for addressing the pressing issues we face. The moment for a new conception of capitalism is now; society's needs are large and growing, while customers, employees and a new generation of young people are asking business to step up.[27]

For me, Porter presses every button. In order to produce social benefits like providing more employment for disabled people, we don't need to temper the drive for economic success as neoclassical economists tell us, he says, while also rejecting the complacency that says that externalities such as pollution are dealt with through taxation and can thus be 'ticked off' rather than tackled at source. It's not about redistributing economic value alone away from the rich and towards the poor, but growing an ever larger pool of both economic and social value which will benefit all. Three shared value tools in particular are worthy of mention (with my added examples, which are easier to find in corporate Africa than in Europe or the USA as yet):

- re-conceiving products and markets (Unilever creating smaller packages of cleaning products in Africa so they can sell at a more accessible price);

- redefining productivity in the value/supply chain (Nestlé using fair trade chocolate in its mainstream brands);

- building supportive industry clusters at the company's locations (as Anglo American does in Africa).

At the heart of it, as there has to be, is the business case:

The concept of shared value resets the boundaries of capitalism. By better connecting companies' success with societal improvement, it opens up many ways to serve new needs, gain efficiency, create differentiation and expand markets.[28]

In the Oxfam report on global food businesses mentioned earlier,[29] the most sustainable large food company in the world, using triple bottom line criteria,

---

27 Ibid. See also http://www.youtube.com/watch?v=aUdPDVO-toM.
28 Ibid.
29 http://www.theguardian.com/sustainable-business/oxfam-multinational-companies-failing-csr?INTCMP=SRCH.

was a multinational which explicitly espouses Porter's philosophy: Nestlé. Once regarded as a corporate pariah because of its controversial approach to marketing baby milk substitute in the 1960s and 1970s, Nestlé has complied with the robust ethical standards in this field established thirty years ago by the World Health Organisation. In the last decade it has come to be regarded as a leading exponent of Creating Shared Value (CSV), which it defines as follows:

> Creating Shared Value begins with the understanding that for our business to prosper over the long term, the communities we serve must also prosper. It explains how businesses can create competitive advantage, which in turn will deliver better returns for shareholders, through actions that substantially address a social or environmental challenge. Specifically, business will thrive and society will benefit if business can:

> - Develop products and services that meet societal needs in developed and developing countries
> - Use resources more efficiently across the entire value chain, and
> - Improve the conditions for local economic and social development.

Nestlé's expertise is in the fields of nutrition, water and rural development. That CSV encompasses a change in attitude is acknowledged on the Nestlé website:

> In the past, corporate investments in community and environmental initiatives were often seen as 'obligations' or simply philanthropy: added costs that had to be borne to minimise operational risks and protect reputation. Creating Shared Value redefines many of these obligations as opportunities to strengthen the business long-term – adding value for shareholders and our stakeholders.[30]

Or, in the words of CEO Paul Bulcke, 'The company behaves like a citizen, in the same way, with the same responsibilities.'[31] Nestlé also publishes regular updates on its progress as a shared value practitioner.[32]

Notwithstanding the fact that 'shared value' is a process and 'social value' an outcome the two concepts can be regarded as comparable.

---

30 http://www.nestle.com/csv/what-is-csv/csv-explained.
31 http://www.youtube.com/watch?v=6dMEi6IqDds.
32 http://www.nestle.com/media/newsandfeatures/csv-report-2012.

Sustainable Capitalism?

> *Sustainable Capitalism is a framework that seeks to maximise*
> *long-term economic value creation by reforming markets to*
> *address real needs while considering all costs and integrating ESG*
> *[environmental, social, governance] metrics into the decision-making*
> *process.*[33]

Sustainable capitalism is most widely associated with the later incarnation of former US Vice President Al Gore.[34] It originates in the 'inconvenient truth' of climate change which he championed in the hard-hitting and influential 2006 film of that name. It's applicable to the entire investment value chain, from entrepreneurial one-person ventures to large publicly traded companies, from investors providing seed capital to those seeking opportunities for growth, from employees to CEOs, from activists to policy makers. Sustainable capitalism transcends borders, industries, forms of ownership and asset classes, and involves stakeholders of all types.

Sustainable capitalism is a practical approach which doesn't play on the heartstrings, but appeals directly to business rationale. It's couched in business terms, and it makes sense in anyone's language. It's 'responsible capitalism' personified. Let's delay further consideration of this to the final chapter, where, as is traditional, we'll look to the future.

Meanwhile …

Is business open to playing a greater role in creating a better society? Yes, say Jake Hayman and Rachel Linn of The Social Investment Consultancy. They report that:

- 91 per cent of UK senior business leaders believe that businesses using their core strengths would be more effective in creating social change than is giving to charity; only 9 per cent felt charity donations were the best way for businesses to contribute;

- 93 per cent believed that their company could 'create economic value by creating social value';

---

33 http://www.generationim.com/media/pdf-generation-sustainable-capitalism-v1.pdf.
34 Al Gore and David Blood, 'We Need Sustainable Capitalism', *The Wall Street Journal* (5 November 2008).

- 84 per cent agreed that 'companies need to evolve their giving programmes from simply giving money to broader social innovation';

- however, only 64 per cent reported they were currently using their business's resources in this manner.

This suggests that while some doors are open, not all the tools are yet in the toolbox.

Towards a Theory of Responsibility

The industrial private sector of the economy could be said to have begun in the sixteenth century, and became the major player by the nineteenth, when some of the best examples of paternalist corporate citizenship (prompted as much by necessity as compassion, one suspects) can be found. The word 'capitalism' came into common usage in the mid-nineteenth century, being referred to just twice by Karl Marx in *Das Kapital* of 1867 (he preferred the phrase 'capitalist system'). In the twentieth century capitalism grew more ruthless, weakening its links to family businesses as companies grew larger, and took advantage of the opportunities for exploitation of emerging globalisation. Over that time the consensus around the purpose of private business has changed; the task for the rest of the twenty-first century is to change it further.

So what is the purpose of business? What started as the Friedmanite position:

To create profit for the owner/shareholder

... came to acknowledge that the market was not truly 'free':

To create profit for the owner/shareholder	To discharge responsibilities to wider stakeholders

A more specific definition of 'responsibility' developed through greater understanding of market forces and the growing reliance on taxation to fund 'public good':

To create profit for the owner/shareholder	To create goods and services for the market/consumer	To create tax revenue for the government/society	To create jobs for individuals and the economy

The theory of shared value brought in a fifth consideration:

To create profit for the owner/ shareholder	To create goods and services for the market/ consumer	To create tax revenue for the government/ society	To create jobs for individuals and the economy	To be a good corporate citizen; to create benefit for the community

Whereas the relative size of each box will be different in different circumstances, all five are genuine, accepted fields of responsibility. Mohammed Yunus's model of social business would see the fifth box, on corporate citizenship, dominate the model, but this is unrealistic in a capitalist company. However, that box will certainly need to grow if 'social return on investment' were to replace at least some of the financial return:

To create profit for the owner/ share-holder	To create goods and services for the market/ consumer	To create tax revenue for the government/ society	To create jobs for individuals and the economy	To be a good corporate citizen; to create benefit for the community

Of course, no serious analysis of an economy or company will break its activities down as simply as this, not least because the contents of the boxes are inter-related. Reputation management through being a good corporate citizen can generate market share, and with it jobs, taxation revenue and dividends. 'Community' may be a local or virtual group of people, or even a distant one, spread along a supply chain.

As we shall see in the later chapters on investment, a sixth box needs to be added: 'To respect and plan for the long-term future'. That means managing natural resources, limiting carbon emissions, planning to provide the next generation of required skills and simply ensuring that the business can be handed on in at least as sound a condition as it was inherited. Planning for the future is the classic dilemma of the pension fund: the obvious need to maximise profits now, to pay today's pension claimants, must not be allowed to jeopardise the needs of their children and grandchildren who will need sustainable pensions in fifty or a hundred years' time. This dilemma is made ever more acute by changing Western demographics, but in a less stark form it's a dilemma which faces every company.

We have seen that the different purposes of business are not in fact alternatives, but are complementary in a sustainable, socially engaged plan. Yes, the obligations to owners and to the market are fundamental; people set up businesses primarily to make a living, and they earn money by creating what the market can bear. The nation depends on the taxation revenue of business, and business depends on the commitment and engagement of its employees, customers and suppliers. But the true corporate citizen realises that being a good neighbour, behaving in ways which generate respect among peers and stakeholders, and planning to minimise the problems that our children and grandchildren will face actually makes good business sense too.

Figure 2.1 shows a maturation from Level 1 (basic or internal duty) to Level 2 (standard or external duty) and to Level 3 (advanced or global duty); most companies will be in transition (from Level 1 to Level 2, fewer from Level 2 to Level 3). It's important to stress that transition adds new duties and responsibilities rather than replacing others: a Level 3 company will respect all six of the responsibilities this scenario imposes on them.

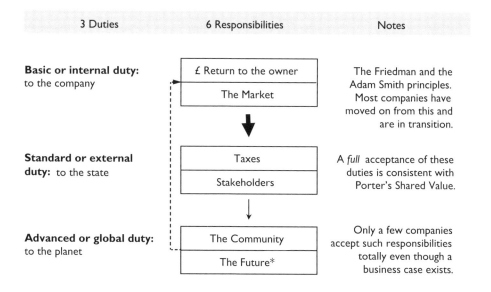

Figure 2.1   The duties and responsibilities of business

Notes:

*   This includes long-term investments as well as carbon and resource management.

-→ The business case for this duty generates a financial return.

At level two, for example, paying taxes – even willingly – is not enough: the attitude of seeing it as a duty and responsibility for the corporate citizen to generate taxation revenue to fund the common good is a state of mind. Those who create offshore subsidiaries with the specific purpose of avoiding legitimate demands for tax payments may be acting within the letter of the law but are not within the spirit of corporate citizenship. Very few for-profit companies are actively engaged in Level 3 and making the most of it. This is short-sighted, as investing in the 'Future' element makes good business sense and the 'Community' element leads, if transacted without hypocrisy, to innovation, new markets and enhanced reputation. Through this, more profits (see Level 1) can be generated.[35]

In short, there's a business case for high standards of corporate citizenship of which too few mainstream companies are taking advantage. We'll celebrate some for-profit companies that are leading the field of community engagement and benefiting from it in Chapter 8, 'The Good Guys'.

Business in Society

Whether capitalism is to be conscientious, responsible, social, progressive (Sainsbury, 2013), transitionary, breakthrough or sustainable, there are sufficient expert business thinkers at work to keep alive and thriving the idea that there can be a 'better way' for this massive force in society to be a massive force for good. But it does depend on awareness of long-term, triple bottom line responsibility and – perhaps most difficult of all – behaviour change. We have looked at the supply side of responsible capitalism – let us now examine the demand side of this new economic equation.

The fabric of British society in the twenty-first century faces crisis on several fronts. People disagree as to what proportion of blame is assigned to each of the two most commonly blamed causes, largely according to where they stand on the political spectrum. They are:

- the consequences of the global financial crisis of 2007–8, and our preparedness and response as exhibited by, for example, pendulum swings in bank lending;

---

35 My three levels reflect the 'breakdown, change-as-usual and breakthrough' stages of capitalism of John Elikington, which we met earlier in the chapter.

- the UK Coalition's economic policy of 'deficit reduction at all costs', prioritising austerity measures over measures to stimulate longer-term economic growth.

There were underlying imbalances already in post-Beveridge Britain which questioned the whole model of services to care for the weakest and most isolated in society. This has never been seen as a proper responsibility of the private sector, although some – Cadbury, Rowntree and others of the nineteenth century – adopted a paternalistic approach to their workforce and their communities. Nobody claims today that this onus should be the responsibility of the private sector alone, and many distrust the motives, track record, ability to collaborate or capacity to care of multinational corporates and are sceptical whether smaller enterprises can make a difference.

Yet in the second decade of this millennium our services are not working as they should: both the state, historically the principal provider, and the voluntary sector, which has always contributed informally or in partnership with the state, have struggled to meet demand comprehensively.

Albert Wenger, a partner at Union Square Ventures, New York-based investors, lays out what he sees as the critical challenge for capitalism today:[36]

> *Our problem as society is no longer how to make more stuff. Cars, clothes, computers are all becoming better and cheaper. Our biggest remaining problems require social innovation: how to distribute the benefits of progress more widely, how to live in better harmony with the environment and how to provide affordable access to education and healthcare for all.*

The simple answer is that the way to improve state services in the past has been to increase taxation income from business. Making business more profitable, growing the taxation base by creating jobs (and reducing the public cost of unemployment) is better than raising the tax rates for both businesses and individuals. But 'more of the same' is generally not the answer.

Five crucial trends are converging.

---

36 http://www.nytimes.com/2013/07/19/us/19iht-letter19.html?_r=2&.

I. WE HAVE REACHED THE LIMIT OF WHAT THE CENTRALISED STATE CAN PROVIDE

At the height of public spending, under Britain's Labour government, the number of people and communities that were socially isolated remained far too high for economic sustainability. In such cases communities don't feel in control of local environments and people are excluded from support through geography, poverty, disability, ignorance, old age, lack of opportunity, dependence on the informal economy or some combination of the above.

For evidence that the fringes of society have not been engaged by the sum of government community support programmes over generations, go to a council estate in one of Britain's poorest areas and see how long it takes to find each of these, for they are all there:

- a pensioner on a basic pension who won't accept money to which she's entitled because 'I don't accept charity';

- a young man who won't register to vote because he doesn't want the tax man to know where he lives;

- a teenage mother who is the daughter of a one-time teenage mother;

- an unemployed person with a disability who risks losing benefit unless he undertakes training for a job that isn't available;

- a benefit advice worker whose case load is too high to do the job properly;

- a person with mental health problems who doesn't receive the level of support he needs;

- a pensioner who leaves her home no more than twice a week;[37]

- an adult with a reading age in English of under 12;

---

37   The Calouste Gulbenkian Foundation commissioned interesting work from Demos on the role of the private sector in helping tackle loneliness, with some excellent small-scale examples (Bazalgette et al., 2012).

- a home that shouts out 'poverty' – broken furniture in the garden, no curtains, an ill-fitting or broken window;

- an ex-offender who receives no community support and is without a job or a permanent home.

Such shortfalls are not principally due to lack of government funding, nor is there a lack of political will to tackle them. The lack of success is caused by an innate inability of central government to function well at the fringes of its influence. Local councils have been emasculated as they are seen by Whitehall as an alternative power base, posing a threat to central government rather than creating an opportunity. Personalisation and localisation of services – two concepts which command wide consensus and are at the heart of the government's professed 'Big Society' ethos – have made operational challenges even stronger. Emasculating councils was wrong, but personalisation and localism are right, popular and essential, and they can't be delivered effectively from the centre.

2. SERVICE-PROVIDING CHARITIES ARE SUFFERING FOR NOT HAVING ACHIEVED GREATER DIVERSITY OF FUNDING

For generations, charities depended on individual and philanthropic giving. Such public services as they came to provide naturally complemented or extended those of the state, thus it was perfectly natural for the state to look to the voluntary sector when seeking to diversify, extend or deepen its capacity to serve. Indeed, such funding was seized upon with alacrity, to the extent that charities' lack of historical need to protect themselves against funding 'shock' left them highly vulnerable in the new era of austerity. In the good times they should have better prepared a broader funding base and reduced dependence on the taxpayer – a caution that applies to both the giants and the minnows who have taken the Queen's shilling over the years.

There are risks inherent in being funded from diverse sources: individual funders (such as foundations linked to private sector corporations or high-net worth individuals) may have their own agendas which can pervert the purpose of charitable activity, however well-intentioned; the quality, pace and scale of activity funded in this way may not complement state-provided services as well as they might, and the worst aspect of the postcode lottery may be exacerbated, namely that areas with most need may not get the most appropriate provision. This is demonstrated dramatically in recent research on company giving (Walker, 2013), which shows that most of it relates to the location of the giver, and not the level of need.

This situation demands a new and imaginative role for councils as commissioners and arbiters of standards, equity and fairness while being friends of both beneficiaries and the broad diversity of providers.

3. THE PRIVATE SECTOR IS THE NATION'S BIGGEST UNTAPPED POOL OF RESOURCES

Taxation is the extraction of cash (largely) from the private sector for public good, yet a whole industry has grown up around tax avoidance, and the line between avoidance and evasion has become blurred, to say the least. As capital is now truly global, it's unlikely that taxation can wring much more blood out of this particular stone.

However, private business isn't just a cash cow; it encompasses employees and other potential community resources. Just 3 per cent of UK employees undertake payroll giving – a tenth of the US figure. Just one UK employee in every 14 has been a community volunteer on their employer's time, whereas in the USA it's one in three. Skills, especially for growing capacity or running a business, are among the most powerful things that business can donate to the voluntary sector of the future if public services are to be delivered collaboratively and sustainably. The systematic, strategic and purposeful donation of products, goods, time, skills and services has grown from a one-off exercise corporations carry out at times of natural disaster to an everyday occurrence.

At its most superficial, this is done to tick CSR boxes. At its most profound, it defines the relationship of the corporate citizen to society, as we shall see in Chapter 8.

4. DEMANDS ARE GROWING FOR BUSINESS TO BE BOTH RESPONSIBLE AND ETHICAL

'Irresponsible' sums up the corporate behaviour that triggered the 2008 banking crash. Today Barclays, Google, Amazon and Starbucks – among the best private sector supporters of UK communities through their donations of hours, skills and in kind – must respect the public belief that excellence in social responsibility isn't an alternative to paying 'fair' taxes, but its partner. At the other end of the scale, Unilever has switched to annual rather than quarterly financial reporting to make it more attuned to long-term sustainability, while Serco has embarked upon genuine partnerships with charities designed to increase their operating capacities. Investors generally are moving slowly towards achieving social outcomes rather than purely financial returns.

If we really are 'all in this together', then there are green shoots in the field of responsibility.

5. THERE IS A BUSINESS CASE FOR GOOD CORPORATE CITIZENSHIP

In international conglomerates and corner shops, staid family businesses and pulsating e-commerce, company engagement with local communities, perhaps through the medium of charity, is good news. Community involvement is the conjoined twin of employee engagement, itself a stimulus for greater worker satisfaction, loyalty and productivity. Volunteering generally, including employee volunteering, is known to support good mental health leading to reduced time lost through sickness. A meaningful corporate responsibility policy, integrated into mainstream business practice, can promote innovation, attract investment, help develop employee skills, loyalty and sense of purpose, increase shareholder return, build reputation and protect against market shock.

Some people in all three sectors and across the political spectrum recognise the power and potential behind these five truths. Many in business are ready to come on board the responsibility bus and accept that 'stakeholder' means more than 'shareholder'. Big corporates like Marks & Spencer demonstrate that thoroughly ethical behaviour in the community, the environment and supply chain can be profitable while helping society meet the myriad challenges ahead. We can't be far from having a business observing a community challenge and recruiting a charity partner to help address it, rather than the other way round.

Traditional views of the public, private and voluntary sectors, each in its place, helped us throughout the twentieth century. They will hold us back in the globalised, interdependent world of the twenty-first.

The last word goes to Sir Roger Carr, President of the CBI and Chairman of Centrica. Writing in *The Guardian* in October 2012, he neatly brings all of these issues together in a single passage. Its significance lies not in its content – succinct, to the point and acutely relevant it may be – but by the fact that it was delivered not by an academic, a politician or a bleeding heart optimist, but by a captain of industry:

> *All industries are wresting with similar challenges as we seek to balance the pursuit of prosperity in our economic world with desire for a healthy and long lasting planet.*

The challenges for business are not simply environmental, but also about the need for an overriding commitment to responsible capitalism. It is clear that unless we sustain business as a force for good in society we will lose the glue that binds people with the wealth creating bedrock on which society depends.

All businesses are increasingly judged not just on how much money they make, but how they make money; business behaviours and business performance are increasingly inseparable.[38]

Let's explore further what this might mean.

---

38 http://www.guardian.co.uk/sustainable-business/responsible-capitalism-businesses-reputation.

Chapter 3
A Very Social Enterprise

Corporations not only have citizens, they are citizens. They have rights in the societies where they operate, but they also have responsibilities which law and custom impose upon them. We increasingly expect our corporate citizens to act decently. At the very least they need an informal licence to operate ....

Charles Handy[1]

Imitation is the sincerest form of flattery.

The way in which supporters of 'good causes', 'progress' and 'equality' have embraced the tools and processes of the private, for-profit sector since the latter years of the twentieth century has been phenomenal; and the phenomenon of social enterprise, which employs people, produces goods and services and sells them into a market just like the traditional capitalist model does, deserves a chapter of its own. Often the only observable way to distinguish a social enterprise from a for-profit company is the replacement of profit with a different, 'responsible', motive. It's relatively easy to recognise a not-for-profit business with a social or environmental purpose when you see one, but it can prove very difficult to define 'social enterprise' in the abstract. Indeed, no two countries in which the concept is recognised define social enterprise in the same way. In France it's only a generation since the concept of a registered company designed to do something other than make a profit was as good as illegal.

The best comprehensive definition of social enterprise is Australian. It says:

Social enterprises are organisations that:

- *Are led by an economic, social, cultural, or environmental mission consistent with a public or community benefit*
- *Trade to fulfil their mission*

---

1   C. Handy, *The Hungry Spirit: New Thinking for a New World*, Arrow, 1998.

- *Derive a substantial portion of their income from trade and*
- *Reinvest the majority of their profit/surplus in the fulfilment of their mission.[2]*

There are perhaps 20,000 social enterprises in Australia, approximately one fifth of the country's not-for-profit organisations. Social Business Australia is an active organisation which supports all forms of 'values-led business', including social enterprises and co-operatives; since 2012 the Australian government has carried out a root-and-branch review of support for the not-for-profit sector designed to grow its capacity and potential.[3]

The definition used in the 2002 UK Department for Trade and Industry report *Social Enterprise: A Strategy for Success* has the advantage of brevity:

> *A business with primarily social objectives whose surpluses are principally reinvested for that purpose.*

Brevity, 'primarily' and 'principally' are all ingredients of ambiguity, but in the confusion stakes the British are amateurs compared to this American attempt:

> *Social enterprises directly address social needs through their products and services or through the numbers of disadvantaged people they employ.*
>
> *Social enterprises use earned revenue strategies to pursue a double or triple bottom line, either alone (as a social sector business, in either the private or the non-profit sector) or as a significant part of a non-profit's mixed revenue stream that also includes charitable contributions and public sector subsidies.*

Employing people with disabilities is not an 'or', as it does not in itself bestow any of the economic criteria of social enterprise; nor are 'charitable contributions and public sector subsidies' necessary parts of the definition (nor should they be, though they may be present).

Many countries have no legal definition of social enterprise, while in India all non-governmental organisations (NGOs), of which there are two million,

---

2   http://www.socialtraders.com.au/finding-australia%E2%80%99s-social-enterprise-sector-summary-report.
3   http://acnc.gov.au/ACNC/Pblctns/Rpts/NFP/ACNC/Publications/Reports/NFPreport.aspx.

are regarded as the same in law and all are allowed to raise funds for 'non-business activities'.

The term 'social enterprise' may have been first used around 1978, and in 1983 the first registered British social enterprise may have been Community Routes, a co-operatively owned minibus company in Greater Manchester, a company limited by guarantee. Judging by the number of American dissertations with the word 'non-profit' in the title, the late twentieth century was a Golden Age: 1 in 1959, 7 in the 1960s, 49 in the 1970s, 238 in the 1980s – though 'non-profit' in America includes charities and foundations. In Italy a movement of not-for-profit co-operatives employing people with disabilities grew in the early 1990s, dedicated to the workers' rehabilitation and training rather than to making a profit from their products, prompting the use of the term 'social economy'.

The Skoll World Forum is an annual three-day conference including workshops hosted by Oxford University since 2004, involving 1,000 social entrepreneurs, researchers and others with an interest in social enterprise. Its claim that 'Social entrepreneurs are society's change agents, creators of innovations that disrupt the status quo and transform our world'[4] may sound like hyperbole, but isn't without merit. Certainly social enterprise today isn't just about doing things differently, but about doing different things. It can be an agent of empowerment of individuals and communities, a tool of sustainability at a time of economic stress, and ultimately a way of changing the balance of values in society towards a greater spirit of common cause.

In the early days there was a risk that what is essentially a simple concept – the not-for-profit company with a social purpose – could become ever more complex. Was an organisation which sold ethically produced or fairly traded goods different in character from one which was more mainstream in its output? Was a social purpose adequate, or should it have to demonstrate social impact? Would 'democratic ownership' of the enterprise make it more authentic than if it were owned by a social entrepreneur?

Even today there's debate about some of the finer features of social enterprise. Should advisory or grant-giving functions be removed from the definition so that it only includes organisations producing and/or selling goods and/or services? Should there be a minimum requirement in respect of the number of paid employees? The idea that owners of a given social enterprise

---

4   http://skollworldforum.org/about/what-is-social-entrepreneurship/.

ought to be associated with the specific community of interests that it was established to further, that it should be self-help in character, has been mooted, but this would be exclusive and thus outside the spirit of the movement. All of these questions could divide the social enterprise movement by creating artificial and unhelpful distinctions.

None of these additional criteria matter if the social enterprise is a Community Interest Company (CIC). The legal form of CIC was established in Britain in 2005 as a way of bestowing legal recognition on the social enterprise model, and in 2010 the newly emboldened movement created the Social Enterprise Mark (SEM) as an internationally recognised certification scheme with defined criteria.[5] The SEM, developed in the south-west of England, no doubt also serves as a marketing device. By this time it was clear that social enterprise had developed a kudos which gave it access to low-interest loans (from social investors) for delivering goods and services in a cost-effective way. It helps that people who work for them tend to be satisfied with generally lower rates of pay than in the private sector. Even in the sale of goods on the high street customers like to think that their money is going to a good cause rather than to line the pockets of the rich, as the charity shop movement is well aware. The SEM was also a useful precursor to the Social Value Act 2012, of which more later; in some respects it's a version of the American B Corp (see Chapter 6).

The idea behind the CIC is credited to Stephen Lloyd, senior partner at charity lawyers Bates, Wells and Braithwaite. While a social enterprise can be a company limited by shares or by guarantee, a mutual or privately owned, its operations are limited by CIC status to ensure that it stays 'on mission':

- A maximum of 35 per cent of any profits can be paid to owners as dividends (to ensure that most profits are available to 'the cause').

- Investors may be paid a return on their investment at no more than 4 per cent above base rate (to emphasise that they are committing to a cause, and not principally to a return).

---

5   The Social Enterprise Mark is awarded to any company that registers itself according to the following criteria: it has social and/or environmental aims, has its own constitution and governance, earns at least half of its revenue from trading (or as a new start-up, plans to), spends at least half of its profits on its social and environmental aims, will distribute residual assets to social/environmental causes if dissolved, and demonstrates social value as defined by the Social Value Act 2012. See http://www.socialenterprisemark.org.uk.

- The CIC is subject to an 'asset lock' to ensure that assets (including surplus profits) are retained for 'the cause' and can only be transferred, should the company fail, to another appropriate asset-locked CIC or charity.

A charity can't be a CIC; a CIC can't have 'political' aims or engage in political activities. However, it's becoming common practice for charities to own a subsidiary CIC. Equally, it's not necessary for an organisation to qualify as a CIC to be recognised as a social enterprise.

The two figures laid down as maxima in the CIC definition above are arbitrary, but they are appropriate and proportionate: 35 per cent profit distribution is unlikely to amount to a lot when divided between dozens or hundreds of co-operative members, but (as my mother used to appreciate when quoting her Co-op 'divvy' number of 6185) small tokens of appreciation do help to keep people on board. The market for social investment is growing, yet access to finance remains the principal barrier to the growth of social and community enterprise. The base plus 4 per cent maximum return on investors' contributions forges a balance between the pressures of supply and demand in the social investment market.

The status of Industrial and Provident Society (IPS) has been recognised in British law for 150 years, and also exists in Ireland and New Zealand. An IPS can carry out any business function except investment for profit. It can be either a bona fide co-operative or have a community benefit purpose; the movement gave rise to building societies and credit unions, and today many housing and agricultural co-operatives and social clubs still have the status. The CIC can be thought of as a modern and more flexible alternative to the IPS. In the USA the L3C is roughly of equivalent status to the CIC, although the main purpose of an L3C is to ensure that investments from foundations and other social ('programme-related') investors are kept 'on mission' and tax-compliant rather than restrict how the company's profits are used.

In Australia they have tried to define subsets of social enterprise. This is of questionable purpose, but it's interesting to get an idea of the diversity of forms.[6] Of 20,000 social enterprises, 62 per cent were more than ten years old (in 2007–2008), they had from zero to 4,500 paid employees, and unpaid volunteers ranged from zero to 56,000; 85 per cent of their income was 'earned' (either through open market sales or through service delivery contracts),

---

6   http://www.socialtraders.com.au.

and most retained and reinvested profits, with a small proportion distributing them among members, passing them to a parent organisation or donating them to charity. Their purpose falls into three categories – employment of disadvantaged or marginalised groups, service delivery or fundraising for charity – and into nine categories for structure: Co-operatives and Mutuals, Fair Trade Organisations, Intermediate Labour Market Companies training disadvantaged job seekers, Charitable Business Ventures, Community Enterprises (such as a local service spin-out), Community Development Finance Institutions and hybrids, along with two other types that primarily employ people with disabilities.

The City of London Corporation is active in maximising the social value generated by its supply chains in a way which it hopes will be attractive to private businesses. This includes a major expansion in the number and value of contracts awarded to social enterprises by both the Corporation and businesses in the City. Such initiatives are promoted by campaigns like Heart of the City,[7] and are close to the heart of Fiona Woolf, only the second woman in half a millennium to be Lord Mayor of London, in 2014.

The '50 in 250' campaign[8] was pioneered by the Corporation to recruit 50 companies operating locally to include at least five social enterprises in their supply chain within 250 days (a working year). Each early adopter would be a 'forward thinking, socially sustainable company that will help pave the way for a new change in business', and their number included KPMG and BITC's 2011 Business of the Year, the Wates Group. 'Social Enterprise' was defined as a company holding the Social Enterprise Mark. The campaign is universally applicable, and every procurer should consider joining it.

Social Enterprise UK (SEUK) publishes a helpful primer on social enterprise which celebrates diversity within the movement and reports growing interest in the sector.[9] There are hints for those considering a career as a social entrepreneur, whether motivated by experiencing the thrill of leadership, chasing the goal of social or environmental benefit, running an existing public service better or opting out of the 'rat race'.

Peter Holbrook, Chief Executive of SEUK, is, as ever, passionate about the cause:

---

7   http://www.theheartofthecity.com/about-us.
8   http://www.socialenterprisemark.org.uk/50in250/.
9   http://www.socialenterprise.org.uk/uploads/editor/files/Publications/Social_Enterprise_
     Explained.pdf.

> *The old ways of getting things done – public services versus charities,*
> *versus private enterprise – are starting to merge, and the future is*
> *hybrid. One of the ways we can see this is that Social Enterprise UK*
> *is getting a constant stream of delegations visiting from emerging*
> *economies like South Korea and India. They need public services and*
> *they have their social problems but they don't want to find themselves*
> *in ten or twenty years having to service a large bureaucratic public*
> *sector or unsustainable charitable sector. They're going straight for*
> *social enterprise. It's a bit like countries who don't have a landline*
> *infrastructure for phones leapfrogging straight to mobile technology.*

SEUK also sees the value and attraction of integrating social enterprise into the supply chain of 'traditional' public and private sector bodies, and it promotes a website to further that end.[10]

The whole variety of legal forms adopted by social enterprises, mutuals and businesses with a social purpose falls within our concept of 'social business'. 'Social business' has no broadly agreed definition, other than that at least some of the company's activities should have a primarily social purpose. This definition would not exclude a for-profit company behaving in part in a socially conscious manner.

The State of Social Enterprise

The social enterprise movement in Britain has grown rapidly in recent years – negligible in 2004, it grew to 68,000 businesses in 2011, employing a million people and with a combined annual turnover of £24 billion.[11]

The People's Business is the State of Social Enterprise Survey for 2013, conducted by Social Enterprise UK and sponsored by Royal Bank of Scotland (RBS) Banking Group.[12] It found that three quarters of social enterprises had trade as their main source of income, a third principally traded with the general public, and a quarter with public sector institutions. Over half traded with the public sector, compared to just a quarter of SMEs, and while public procurement policy is thought to be a growing barrier to trade, there was little confidence (albeit based on only a few months experience) that the

---

10 http://www.buyse.co.uk.

11 http://www.bis.gov.uk/assets/biscore/enterprise/docs/b/12-566-business-support-for-social-enterprises-longitudinal.pdf.

12 http://www.socialenterprise.org.uk/uploads/files/2013/07/the_peoples_business.pdf.

Social Value Act would address this effectively. This was especially true for smaller social enterprises.

Social enterprises were more optimistic about future trade than they were two years previously or than SMEs currently were. This isn't surprising, as more social enterprises were growing and fewer were shrinking than SMEs in general, and social enterprise start-ups were running at three times the figure for SMEs. One in nine had a turnover of under £10,000, while just one social enterprise in 12 had a turnover of more than £5 million per year.

Half had sought access to external finance in the previous year – twice the level for SMEs, though access to finance was identified as the biggest barrier to growth. The mean figure sought was £58,000, well below the threshold for either conventional or specialist social enterprise investors. Hopefully this will be addressed by the future financing programme of Community Development Finance Institutions through Big Society Capital and the Chancellor's announcement of a tax incentive for investment in social enterprise from 2014.[13]

Social enterprises were more likely than both SMEs and FTSE100 companies to have female or ethnic minority leaders and to work in deprived communities; newer social enterprises were more likely to be engaged in health, social care and education than older ones. One social enterprise leader in three had a public sector background, and one in three was from the private sector. Only one in 20 was a complete novice.

However they are defined, their social purpose and the low priority they accord profit distinguish social enterprises from mainstream capitalist hegemony. Some, like *The Big Issue* in Britain and Greyston Bakery in USA, have already graduated from being a stand-alone enterprise to fostering a charity to work with the most excluded and vulnerable people. The Eden Project and Divine Chocolate have become household names. Hackney Community Transport may not yet be that, but from being a local supplier of minibus services for elderly and disabled people a few years ago it has become HCT Group, its big red buses providing over 12 million passenger trips each year across London. HCT reinvests profits from its commercial work into transport services and projects in local communities. Jamie Oliver's Fifteen is a splendid restaurant convenient for the City of London, employing apprentices from challenging backgrounds and donating all profits to the company's

---

13 http://www.theguardian.com/social-enterprise-network/2013/mar/20/social-enterprise-investment-leaders-budget-tax-relief.

Food Foundation. The Brigade restaurant, a former fire station at London Bridge, recruits homeless people and trains them in catering and hospitality skills.

A new feature in the not-for-profit world is also borrowed from the private sector: franchising. The title of Dan Berelowitz's article 'The McDonald's Template for Social Change'[14] would have been heretical a few years ago, but he draws astute and insightful parallels between the way the burger chain has grown and the rapid recent rise of the Trussell Trust in response to the growing need for food banks in Britain during the current decade: the two work on comparable franchise models.

This was the advice McDonald's offered on franchising:

> *Pick your franchisee wisely, invest in them, create a network and connect the people within it to each other, create clear shared financial agreements – money is where the most discomfort comes for franchiser and franchisee. Importantly, be sensitive to the local environment and need and don't standardise at the expense of cultural sensitivity. This is no 'project in a box' quick win, but a different approach.*

The Trussell Trust gave its first franchise permission in 2004. There were 55 food banks in 2010 and over 350 in 2013, with three new ones opening each week as demand grows.[15] Franchising in the social sector is slightly more complex than in the private sector as franchisees are usually community groups and organisations rather than individuals, often church groups. A franchise 'start-up pack' can be purchased from the Trussell Trust; the quality of its service and the strength of its brand – voted Britain's most admired charity in 2013 – gives the franchisee confidence in the product.

The Social Value Act

The UK Public Services (Social Value) Act 2012 calls upon all public bodies, local government and government agencies to consider how local economic, social and environmental factors could be enhanced through their own commissioning and purchasing policies. For example, if two bids for a tender were similar but one company took on more apprentices than the other,

---

14 http://www.socialenterpriselive.com/section/comment/management/20121122/the-mcdonalds-template-social-change.
15 http://www.theguardian.com/society/2013/apr/24/number-people-food-banks-triples.

or actively sponsored a local good cause, or promoted employee volunteering more, or were better at recycling, then they could be said to bring additional social value compared to their competitors and be awarded the contract – even if theirs wasn't the lowest tender. It's seen as offering opportunities for social enterprises to win public sector contracts, even though the Act is weaker than its author initially intended.

The bill which delivered the Act had the longest gestation of any private members' legislation in recent history; it practically disappeared several times as it laboured its way through the legislative process. Sponsored by the then newcomer Conservative MP Chris White, the bill should have sailed through both the Commons and Lords with little problem as it both embodied the Prime Minister's flagship 'Big Society' idea and built upon many of the measures the previous Labour government had brought in. White launched it in October 2010 and it received Royal Assent in March 2012 – a feat of patience only made possible (for a private member's bill) because of Parliament's long sitting between one state opening and the next, unprecedented in modern times. (Private members' bills usually succeed, or more often fail, within nine months). The Civil Society Minister Nick Hurd had, as an Opposition MP in the previous Parliament, seen his own Sustainable Communities Act become law with all-party support, but it fell to him to chaperone the White Bill without – and this was the stumbling block on the Conservative benches – appearing to add to red tape and as a result 'distort' markets.

The solution was to make it a permissive bill, to allow councils and others to assign tenders according to social value criteria without obliging them to do so. On that basis the MP got his bill through, Labour acknowledged that some progress had been made, and the government could live with an Act to which its opposition would justifiably have generated accusations of hypocrisy.

It came into force in January 2013. Already some local authorities, such as Birmingham City Council and the London Boroughs of Camden and Croydon, are using the procurement provisions of the Act to enhance their communities for all they are worth.[16] Birmingham in particular has laid down a code of social

---

16 http://bssec.org.uk/birmingham-city-council-adopts-social-value-policy/. Social Enterprise UK publishes its own guide to the Social Value Act – http://www.socialenterprise.org.uk/uploads/files/2012/03/public_services_act_2012_a_brief_guide_web_version_final.pdf –and the Cabinet Office publishes the official guide: https://www.gov.uk/government/uploads/system/uploads/attachment_data/file/79273/Public_Services_Social_Value_Act_2012_PPN.pdf.

value conduct, a standard of corporate citizenship, to which all organisations seeking to trade with the council should adhere.[17]

As presently constituted, the Act only applies to public service procurement and does not alter European Union procurement rules. As it's only permissive, what are the prospects of extending it to cover private sector procurement?[18] Now that really would make a difference – and some leading businesses would actively support such a move.[19]

Charity Shops

Good causes raise £1.2 billion a year from Britain's network of charity shops, with a 25 per cent profit margin. Against economic trends, the number of such shops has recently risen to over 10,000; one in ten support the British Heart Foundation, and Cancer Research UK has the second largest chain, of over 550. They 'employ' 200,000 volunteers and recycle or reuse 360,000 tons of textiles each year. They are increasingly used by charities as campaign centres or advice surgeries on the high street. They are generally, but not exclusively, found where there's high demand for low retail prices: over half of us use them, averaging nine purchases each year, with value for money on a tight budget being a major driver. Three quarters of households donate goods to them.[20]

Charity shops are not normally regarded as social enterprises, but they meet any such definition to a tee: they trade by selling products, they employ people, and their aim is primarily to maximise income for a good cause – a charity – rather than line the pockets of an individual owner. While most will be managed by one or more paid professional staff, they rely heavily on volunteers as sales assistants and back-room sorters and on paying nothing for their wares, relying almost totally on books, clothes and household goods donated by the public. Specialist charity shops are a recent trend, especially for second-hand books (Oxfam) and used furniture in large high street stores (British Heart Foundation). The shops even make money from selling surplus

---

17 The government has published a positive assessment of the Act after its first year of operation: https://www.gov.uk/government/publications/public-services-social-value-act-2012-1-year-on.

18 I contributed this suggestion, among others, to a 2013 UK government consultation on improving levels of CSR and I agreed to be quoted in the resulting document which was to be published in December 2013. This did not happen. As of April 2014 publication is, inexplicably, no longer scheduled.

19 Personal conversations.

20 Personal communications with the Charity Retail Association.

materials in bulk to the recycling industry when they have been unable to sell them otherwise. But the way they work is unfair and anti-competitive, say some high street traders.

One bone of contention is the 80 per cent relief in business rates charities are entitled to claim from local councils, which for-profit retailers in the same marketplace can't claim. Given charity shops' low overheads, they say, other small retailers are being put out of business. Is this chicken or egg? The Charity Retail Association claims that 'unfair competition' is a false analysis,[21] as even in places like Rochdale (where there are eight charity shops within the 100-metre main street) the charity shop isn't displacing a thriving boutique, but an empty store which earns nothing for anyone.[22] They have a point: more than one town centre shop in nine was empty in 2012. This was due to a number of complex causes, among which 'anti-competitive' rate relief is probably insignificant. Other factors include the state of the economy, planning policy and changes in shopping habits, favouring out-of-town or online providers. Mary Portas, called in to advise the government on town centre retail development, was lobbied by the private retail sector to campaign for an end to business rate relief for charities. Instead she sensibly called for it to be extended to cover start-up private sector businesses too.

A charity shop is expected to sell second-hand goods, and is restricted in the range and value of new products it can sell, as these could be in direct competition with shops which do not receive rate relief; Christmas greetings cards are commonly in this category. One way in which charities compete with each other is on the holier-than-thou front: 'When you buy this £1 card, 94p goes directly to feed starving children!' 'But 96p from this £1 card helps rescue disabled donkeys!'

Comparing overheads is an unreal and unhelpful exercise. Having low overheads tells you nothing about the quality of service the charity delivers nor its efficiency on the ground: when choosing between washing powders, we don't ask what proportion of the price goes on overheads, so why should we apply that criterion to Christmas cards? Of course we want the maximum amount of our donation to reach the cause for which it was intended, and we don't want to encourage profligacy, but an enterprise which keeps its overheads unreasonably low may be exploiting its employees, failing to utilise

21 The CRA position is supported by an independent report from the thinktank Demos: http://www.demos.co.uk/publications/givingsomethingback.
22 http://www.thirdsector.co.uk/news/1147855/.

the best professionals available and helping propagate the unfortunate image of charities as amateurish do-gooders.

American professional fundraiser Dan Pallotta bemoans the fact that although businesses have permission to fail in the public mind, often with the expectation that they will 'bounce back', the not-for-profit sector is given no such leeway: if Disney makes a loss on a $200 million film, nobody cares, he says, but a charity or social enterprise which carries out a single initiative which fails to meet expectations would suffer zero tolerance. Here he is again:

> We launched the breast cancer 'three days' [bicycle ride] with an initial investment of $350,000 in risk capital. Within just five years we had multiplied that 554 times into $194 million, after all expenses, for breast cancer research.
>
> Now if you are a philanthropist really interested in breast cancer what would make more sense – go out and find the most innovative researcher in the world and give her $350,000 for research or give her a fundraising department with $350,000 to multiply it into $194 million for breast cancer research?
>
> 2002 was our most successful year ever, we netted for breast cancer alone, that year, $71 million after all expenses. And then we went out of business, suddenly and traumatically. Why? Well, the short story is our sponsor split on us. They wanted to distance themselves from us because we were being crucified in the media for investing 40 percent of the gross in recruitment and customer service and the magic of the experience and there is no accounting terminology to describe that kind of investment and growth in the future other than this demonic label of 'overhead'. So, on one day, all 350 of our great employees lost their jobs – because they were labeled 'overhead'.
>
> Our sponsor went and tried the events on their own, the overhead went up, the net income for breast cancer research went down by 84 percent or $60 million in one year. This is what happens when we confuse morality with frugality.[23]

Every professional fundraiser knows that you have to spend money to make money. Why do we expect risk-taking professionalism in the for-profit sector, and bumbling, risk-free, low-return amateurism in the charity sector? Perhaps the growth of social enterprise – bringing together the values of the third sector with the professional skills of the private sector – is the antidote to this most

---

23 http://www.youtube.com/watch?v=bfAzi6D5FpM&feature=youtu.be.

unsatisfactory state of affairs. Failing that, Pallotta clearly shows that there's a market for professional for-profit fundraisers – as long as public perception can square the circle and accept that this is no contradiction.

Sponsoring Social Enterprise

A number of companies in areas outside the finance industry are using surplus cash to invest directly in social enterprises as a way of helping communities and deprived groups, motivated by both moral and business reasons such as reinforcing a supply chain or growing skills in a community. Sensibly, some such companies have pooled their activities and resources to create The Social Business Trust.[24] Since 2010 this consortium of Bain (consultancy), Clifford Chance (lawyers), Credit Suisse, Ernst & Young (now EY), Permira (private equity) and Thomson Reuters, along with British Gas since 2012, has invested both capital and professional expertise into a portfolio of social enterprises and charities. Since 2010 its investments of £4.2 million (30 per cent in cash and 10,000 hours of professional services) were shared between seven enterprises, generating 46 per cent growth in year one and 95 per cent in year two. A total of 105,000 people used the investees' services in 2011–12, and this doubled in 2012–13.

Qualifying charities or CICs must already be established in the UK, must turn over at least £1.5 million, generated largely through trading, and have a year's audited accounts and at least 1,000 beneficiaries each year. They include Bikeworks, which finds employment for 73 per cent of its trainees and helps over 1,100 people from disadvantaged backgrounds to develop cycling skills each year; the Shakespeare Schools Festival, engaging 25,000 children through schools, disproportionately from disadvantaged backgrounds, and Moneyline, a low-interest alternative to small payday loans. For the London Early Years Foundation, Permira gave financial advice, EY seconded a consultant for six months, Bain helped draw up a business plan, and British Gas advised on customer service as the organisation was restructured and its beneficiary list hit 2,000.[25]

The construction company Wates has a long history of investment in local social enterprise for community development purposes, including the part-time

---

24 http://www.socialbusinesstrust.org.
25 http://www.theguardian.com/social-enterprise-network/2013/aug/07/big-businesses-support-social-enterprises.

seconding of managers; the Co-operative Group provides free banking for CICs with a balance of up to £1 million and access to the Co-operative Enterprise Hub.[26] 'Supporting co-operatives' is one of the group's priorities in its three-year Ethical Plan published in 2011, during which time the Hub will invest £7.5 million; in previous years 521 new and 165 established co-operatives had received advice, support or investment from it. During 2008–10 the 'co-operative economy' of Britain grew by 15 per cent in both value and number of enterprises.

A similar agglomeration to the Social Stock Exchange (see Chapter 2) is sponsored by RBS: the SE100,[27] described as 'a valuable tool for individual organisations which are using an enterprise model to deliver their social mission, to help them manage and build success'. It includes over 3,400 social enterprises, including 761 on the Growth Index, listed according to their percentage growth over three years. RBS also has a community banking unit with a £5 million annual budget aimed at those social and community enterprises which may not qualify for mainstream finance. Working together with the Big Lottery Fund, Lloyds Banking Group provides grants and mentoring for start-up and growing social enterprises, while the School for Startups is a competitive programme run by Barclays bank to support five social enterprises each year led by young people.

While most of these sponsors are finance companies, every major business has spare capacity that could support social and community enterprises in its locality with loans and mentoring.

Deloitte's Social Innovation Pioneers programme is a case in point: a £1 million annual investment produces annual growth in selected social enterprises of over 40 per cent. But it is in procurement that real changes are being made: visit the Deloitte head office and you may see a kitchen worker from Blue Sky, a social enterprise which creates paid work for ex-offenders; use paper provided by Wildheart, where all profits go into microfinance in the developing world, or meet a software tester who has joined through Autism Works. As SEUK points out, for a company like Deloitte with a half-billion-pound procurement budget, diverting half of one per cent through social enterprise would make more of a difference than any known CSR programme.[28]

26 http://www.co-operative.coop/enterprisehub/About-the-hub/.
27 https://se100.net/about#phases.
28 http://www.deloitte.com/view/en_gb/uk/about/community-investment/social-innovation/.

Credit Unions

Banking is, of course, a fundamental building block of capitalism, and the 'tools' of banking are relatively simple: charging interest on loans made against assets comprised of voluntary deposits upon which a lower rate of interest is paid. The difference in interest rates (plus charges for services) creates the profit. Banking has undoubtedly borne the brunt of criticism following the recent crisis, with serious questions being asked about risk aversion and why loans have not been forthcoming to the parts of the economy that need them, such as SMEs. An old joke says that if I owe the bank a thousand dollars, I have a problem; if I owe them a million dollars, *they* have a problem. To which must now be added: if the bank has a debt of a billion dollars, *we all* have a problem.

As poor people feel (and are) alienated from a banking system which is not inclined to help them, they become vulnerable to exorbitant payday loan merchants. This is why the Church of England has chosen to help credit unions by providing premises and other assistance in supporting poorer communities.

It's not surprising, then, that in recent years there has been a tendency to go 'back to basics' to the benefit of the credit union movement.

Credit unions were recognised in UK law in 1979, although their history spans a century before that (as industrial and provident societies). Worldwide, 118 million people are members of 40,000 credit unions. Seventy per cent of Irish people are members, as are 43 per cent of North Americans, but engagement in Britain and Continental Europe is much lower. Credit unions employ basic banking techniques, with the proviso that depositors are active and engaged owners, lending attracts low interest rates, and they are normally linked to a distinct and relatively small geographical area, often one suffering deprivation. A few, larger and more sophisticated, offer chequing accounts and other banking services.[29]

The Dutch banking giant Rabobank started life as a small agricultural credit union.

---

29 For more information about UK credit unions, see http://www.abcul.org/home.

The John Lewis Partnership

One of the country's largest retailers started as a for-profit purveyor of wool, silk and haberdashery. From his small premises and handcart in 1864, eschewing all advertising, John Lewis built what is now the UK's third largest private company (one whose shares are not traded on the stock exchange).

Unusually for a rags to riches story, John Lewis's Oxford Street store is still on its original site, although it has grown considerably in size. Today the John Lewis Partnership has 85,000 partners (employees), 40 stores, 300 branches of its Waitrose supermarket (expanded from the 10 grocery stores acquired in 1937) and a thriving online business.

In 1905 Lewis acquired the Peter Jones store in Sloane Square and gave each of his sons a 25 per cent share in his business. The elder son, Spedan, was convalescing from a riding accident when it struck him how unfair it was that even lying on his bed he was earning as much as the entire workforce of the Oxford Street shop. He set about planning how to make the business more democratic and equitable.

By 1914 Spedan was the 29-year-old manager of Peter Jones. He set up staff committees and discovered the commercial advantages of working more closely with the workforce while improving their conditions of work, eventually granting them profit-sharing status as 'partners'. Partners at Peter Jones were entitled to three weeks' annual holiday, while those in Oxford Street had only two. Lewis senior did not approve of such practices, and the two men were at loggerheads for many years – in 1920 the original store was crippled by a five-week strike when even Queen Mary spoke out in favour of the staff. It was only when Spedan inherited the Oxford Street store upon his father's death in 1928 (having bought out his brother's inheritance) that the extra holidays, shorter hours, greater consultation (not least through the independent *Gazette*) and better perks enjoyed by the Peter Jones employees became available there. Spedan immediately turned the organisation into a public limited company, and then a legal partnership, in which an accountable trust represented employee interests, with profit-sharing built into its constitution.

That constitution is still active, focusing on the pursuit of the happiness of its members, the sharing of profit, mutual respect and courtesy, customer care ('Never knowingly undersold'), honourable business practices and meaningful community contributions wherever the company operates. Spedan Lewis called this 'a better way of doing business'.

In 1950, Spedan handed over all his own remaining shares to the trust and signed the irrevocable second trust document to make the 'partners' the undisputed owners of John Lewis. He remained in day-to-day control until he retired, aged 70, in 1955.

With a pre-tax profit of £410 million in 2012–13, the John Lewis Partnership is not embarrassed about making money. It may be little different in customers' eyes from an up-market company like Debenhams – except that it's known to be owned by its employees. The annual bonus has been 13–18 per cent of salary in recent years (17 per cent, equivalent to nine weeks' pay, in 2013). An attempt to demutualise the organisation in 1999, which would have given a windfall of £100,000 to every partner, failed through lack of support from partners.

In 2000 the John Lewis pension fund helped to establish Ocado, the independent online home delivery outlet for Waitrose, selling its shares in 2009. John Lewis, the Scout Association and Dorset Wildlife Trust together helped the National Trust purchase Brownsea Island in 1962, and the company's staff holiday home is still located there.[30]

The John Lewis Partnership is not, however, unique. For example, Scott Bader is a multi-million-pound company based in Northamptonshire, producing chemical resins and polymers, and employing over 600 people on four continents. Founded by Swiss Quaker Ernest Bader in 1920, it was handed over to the Scott Bader Commonwealth, a charitable co-operative of its workers, in 1951. The Commonwealth still owns it today as the sole shareholder. Free from the threat of ever being taken over, the company has an overtly long-term perspective, an engaged workforce and a high degree of commitment to the communities in which it operates. Each year a sum equivalent to 1 per cent of the salaries bill is donated to good causes supporting children and minority communities through its Commonwealth Global Charity Fund: in 2013 this amounted to £176,000.[31]

A Vision for Social Enterprise

We have already heard how the growth of UK social enterprise has been accelerating to reach parts of the economy not previously contemplated.

---

30 Sources include http://www.johnlewispartnership.co.uk/about/our-history/our-history-text-version.html.
31 http://www.scottbader.com/about-us.

Organisations like Ashoka and UnLtd exist to identify, support and invest in the next generation of social entrepreneurs. Throughout the 1980s Ashoka, dedicated to supporting social enterprises through the injection of venture capital, grew from its origins in Arlington, Virginia, supported by research, publications and projects at several American universities. The first Ashoka 'fellow' (investee) was named in India in 1981, when the organisation had an investment fund of $50,000; today it works on every continent, with an annual turnover of $30 million.

UnLtd[32] offers support packages for different types of social entrepreneur in UK, from the novice idealist who has an idea that is viable, valuable and scalable through to the Big Venture Challenge – up to £250,000 of Lottery funding to grow an established social enterprise with a proven record. In each of the eight streams professional advice, coaching, business planning and/or cash are available. UnLtd also provides a brokerage service enabling social or impact investors to place their money where it will bring about most benefit to the community. Some funding streams are restricted – such as to young people, the university community or digital companies.

In 1997 the idea of the School for Social Entrepreneurs[33] came, like many others in the social policy field, from Lord (Michael) Young of Dartington. It was founded at the Young Foundation's office in Bethnal Green, but later moved to the upper floors of The Brigade, a social enterprise training restaurant on London's trendy South Bank of the Thames. These premises were part of a plot purchased by PwC, one of the world's largest accounting firms, for its new global headquarters. Finding that the former fire station had a preservation order on its façade, PwC decided not to incorporate it into its offices, but to do something different with it: as well as the restaurant, sponsored by DeVere Hotels and training homeless people in catering and hospitality skills, it now houses the head offices of both the School for Social Entrepreneurs and Social Enterprise UK.

Some of the school's courses last a day, others one day a week for six months. No qualifications are required other than a passion for social enterprise and the idea that it might be for you – and no formal qualifications are awarded. Courses range from employment law to franchising, from impact assessment to 'unlocking social finance', and some are delivered in collaboration with other organisations such as Lloyds Banking Group or the New Economics Foundation (nef). There are now nine such schools in UK, two in Australia and

32 http://unltd.org.uk.
33 http://www.the-sse.org.

one in Canada. Enterprises created by the community of over 1,000 fellows who have completed a full programme mostly serve deprived areas; their five-year survival rate is significantly better than 'traditional' UK start-up businesses. Working with fellows is a key part of the learning of the school's students and novice social entrepreneurs.

Both UnLtd and the School for Social Entrepreneurs, plus around twenty others (SEUK, charities, social enterprises, universities, the Impetus Trust and Unity Trust Bank), are partners in the Social Economy Alliance, a group brought together to campaign to increase the impact of the social economy on politics before the 2015 UK general election. Contrasting social enterprise with the spectre of corporate greed which continues to make headlines, SEUK's Peter Holbrook justifies the campaign in this way:

> *The last decade has seen massive progress in the social sector in the UK. Social enterprises and co-operatives are outperforming just-for-profit businesses; alternative banks have better returns on assets, lower volatility and higher growth; and a growing proportion of start-ups are socially driven. A shift in the plates of the UK economy is happening.*[34]

Bringing It All Together – Saath

'Of course spirituality is important in our work,' says Rajendra Joshi, founder and continuing inspiration for Saath, a one-stop integrated services organisation working on a daily basis with over 100,000 occupants of illegal slums in Ahmedabad in the Indian state of Gujarat, 'but it is not the be all and end all.'

Over 18 years Saath has built a co-operative, collective ethos and many cross-sector partnerships. This, says Joshi, is the key to success in leveraging support from donors. There's no doubt that the outcomes – health and education services, employment and skills, industry, microfinance and affordable housing, largely delivered through one-stop shops – are creating happier and more sustainable communities.

Joshi, 52, was inspired by Julius Nyerere, whose practical approach to governance in his native Tanzania promoted the idea of a broader, less tribal

---

34 http://www.independent.co.uk/news/uk/politics/the-power-of-social-enterprise-fed-up-with-your-money-lining-the-pockets-of-companies-that-avoid-tax-money-talks-and-now-big-business-must-listen-8660458.html.

identity. Returning 'home' to India for the first time in the 1970s and finding he disliked working in the private sector, he joined a slum education programme under the tutelage of a Basque Jesuit priest. When his mentor died in 1986, Joshi resolved to move forward, creating Saath as a social enterprise in 1989 and dedicating it to the creation of 'inclusive and empowered communities and individuals'.[35]

His first strategic decision was to work with, not independently of, local government, and the second was to persuade private business to take its first steps towards corporate citizenship. In recognising that some essential services were only available from the private sector, Joshi acknowledged that progress could only be delivered by creating a business case, a market-based solution to a community problem. These two approaches delivered vocational training and mains electricity to the slums in the first instance, and many more services followed.

In 2002, following an earthquake and inter-communal riots which led to 1,200 Muslim households needing relief and rehabilitation, Saath realised that the old model of government providing funding for charities to deliver solutions was not going to deliver sustainable outcomes. Such funding was always subject to uncertainty, and NGOs were clearly uncomfortable about growing to any size that could make a real difference, so a new model had to be found that could service the needs of 100,000 people in Ahmedabad and countless more elsewhere – entrepreneurship.

Although traditional finance was not appropriate for these new models of working, microfinance could contribute to social change and sustainability through Saath's bottom-up entrepreneurial approach. Joshi found that the scaling up of pilot projects was the greatest challenge for his new regime, but that overheads could be reduced by 80 per cent through proper business planning. In this way private partners such as the power companies could still make a profit when servicing shanty towns by sharing the otherwise huge capital cost of electricity infrastructure between ever greater numbers of customers.

Scaling up, he has realised, is a human resource issue, not an economic one, as the sums are relatively simple. Bright young people such as Keren Nazareth, Joshi's successor as Saath's CEO, are key to the organisation's success, as those hidebound to old ideas and ways of working find it difficult to cope with change, he says. Change must be sustainable and gradual, he warns her:

---

35 http://www.saath.org.

don't make commitments too early. Educate your funders and donors to understand the process, to be patient, and don't interfere unreasonably – then funding will follow, he claims confidently. Above all, do not fear failure; but do manage risk.

Saath has won international recognition for its work with neglected communities. Its 'all for one' philosophy is a binding ethos, while its work, in a city once renowned for inter-communal riots, is overtly secular. But Joshi is adamant that 'we cannot do everything ourselves'. The alignment of values with those of partners – not necessarily persuading them to adopt common ones – is at the heart of its success, while issues like the management of expectation, the process of inclusion and the celebration of diversity are the human characteristics of what is now a very large and effective organisation.

Throughout my stay in India with Journeys for Change[36] in 2011 I saw many inspiring projects and passionate and capable leaders. Their achievements in that country would lead many Western social entrepreneurs to stagger in amazement and rethink their ambitions. Although our visits to Saath's Urban Resource Centre and microfinance managers were brief, and our lunch with Rajendra Joshi even more so, his approach stays with me – it was profoundly impressive.

In short, everything I have chosen to believe since establishing myself as a writer and consultant on cross-sector partnerships, my commitment to a new vision of a socialised economy, was borne out by Saath. The opportunities for empowering communities and individuals that exist through entrepreneurship, the clear necessity of reducing reliance on state funding for services, and the need to make available the resources and tools of the private sector through a greater sense of corporate citizenship are as real everywhere as they are in India.

---

36 http://www.journeysforchange.org.

Chapter 4

The Power of Investment

The challenge to us all is to create a society which is productive and
prosperous, but which shares its wealth with a sense of social justice.
John Smith, UK Labour Party leader 1992–4

With perhaps a similar attention to historical detail as that for which the poet
Phillip Larkin is renowned,[1] it has been claimed that private equity finance
began in 1901. That was the year when J.P. Morgan bought the Carnegie
Steel Company from Andrew Carnegie and Henry Phipps for half a billion
dollars. Phipps set up the Bessemer Trust with $50 million to invest in private
businesses – and his family's future. That fund still exists, worth a thousand
times more than the original stake. Carnegie's bequest lives on too, in both
concrete and philosophical terms: his foundation endowed over 2,500 libraries
in his lifetime, starting in Scotland in 1883. When he died in 1919, half of all
the libraries in the USA had been funded by him. The man who argued (in
The Gospel of Wealth, 1889) that businesses are the trustees of societal property
that should be managed for the public good could be said to be the father of
modern corporate social responsibility.

Following the Second World War capitalism blossomed: other giants came
into the American market, including George Doriot's ARD, which epitomised
the power of investment by buying Digital Equipment Corp for $70,000 and
selling it for $37 million – an increase of over 52,000 per cent – using money to
create money.

By then the first and largest giant of privately owned monopoly
capitalism was long gone. The first company ever to issue public shares
was the Dutch East India Company (Vereenigde Oost-Indische Compagnie,
VOC) an amalgam of many existing Dutch private trading companies. It was
formed in 1602 in recognition that it was more effective to insure all voyages
of trade and discovery together than each one individually, given the risks

---

1   'Sexual intercourse began in nineteen sixty-three … Between the end of the Chatterley ban and
    the Beatles' first LP'; 'Annus Mirabilis' by Philip Larkin.

they ran of shipwreck, piracy and starvation. Its purpose was both to trade and carry out 'colonial activities' in newly discovered parts of south-east Asia, including the administration of law and order and even the waging of war, where necessary, on behalf of the government of the Netherlands. VOC exerted more influence on some parts of the world than the most powerful governments of the day, helping the Dutch compete against growing British trade with the East.

The ambition of shareholder power was also born: religiously minded share owners tried to dissuade VOC from utilising violence, piracy, assassination, warfare, slavery and bribery. They organised boycotts and collected notarised petitions. They sold off their shares publicly in the street. The move failed: the conscientious were out-voted by wealthy men who justified the company's use of intimidation and physical force to protect their investments.

The largest of the initial shareholders, owning a quarter of the company's stock, was a trader in insurance, fish, grain, timber and caviar named Isaac Le Maire. He became the company's first governor (today's Chairman of the Board), but fell out with the management over mutual allegations of malpractice and by 1605, with shareholding still in its infancy, he appears to have created the practice of short selling: selling shares he didn't yet own in the belief that their value would fall. This practice, which we now know to be destabilising, was made illegal in Holland in 1610 and in many other countries, for a time. Although Le Maire left VOC and sold his shares, he was never reconciled with his former colleagues. His son, Jacob, discovered a route to the East around the tip of South America – predictably now known as the Le Maire Straits – which didn't infringe VOC's monopoly on the toll-controlled Magellan Straits. Despite this, VOC impounded his boat in Chile. Although Isaac eventually succeeded in getting his property back 18 months later, in the mean time Jacob had died on his journey back to Holland.

At one point, at the height of the 1637 tulip bulb mania, VOC became the most highly valued private company of all time, worth $7.4 trillion – long before the modern idea of companies being 'too big to fail'. For two hundred years VOC monopolised the Far Eastern spice market with its 5,000 vessels, carrying two million people to work in Asia, employing up to 50,000, trading 2.5 million tons of goods. Then several factors combined to cause the giant's downfall: changing markets, corruption, lax management, high employee mortality – and over-generous dividends of up to 40 per cent of annual return on investment. The crash must have been heard the world over.

The essential difference between venture capital and hedge funds is one of timescale; a hedge fund looks for shorter-term gains, veritably 'playing the market'. For many, the epitome of the casino economy is the image of hundreds of young men in brightly coloured jackets screaming, shouting and waving slips of paper – or today's digital equivalent – to maximise the advantage gained from minute-by-minute changes in prices, buying and selling money, shares and futures – including (it sometimes feels) yours and mine.

An American website lists what it calls 'Seven Timeless Principles of Investment'.[2] One doesn't have to be a sceptic to wonder at the definition of 'principle', so I've added my interpretation in parentheses below. They are:

- Don't entrust Wall Street with your financial future. (Insiders and brokers are there primarily to make money for themselves.)

- Do it yourself, but don't go it alone. (Subscribe to our magazine to guide your way to profit through investment without paying fees.)

- Don't follow the herd. (Remember that most investors are wrong in their judgments most of the time. Isn't that reassuring?)

- Always maintain your balance. (Don't put all your eggs in one basket.)

- Never lose your shirt on an investment. (Still don't put all your eggs in one basket.)

- Always focus on the fundamentals for the long term. (This doesn't mean 'don't be short-termist' – it means understand the risks you are proposing to take.)

- Cut your fees and expenses to a minimum. (Have you subscribed to our very helpful magazine yet?)

This is value-free investment, and it isn't restricted to the USA; investors' guides available on railway station newsagents' shelves across the UK employ similarly narrow blinkers. It ignores all of the consequences of investment other than financial return, reflecting the basis of Western business for the last hundred years.

---

2 http://www.investmentu.com/investment-u-fundamental-principles-of-investing.html.

The Value of Values: Engaging with Business to Create Social Change

The first vocal proponent of 'ethical investment' was perhaps John Wesley (1703–91), the father of British Methodism, who was, along with Luther and Calvin, associated with the 'Protestant work ethic'. He believed that it wasn't enough to 'be' a Christian: Christians should 'do' Christianity, too – behave in ways that conform to their moral code, not least at work. In his sermon 'The Use of Money' he preached against harming your neighbour through your business practices and cautioned against involvement in industries like leather tanning, which has since been linked with carcinogenic and other harmful effects of chemicals such as chromium on workers. Many of the early applications of socially responsible investing were religiously motivated, as investors were urged to avoid 'sinful companies' associated with guns, alcohol and tobacco. While many people of conscience have argued that the Bible forms the basis for an ethical course for business, R.H. Tawney argued the opposite: that religion played an essential role in the rise of commerce and individualism (Tawney, 1926).

In 1672 the Royal African Company was established to grant the Port of London a UK monopoly on the slave trade. In 1698 that right to trade in humans was extended to Bristol and Liverpool, prompting a fifteenfold growth in the latter's population over the next century. Anticipating the huge impact of slavery on the economy prompted the establishment of the Bank of England in 1694: there was hardly an element of British trade and industry, the sugar trade in particular, which didn't benefit economically from slavery. It powered the Industrial Revolution in Britain. Between 1750 and 1780 no less than 70 per cent of the British government's tax income came from the colonies.

In 1758 the Religious Society of Friends (Quakers) banned its members from participating in the slave trade, and by 1783, following British defeat in the American War of Independence, many English families were returning to Britain with their domestic slaves, heightening awareness on both sides of the abolition debate. That year a skipper threw 133 sick slaves overboard and made an insurance claim for compensation. Spurred on, in 1787 the Quakers formed an ecumenical group, the Committee for the Abolition of the Slave Trade, and petitioned Parliament. The intellectual case against slavery started to grow. From 1790 to 1792 the import of sugar from non-slave sources in India grew tenfold in response to consumer boycotts of West Indian sugar. However, the campaign to ban slavery didn't succeed until 1807 in Britain and across the Commonwealth in 1833.

The West India Lobby was a group of business campaigners who tried to preserve slavery and the wealth it brought to the country – not least to themselves. But their position weakened as parliamentary reform removed many of their supporters from the corridors of power, while the Industrial Revolution outgrew its economic dependence on slavery. With a few honourable exceptions, business was silent on the issue: Josiah Wedgwood was a prominent business opponent of slavery, producing a famous brooch and tea sets in support of abolition. A handful of other professionals with experience of the conditions slaves had to endure rallied to the campaign – former slave traders, ships' doctors – which was also joined by Quaker business people, ex-slaves and social campaigners.[3]

We saw in Chapter 2 that British Prime Minister David Cameron has claimed that the abolition of slavery in Britain, a decade after its abolition in France, was an example of responsible business seeing sense; but the evidence for this is very weak. As the Chartered Institute for Professional Development says: 'The slave trade did not end because of a convincing business case, but through moral persuasion.'[4]

Abolition of the slave trade and associated changes in the international sugar market led to the exploitation of a new resource by landowners in the West Indies and elsewhere and the coming to prominence of a new world power: the modest and impotent banana, now the planet's fourth largest agricultural market.

Through his work on *The Wealth of Nations*, Adam Smith is regarded as the father of modern capitalism, but this volume of 1776 contrasts in some ways with his 1759 study *The Theory of Modern Sentiments*. Smith as an adult was, unusually for his time, a man not swayed by the influence of religion, and especially not by the Church. Although in *The Wealth of Nations* Smith did argue that competition and self-interest in a free market with the minimum of regulation produces benefits such as lower prices and wider access to goods, he also argued that anti-competitive trends such as price-fixing were wrong and warned that government, politics and legislation were becoming dominated, even then, by business interests in a 'conspiracy' against consumers. In *The Theory of Modern Sentiments* he had suggested that conscience arises from experience of social relationships, and that observing others is the basis of making judgements about one's own moral behaviour. In the human

---

3   http://abolition.e2bn.org/people.html.
4   http://www.cipd.co.uk/comment-insight/comment/understanding-bigger-picture.aspx.

personality the pursuit of self-interest is natural, said his later work, but it has to be balanced against more sympathetic emotions.

This softer side of Adam Smith's work, in which he envisages a social role for the movement that would later be known as the private sector, is very often overlooked by his supporters and detractors alike.

In the nineteenth century Marx argued that capitalism only worked by exploiting labour, and was devoid of moral justification. If workers were paid the proper rate for the job, the profit motive would no longer exist and major elements of the emerging capitalist system wouldn't survive. Throughout most of the twentieth century Catholic popes railed against both the command economy of the Eastern bloc and laissez-faire capitalism in equal measure, arguing that our economic system should be informed by Christian principles designed to improve the lot of the world's most disadvantaged people and in 2012 the Catholic bishops' conference in London promoted an ongoing debate on 'A Blueprint for Better Business?',[5] a debate no doubt finding the approval of the relatively new Pope Francis, a champion of social justice. (In 2008 the Catholic Church admitted that it didn't know how wealthy it was.[6])

In the 1960s Dr Martin Luther King sought support from professional investors for Operation Breadbasket, designed to improve economic conditions for black people in the southern USA through measures such as community banking. The young Reverend Jesse Jackson was a key figure in his Chicago outpost when civil rights, union rights and women's equality were added to the conscientious investor's agenda. The 1964 Civil Rights Act and the 1965 Voting Rights Act were a watershed in the USA.

Although the USA had banned practices like child labour in the 1930s, from the late 1960s a legal framework for ethical corporate behaviour emerged, leading to the first global conference of academics on business ethics in 1974 and the Foreign and Corrupt Practices Act 1977. This was the first piece of US legislation to influence the behaviour of American companies abroad, following the fall of the Japanese government in the Lockheed bribery scandal.

The Vietnam War polarised views, including a negative investor response to Dow Chemicals, producers of napalm, following the 1972 publication

---

5   http://www.blueprintforbusiness.org/Home.
6   http://news.nationalpost.com/2013/03/08/wealth-of-roman-catholic-church-impossible-to-calculate/.

of an iconic photograph of a young and naked Vietnamese girl whose back was burning from contact with it following its military use. By the late 1970s environmental issues, such as nuclear power and vehicle emissions, had become targets of ethical investor campaigns.

Leon Sullivan

Following the Sharpeville massacre of 1960 many faith-based, union and other investment funds with an ethical edge avoided direct investment in apartheid South Africa. However, it was difficult to avoid indirect investment in businesses with interests there, so in 1971 an American, the Reverend Leon Sullivan, drew up a code of practice to govern business engagement with South Africa.

Like Luther King, his contemporary, Sullivan was a black man who had experienced discrimination from an early age. Born in West Virginia in 1922, by 18 he was working in a steel mill, active in the civil rights movement and already a Baptist minister. By 1958 he was organising the black fifth of the Philadelphia population to boycott businesses which refused to employ black people, giving Luther King confidence that Operation Breadbasket could work. In 1962 Sullivan encouraged his congregation to become community investors by starting a fund to invest in scholarships, community health and even small businesses – based on 50 people each loaning $10 to the cause over 36 months. On its first day the '10–36 Plan' attracted 200 shareholders for the private company Progress Investment Associates (PIA). PIA's early investments included apartments for black people in former white neighbourhoods. It's still active today, leveraging millions of dollars of state and private capital into community development across the USA, still a mutual, directly accountable to its members.

In 1971 Sullivan became the first black American to join the board of any major US company, General Motors (GM), one of the largest employers of black people in South Africa. The United Nations had condemned apartheid in 1962, and in 1973 it was designated a crime under international law. With such a large economic stake it was clear that immediate and total disinvestment by GM from South Africa was unlikely to happen. This led Sullivan to draw up the Sullivan Principles on racial equality in the workplace in 1977:

- non-segregation of the races in all eating, comfort, and work facilities;

- equal and fair employment practices for all employees;

- equal pay for all employees doing equal or comparable work for the same period of time;

- initiation of and development of training programs that will prepare, in substantial numbers, blacks and other nonwhites for supervisory, administrative, clerical, and technical jobs;

- increasing the number of blacks and other non-whites in management and supervisory positions;

- improving the quality of life for blacks and other non-whites outside the work environment in such areas as housing, transportation, school, recreation, and health facilities;

- working to eliminate laws and customs that impede social, economic and political justice (added in 1984).[7]

Over the following years 125 American companies adopted the principles and over 100 of them disinvested from South Africa completely.

In short, the Sullivan Principles were designed to give black people the same rights at work in South Africa as they enjoyed in the United States. In his preamble, Sullivan wrote:

> *The objectives of the Global Sullivan Principles are to support economic, social and political justice by companies where they do business; to support human rights and to encourage equal opportunity at all levels of employment, including racial and gender diversity on decision making committees and boards; to train and advance disadvantaged workers for technical, supervisory and management opportunities; and to assist with greater tolerance and understanding among peoples; thereby, helping to improve the quality of life for communities, workers and children with dignity and equality.*[8]

In 1977, at the launch of the Principles, Sullivan said: 'I threatened South Africa and said in two years Mandela must be freed, apartheid must end and blacks must vote or else I'll bring every American company I can out of South Africa.'[9]

---

7   http://www.marshall.edu/revleonsullivan/principles.htm.
8   Ibid.
9   http://www.marshall.edu/revleonsullivan/principled/principles.htm.

But Sullivan was frustrated: even though the principles may have contributed to the fall of apartheid in the early 1990s, the regime itself survived for many years after the start of the disinvestment campaign. A stronger version, dedicated to demonstrating an ethical basis for business behaviour in all circumstances, was required. It wasn't good enough to focus on one evil at a time; there had to be standard guidelines for responsible business.

Many other Sullivan initiatives grew across the USA and Africa over the years, including training for unemployed black people, investment in black entrepreneurs (the Zion Investment Association) and projects to help fight disease, poverty and ignorance.

In 1992 Sullivan received the Presidential Medal of Freedom from President George H.W. Bush for his work with the world's most disadvantaged people. In December 1999 he received the Eleanor Roosevelt Award from President Clinton for his humanitarian work. In the same year, with apartheid dead and well buried, Sullivan launched his Global Principles with the support of United Nations Secretary General Kofi Annan. Their purpose was to enable companies to 'support economic, political and social justice', and they are widely regarded as a definitive statement of modern Corporate Social Responsibility:

> As a company which endorses the Global Sullivan Principles we will respect the law, and as a responsible member of society we will apply these Principles with integrity consistent with the legitimate role of business. We will develop and implement company policies, procedures, training and internal reporting structures to ensure commitment to these principles throughout our organization. We believe the application of these Principles will achieve greater tolerance and better understanding among peoples, and advance the culture of peace.
>   Accordingly, we will:
>
> 1. Express our support for universal human rights and, particularly, those of our employees, the communities within which we operate, and parties with whom we do business.
> 2. Promote equal opportunity for our employees at all levels of the company with respect to issues such as color, race, gender, age, ethnicity or religious beliefs, and operate without unacceptable worker treatment such as the exploitation of children, physical punishment, female abuse, involuntary servitude, or other forms of abuse.
> 3. Respect our employees' voluntary freedom of association.

4. *Compensate our employees to enable them to meet at least their basic needs and provide the opportunity to improve their skill and capability in order to raise their social and economic opportunities.*

5. *Provide a safe and healthy workplace; protect human health and the environment; and promote sustainable development.*

6. *Promote fair competition including respect for intellectual and other property rights, and not offer, pay or accept bribes.*

7. *Work with governments and communities in which we do business to improve the quality of life in those communities – their educational, cultural, economic and social well-being – and seek to provide training and opportunities for workers from disadvantaged backgrounds.*

8. *Promote the application of these principles by those with whom we do business.*

We will be transparent in our implementation of these principles and provide information which demonstrates publicly our commitment to them.[10]

Although Leon Sullivan died of leukaemia in 2001, his spirit lived on for a while in the form of the Leon H. Sullivan Foundation, run by his daughter, Hope, and its annual summit, held in a different African country each year. Unfortunately the foundation became better known for its lavish parties featuring controversial African leaders past and present than for its good deeds. Its decision to hold its 2012 summit in Equatorial Guinea was the last straw for many corporate and other sponsors (Coca-Cola, GM, President Clinton), who deserted it. Its cupboard was then found to be bare.[11]

* * *

The exercise of shareholder power has matured over the years. While the Sullivan story hints at the exercise of great influence through investment, it's fair to say that shareholding has never achieved its potential of empowering ordinary people to exercise collective control over those businesses that provide for us in everyday life, let alone those which increasingly influence

---

10 http://www1.umn.edu/humanrts/links/sullivanprinciples.html.
11 http://100r.org/2013/07/fatal-attraction-why-the-leon-h-sullivan-foundation-made-friends-with-african-despots/.

our world. Remember, there are more corporates than countries in the world's top 100 economies.

However, the investor with a conscience isn't a solitary figure, and over the years such people have come together with growing effect, initially through religious organisations, to try to make shareholding a force for good and to bring about positive social and environmental change. The modern story of 'ethical' investment and how it evolved into 'responsible', 'social' and 'impact' investing deserves a chapter of its own, and we'll cover this in Chapter 5.

In July 2013 the UK Parliamentary Commission on Banking Standards published a comprehensive report.[12] It laid to rest the myth that shareholders' role in the financial crisis was merely that of 'absentee landlord', revealing how institutional investors – or their representatives, whether informed by their clients or probably not – had actively pressured banks to pursue more risky strategies.

The campaigning charity ShareAction, which has campaigned on these issues for many years, previously as Fair Pensions, said: 'it is not enough for policymakers to empower shareholders in the expectation that this will promote more responsible corporate behaviour. Instead they must create the conditions for shareholders themselves to be more responsible.'[13] Those conditions, ShareAction rightly claimed, should clarify that 'fiduciary duty' extends beyond short-term concerns, and should include greater accountability and transparency.

The Special Role of Pension Funds

Throughout Chapter 5 there are references to investments made by pension funds and the controlling role which they, as major investors, play. It's worth considering their special situation, with clear obligations to their own investors for both short-term and long-term gain. A pension fund is in effect an insurance and/or savings scheme into which people and/or their employers make contributions during their working life in order to receive a one-off and/or regular payment during their retirement – in short, an investment in a higher standard of living in retirement than one could expect from the state pension and their unimproved savings.

---

12 http://www.publications.parliament.uk/pa/jt201314/jtselect/jtpcbs/27/27ii02.htm.
13 http://www.shareaction.org/response-uk-parliamentary-commission-banking-standards-report.

A pension fund that only pays you back what you have paid in isn't worth having. The trick is to manage the fund such that it pays back more – considerably more – than has been paid in. The only way this is possible is if fund managers invest the resources judiciously. How much the fund is required to generate depends partly on actuarial considerations – how long the retiring generation is expected to live after retirement. Inevitably some contributors will die before they have withdrawn even the amount they put in.

In the last half-century the pension industry has grown as people have had more disposable wealth to invest in it. There have been legal changes in the UK to encourage participation as there's a growing fear that state provision will be insufficient to provide for a 'decent' standard of living in retirement. The demographic and actuarial time bomb that will be exploding before long is that life expectancy in Western countries is now such that hardly any pension funds will be sustainable into the future. Many, even among the largest, are technically in breach of sustainability regulations already – although, put simply, as these anticipate all of a fund's liabilities being called in at the same time, such calculations are based on an unlikely scenario.

The current participation level is also worrying: the total membership of UK occupational pension schemes in 2011 was static at 27.2 million, rising to 27.6 million in 2012.[14] However, the number of active members – those paying money into a scheme themselves or by proxy – actually fell to 8.2 million in 2011 and 7.8 million in 2012 compared to a peak of 12.2 million in 1967; today two thirds of members are only withdrawing funds. This proportion will rise as life expectancy rises, so with statutory support for pension schemes having been increased the only way funds can prompt a big rise in investment is through voluntary contributions – which doesn't look likely, given the predictions for the economy.

Back in the 1960s over half of all shares on the UK stock market were held by individual shareholders. Over the years their influence waned to the extent that wealthy people owned just one share in every six; institutional investors, not least the pension funds, could be said to have owned a significant part of the UK economy. Since then the proportion of shares in UK companies owned by pension funds has fallen considerably – from 21.7 per cent to barely 5 per cent since 1998 alone. This is due not to a resurgence in individual shareholding, but to the intervention of foreign capital into the UK share market.

---

14 http://www.ons.gov.uk/ons/rel/fi/occupational-pension-schemes-survey/2011/stb-opss-2011.
    html and http://www.ons.gov.uk/ons/rel/fi/occupational-pension-schemes-survey/2012/stb-
    opss-2012.html.

And the unique quality that pension funds have is that while they need to make money in the short term to service their retired members' needs, they have an absolute vested interest in long-term planning too: the graduate paying her first pension contribution today needs to know that she will have a pension worth having not only in 40 years' time – the age at which her parents might retire – nor in 50, when she may be facing retirement, but in 75 years' time when, according to actuarial predictions, a quarter of girls born in UK today will be preparing for their hundredth birthday.

The key to sustainability is long-term thinking. So consider the situation:

- Pension funds have to think long-term.

- Pension funds could potentially own vast tracts of private business.

- We own the pension funds.

Pension funds are responsible to their members – which ultimately means to us. Far more of us are pension fund members than are individual shareholders in private business.

Large investors who favour short-term profits, rewarding fund managers with big bonuses for maximising short-term gain, work against the interests of responsible capitalism; they are part of the problem, not the solution. There are alternatives to short-termism, but they must be hard-wired into the rules by which each element of 'the system' works. Shareholder democracy is arguably easier under British rules than those in the USA, where the Dodd-Frank Act tried to re-set the balance in shareholders' favour, but having active shareholders doesn't guarantee more responsible corporate behaviour. If anything, it may have the opposite effect, as a broader constituency of people may feel that making a 'fast buck' from shareholding is now possible for them: witness how quickly the initial tranche of Post Office shares was re-sold in late 2013. *The Economist*'s Matthew Bishop described Dodd-Frank as 'a confused 2,100-page Frankenstein's Monster'[15] (see also Bishop and Green, 2011).

Davis, Lukomnik and Pitt-Watson (2006) argue that a civil economy should emerge in parallel to civil society:

---

15 Matthew Bishop, speaking at a Tomorrow's Finance event for Tomorrow's Company in December 2012.

> *... forward-thinking corporate leaders understand that popular resentment of globalisation, divisions between the shop floor and executive suites and recurring clashes between corporations and social interests cannot help but drain energy from competitiveness, costing jobs and undercutting public confidence in institutions critical to growth.*

The question, they say, isn't whether such a move is happening – it is – but whether it can maintain its direction, grow in momentum and become the driving force of modern capitalism. David Pitt-Watson looks forward to a day when pension funds are governed largely by people without an immediate financial interest (albeit advised by people who do) so that their values remain human ones and their outlook is long-term.[16]

It was the Norwegian government's pension fund which prompted behaviour change at Walmart by disinvesting in 2006. It did so because its own constitution told it to avoid '[i]nvestments which constitute an unacceptable risk that the Fund may contribute to unethical acts or omissions, such as violations of fundamental humanitarian principles, serious violations of human rights, gross corruption or severe environmental damages.'

On climate change alone it has been calculated that global pension fund investment in mitigation and adaptation measures could reach $300 billion by 2015, assuming climate change continues to represent just 5 per cent of fund investments. This dwarfs the 'green bond' market of $16 billion (to which an estimated $1–2 billion is added in new bonds each year).

A recent paper by the International Trade Union Confederation acknowledges a close link between trade unions and pension funds:

> *Pension funds represent an important class of asset owners and one with which trade unions have a special relationship. They have a social purpose, that of financing workers' right to retirement and most often they are established as part of a collective bargaining agreement and include union representatives on their board of directors.*[17]

In 2012 the Smith Institute reported on the possibilities of local authority pension schemes using their substantial resources to deploy their 'patient'

---

16 Personal communication.
17 http://www.ituc-csi.org/what-role-for-pension-funds-in,12358.html.

capital to derive wider economic benefit.[18] It concluded that there was an appetite for pension fund money being used in this way – such as to finance local infrastructure or help meet government energy conservation and waste management targets – but there were concerns about reputational risk and potential conflicts of interest. One is left with the feeling that such an investment policy is more demanding on fund managers than conventional investment decisions, so the undoubtedly welcome practice of making pension fund money work for a good cause while it's waiting to be called upon to provide pensions is subject to Joseph Heller's 'Catch-22': no one will commit to doing it until it has been shown to work.

One method that does seem to work is the Dutch system of 'vertical regulation' of pension management. In Britain regulation is deemed 'horizontal'; agents are regulated, and pensions and annuities are allocated individually, while in Holland they are lumped together, with trustees managing them collectively. If two people of the same age each put the same amount of money over the same period into identical schemes, the one in Holland would receive 50 per cent more than his British counterpart in retirement.[19] We have to ask: are our pension funds being managed in the best long-term interests of their members?

'Shareholders are harmed as consumers and citizens by the very activities that they own in part,' declared the young consumer champion Ralph Nader in 1970 as he sought to raise awareness among shareholders of the power they had at their disposal; they should rise up and 'tame the corporate tiger', he said, focusing his attention initially on General Motors. His aim was to convince pension funds and other big investors to support rebel petitions at the firm's annual general meeting. If the funds themselves didn't rise to Nader's challenge, then he would mobilise the citizen investors who owned the pension funds. Move the citizens and you move the funds, he reasoned; move the funds and you move the boardrooms.

The dominoes didn't fall as Nader predicted: his purely social mission downplayed the interests of shareholders, but the approach of investors and their institutions was innately conservative and the demands of the new consumer movement were a risk too far. But if a dam wasn't broken, then the cracks in it had at least become clear: civil society already knew that changing

---

18 http://www.smith-institute.org.uk/file/local%20authority%20pension%20funds%20-%20 investing%20for%20growth.pdf.

19 RSA research quoted by David Pitt-Watson in a Tomorrow's Finance lecture for Tomorrow's Company in July 2012.

laws was one way to change society, but it had learned that changing the outlook of major investors was another matter.

The question shouldn't be 'Why invest responsibly?', but 'Why not?'

The power of the 'new capitalists', as Pitt-Watson and his co-writers labelled pension fund members with long-term needs, has now been identified, even if it hasn't been activated (Davis et al., 2006). Much of its potential as a force for good remains unfulfilled, though potential there certainly is. Matthew Bishop, as ever, puts the 'new capitalist' agenda in a down-to-earth context:

> Surely the time has come for all of us to hold our investments to the same ethical standards that many of us now apply to the products we consume. Just as ethical consumerism has over time driven significant change in how companies produce, so this responsible investment movement could drive change in how our investment institutions invest on our behalf. This could be a genuinely new 'citizen capitalism'. Built on long term, engaged ownership by the public, this 'popular capitalism 2.0' would be the exact opposite of the 'sell off the family silver cheap' version of popular capitalism pushed in the 1980s by Mrs Thatcher.[20]

It won't happen overnight.

Walking the Talk

In 2000 the British government asked Paul (later Lord) Myners to study the relationship between institutional investors and their clients. Put simply, if a pension fund wanted to achieve certain long-term qualitative outcomes from its assets, how much could it trust the financial intermediaries of London's Square Mile to deliver them?[21]

The outcome of the review was disappointing. Myners concluded that many pension fund trustees lacked the necessary investment expertise to act as strong and discerning customers of the investment consultants and fund managers who sold them services; evaluation of advisers and their advice was poor; only a small number of investment consultants were used,

---

20 Matthew Bishop, speaking at a Tomorrow's Finance event for Tomorrow's Company in December 2012.
21 http://uksif.org/wp-content/uploads/2012/12/MYNERS-P.-2004-Myners-principles-for-institutional-Investment-decision-making-review-of-progress.pdf.

often bundling actuarial and investment advice together; contractual structures were often unclear, creating strong and unnecessary incentives for short-termism, and there was little focus on the potential for adding value through active shareholder engagement. A series of measures was proposed aimed at achieving clarity of objectives, timescales, skill needs, engagement and strategy. In 2004 Myners' proposals were revisited: some progress was found, principally among larger occupational schemes and local authority pension schemes, which together represented nine out of every ten pension funds. Over half of all trustees regarded the principles as best practice, and trustees believed that they were now better informed. Seven out of ten schemes claimed that they were fully or mostly compliant with the principles as a whole: however, figures for compliance for each of the individual principles didn't confirm this rosy picture.

More worrying, the continuing low level of appropriate skills among trustees was clearly hampering progress, and there was confusion between the roles of trustees and advisers. Insufficient time and resources were being spent on fund allocation, there was little clarity between trustees and managers about what constituted an appropriate timescale to work on, and little progress had been made on stakeholder engagement. It was almost as though those responsible for the funds were scared of confronting their advisers for fear of being perceived as telling them how to do their job – and with 80 per cent of funds utilising independent advisers (over half relying on just eight such companies), this was clearly a major barrier to progress. Only one in six pension funds had taken steps to better engage grassroots scheme members two years after the Myners Principles had been endorsed.[22]

Although the 2004 review concluded that progress had been made, it said that funds perceived the progress as being greater than it really was, though appreciation of the need for the principles remained high. Lord Myners made further recommendations on how to address these serious shortfalls by encouraging a more professional approach. There should be proper in-house support for fund trustees; contracts for actuarial asset allocation and fund management advice from independent sources should be obtained through open competition, and reports on performance on all aspects of the fund's management should be available (perhaps through a website) to all fund members.

---

22 UK local authority pension schemes, worth £6.5 billion in 2004, have had a statutory obligation to take independent investment advice since 2002. Their compliance with Myners' Principles was slightly better than that of the private sector.

Ten years later, the jury is still out.[23]

Bridges to the Future

Bridges Ventures recently celebrated its first decade in business, although its founder, the ubiquitous Sir Ronald Cohen, has been involved in venture capitalism much longer than that. Bridges' record demonstrates that share ownership isn't the only way in which the diligent and responsible use of capital can generate public good:

> *Over the last ten years, we have innovated three different fund types, showing how an impact-driven investment approach can be employed across a range of asset classes – from growth capital for ambitious businesses, to investments in properties in regeneration areas and buildings showing environmental leadership, to flexible funding for social enterprises.*
>
> (*Bridges Ventures, 2013*)

The key to successful investment, Bridges says, is to identify an entrepreneurial spirit associated with talented management teams building high-impact, fast-growth schemes. Any investor might say the same: but half of Bridges' investments are made in the most deprived 10 per cent parts of Britain and 85 per cent in the most deprived quarter, while the high impact it's seeking is specifically in the fields of healthcare, education, skills and environmental sustainability. Its sustainable growth fund gave a 20 per cent return on investment in 2012 despite the poor economic environment and the company's policy of exiting from successful clients once they show they can operate at their new, higher level.

The ten-year review lists several lessons learned: one is that where the challenges are greatest, the potential can be highest – both for social impact

---

23 In late 2013 the Co-operative Group, and the Co-operative Bank in particular, faced severe problems arising from years of unfortunate management decisions, epitomised by the demise of the bank's Chairman, the Reverend Paul Flowers (the Methodist minister resigned from his post after being arrested on drugs charges). A £700 million 'hole' in the bank's finances was declared, but on examination the hole was found to be more than double that sum. The involvement of hedge funds in the bank's rescue package alarmed many, and was regarded by some as the possible end of large-scale ethical banking. However, a charter was agreed, with hedge fund support, to retain its historical principles. A further reassurance came with the recruitment of Paul Myners as a non-executive director on a peppercorn fee with the expectation that he may become chairman later: http://www.theguardian.com/business/2013/dec/12/myners-co-op-board-salary-former-city-minister.

(intuitive) and for financial return (counter-intuitive). The Gym is a fitness club with branches in several deprived areas, thanks to Bridges' investment. The Gym charges no fees for membership because local people wouldn't be able to prioritise that sort of up-front payment, so members pay only for usage. But what it loses in monthly receipts it gains in users: 33,000 of its members had never used a gym before. A second lesson is that Bridges' principles can be applied to all asset classes and all investor types: ten years ago Bridges' projects were funded by private investors and government, while today its institutional investors include a host of banks, pension funds, Oxbridge colleges and charities. A third lesson is that investment in property is part of the approach, and not divorced from other sorts of investment: when investing in a retirement home in a deprived part of Gloucester, Bridges paid for its roof to be covered with photovoltaic cells, resulting in a 50 per cent reduction in energy costs which was passed on to residents.

Bridges has demonstrated how success in delivering social impact can influence government policy, how there's always a case for maximising customer satisfaction, and why exiting from a successful investment is as important in the process of growth and maturation as are the initial stages. The Gym won the Venture Exit of the Year Award at the British Private Equity Awards for Bridges in 2013.

The report ends, as it begins, with a question; somehow you feel that the 32-page report has gone a long way to answering it. It is: 'How can capitalism better serve society?'

The Name's Bond …

In 1999 Citylife started to raise money to fund projects to tackle unemployment in inner cities – but this was no ordinary charity. Rather than pass the money on directly to the projects, it invested it in a low-risk social housing project, and the returns from that investment were used to create the employment opportunities. This grew into a bond (in simple terms, an IOU) – a form of debt security – the proceeds of which could be used to fund any charitable venture. Ten years later it had created £10 million worth of bonds; it changed its name to Allia, and four years on another £10 million worth was issued: small investors with patient capital (minimum £100) are able to gain modest returns of income (better than from high street bank deposit accounts) which help them or their chosen charities while the debt generated is repaid at the end of the agreed term.

Early in 2013 Allia created a new bond called Future for Children. It was a trial product designed to support a Social Impact Bond (SIB) for Essex County Council. Although that SIB was fully subscribed, one social investor agreed to reduce its contribution by up to £200,000 to allow the Allia model to be tested. It would work like this, using a £100 investment as a very simple example, although the minimum laid down for this product was £15,000 per investor:

- An investor buys a £100 bond from Allia, from which Allia takes a £2 administration fee.

- Allia invests £78 in a low-risk social housing project, at an agreed rate of interest which will pay back the principal (£78) plus at least £22 in interest by the end of the eight-year term.

- Allia invests the remaining £20 in the Essex County Council SIB. The SIB helps children on 'the edge of care' by paying the charity Action for Children to help prevent the children having to enter care. The more children are kept out of care, the lower the cost of the process and the greater the saving to Essex County Council. The greater the saving, the more money can be repaid to the SIB's contributors, including Allia.

- After eight years Allia repays the bond to the investor:

  £78 – repaid by the social housing provider ⎫ thus repaying
  £22 – (at least) interest from the social housing ⎬ the £100 bond in
      provider ⎭ full (at least)
  £? – *plus* the share of the saving generated
      by the SIB

Unfortunately Future for Children couldn't raise sufficient funds quickly enough to make partaking in the SIB worthwhile, so it was abandoned; the SIB went ahead without Allia. But this had been a 'trial run' for the bond merchant, and Allia wasn't unhappy with the experience. NPC was commissioned to examine why the model hadn't worked (Rotheroe et al., 2013);[24] It concluded that there were few, if any, insurmountable obstacles to such bonds working.

---

24 http://www.thinknpc.org/publications/the-future-for-children-bond-lessons-learned/.

The bond's offer period had been too short and poorly timed, being launched at the end of the financial year, when financial advisers were especially busy. The name Allia and the type of bond were unfamiliar to financial advisers, which meant that advisers who were asked to consider them had to spend time investigating, highlighting the need for better marketing. Unhelpful regulations on social investment hadn't yet been lifted by the government, NPC said, nor had the promised tax relief on such bonds yet seen the light of day; the commercial terms of the SIB made it impossible to indicate to investors even a range of return they might expect from their investment. Eight years was thought to be a long return period for such a bond, and in future Allia ought to consider a more diversified product rather than linking it to a single SIB.

In fact Allia has diverse products on its shelves; they are the bread and butter of the nascent social bond industry: charitable bonds, retail charitable bonds and capital plus bonds, of which Future for Children was one. The first and best-known of its charitable bonds was for the disability charity Scope. It works like this:

- An investor spends (say) £100 on a charitable bond from Allia and chooses from a range of returns; the lower the rate chosen, the more money Scope will get.

- Allia immediately makes a one-off donation to Scope of £12–18, depending on the rate of return chosen. The initial investment is passed on by Allia in full as a low-risk fixed-interest five-year loan to a social housing provider. Five years later the £100, plus interest, is returned to Allia, which passes the £100 plus the agreed interest (less the Scope donation) on to the investor, with Allia keeping any surplus.

Thus investors' money makes money for them in the manner of traditional capitalism, but along the way, in a somewhat Heath Robinson manner, it generates 'good', both by creating a donation to charity and providing longer-term security for a social housing project. Missing from the equation is the rapacious middle-man, replaced by the bond manager who has a dedicated social purpose. While there are few guarantees in economic life, anyone who plays the capitalist investment game must understand the difference between a high-risk investment – a chance of high returns but a risk of loss – compared to a low-risk investment, with the probability of lower returns tempered by a lesser risk of loss.

Some philanthropists acquired their capital not through their skills, but through chance windfalls of inheritance or lottery; others played the markets or took advantage of buying and selling property when the market was fortuitous. The 'casino economy' – a phrase which came to prominence twenty years ago – is where money begets money, outcomes are defined more by chance than strategy, and a few make wholly disproportionate gains while most punters lose. If this image endures in the twenty-first century, then hope is lost.

And yet there is hope: some of the best financial returns for the small British investor can be obtained through a sort of investment crowdfunding which disintermediated Internet technology makes possible: Funding Circle is just one of several examples.[25] Here the small investor with as little as a few hundred pounds to spare chooses specific SMEs in which to invest (allowing the use of ethical criteria, for example) and disperses their risk by making many very small investments across a variety of risk bands. In this way an SME may receive a £50,000 loan from hundreds of participants in the Circle. Even the lowest risk band is likely to return over six per cent over two years, twelve times more than a bank deposit account in 2014, and the investor can sell their investment at any time – usually being able to do so within minutes. There is, in effect, no middle man to create costs, pervert investor intention or obstruct a genuine sense of collaboration and purpose.

Investment is a fundamental tool of capitalism: if I have a lot of money, I can change things – certainly enough to make a difference in my own life, and probably (for good or ill) in the lives of others. Most of us don't have that sort of money, and never will. But collectively we can make a difference, both through the ballot box and through millions of small investments for the common good, often made on our behalf through savings, pensions and insurance policies or through crowdfunding in the future. Investing for good is the subject of the next chapter.

---

25 www.fundingcircle.com.

Chapter 5

Ethical, Responsible, Social, Impact

The test of our progress is not whether we add more to the abundance of those who have much; it is whether we provide enough for those who have too little.

Franklin D. Roosevelt, US President 1933–45

Over the years the expression of our values through engagement and, where appropriate, investment in business has matured. As we have seen, shares – the icon of ownership and the obvious tool of engagement – have existed for 400 years, but the number of people for whom direct share ownership is feasible, let alone actual, has been small. In 1963, for example, 54 per cent of all shares in UK companies were owned by individuals; today institutions own 85 per cent of them. Popular share ownership has come about not through mass ownership of shares, but through mass ownership of interests in intermediaries such as pension funds, savings accounts (such as shares ISAs) and life assurance policies. Most share ownership has been non-philanthropic in nature, intended to produce a financial return in dividend receipts, profit on sale, or both; shares can also be given away as gifts or through inheritance. Philanthropic giving pre-dates share ownership by some 2,000 years, the first known reference to 'philanthropy' being the gift of fire to mankind in the story of Prometheus.

Alongside changes in the nature of share ownership, concerns about ethical business behaviour have grown; the use of shareholding to influence corporate behaviour for 'the good' has matured, too.

It will help us to define a few terms at this stage – see Table 5.1.

A much-used modern term which describes the subject of ethical, responsible, social and impact investment is ESG: environmental, social and governance issues. Governance is often overlooked, but without focused governance within the investee organisation it won't be possible to maximise the environmental and social returns being sought.

Table 5.1   Modes of influence through investment

Investment mode	Activity	Significant dates
Philanthropic giving	Donations to a chosen good cause, not an investment, no financial return	460 BC – first reference nineteenth century – modern usage began
Traditional	Financial return is only or main criterion	1600s – share ownership 1901 – private equity finance
Ethical	Using a 'sieve'; declining to invest in unsuitable companies	USA – 1900s UK – 1960s
Responsible	Wider investment, engaging with business policy as shareholder/owner to change company policies where desirable	USA – 1980s UK – 1999 United Nations Principles of Responsible Investment – 2005
Social or Socially Responsible Investment	Investment in companies with a social purpose which may yield a smaller or longer-term return on investment	USA, 1981 –Social Investment Forum UK, 2001 – Social Investment Task Force
Impact	Priority given to the social element, but may create a market level of return; impact assessment is integrated into investment	2007 – term gained widespread currency 2009 – Global Impact Investing Network created

Ethical Investment

Until 100 years ago the Methodist Church in the USA believed that the sale and purchase of shares, in which financial gains were subject to an element of chance, was a form of gambling, and thus condemned by its ethical code. It started to buy shares as a way of protecting its assets, unsurprisingly vowing not to invest in companies with alcohol or gambling interests. Its example was followed by the Quakers, who added the manufacture and sale of arms to the banned list. Their first independent ethical investment fund, the Pax Fund, was set up in 1971 as a public response to American use of Agent Orange, a toxic defoliant, in Vietnam, establishing the principle of ethical investment in the public realm. Britain was somewhat behind the curve: although another Methodist, Charles Jacob, established the first British ethical investment fund in 1973, it took several years for the UK Department for Trade to grant approval for it to operate.[1] Ten years later Friends' Provident, the 150-year-old Quaker-inspired life assurance fund, offered Britain its first publicly available ethical fund.

A major boost came in 2000, when UK law demanded that occupational pension schemes should state what account they took of social, environmental and ethical factors when deciding where to invest. There is now around

---

1   http://gaeia.co.uk/making-difference/history-ethical-investing/.

£9 billion invested in almost 100 ethical funds in the UK – a decade ago there were a couple of dozen.

To the original three 'sins' of alcohol, gambling and arms, the ethical investment movement added tobacco, products tested on animals and, latterly, pornography to the sieve of products which would lead to non-investment or disinvestment.

However, life's not that simple – as the Church of England recently found.

In July 2013 Justin Welby, Archbishop of Canterbury, spoke out against the high interest rate policies of payday loan companies which were making disproportionate amounts of money – an APR equivalent of up to 6,000 per cent – from the most vulnerable members of society. His plan wasn't that the Church should compete with payday loan companies, but it should facilitate those that do by making church premises available, free of charge, to organisations such as credit unions (whose equivalent loan fee was nearer to 70 per cent). He thought he was on solid ground: the Ethical Investment Advisory Council, his Church's adviser on where its pension fund and the Church Commissioners should best invest over £8 billion of assets, had strict rules. These forbade investment in any company, directly or via an intermediary, where military products and services comprised more than 10 per cent of its activity, or where tobacco, gambling, alcoholic drinks, high-interest lending or human embryonic cloning accounted for more than 25 per cent of revenue, or where more than 3 per cent was from pornography. In addition to the ethical sieve, a positive 'responsible investment' element directed investments towards enterprises that supported Church policy on the environment, climate change, supply chain ethics and HIV/AIDS. The ethical sieve also ruled out companies with 'unacceptable' management practices, judged on a case-by-case basis – including, presumably, massive levels of tax avoidance.

Low levels of 'sin' were tolerated in order to avoid an absolute ban on investing in, let us say, the newsagent WHSmith simply because its top shelves carry pornography or a clothing company where 1 per cent of its socks might be military supplies.

In the story that follows there's no evidence that the Church or its agents were acting outside the rules they had adopted for themselves to guide their investments.

Justin Welby – a former financial executive in the oil industry and clearly a man of the world by primate standards – had been a member of the Parliamentary Commission on Banking Standards both before and following his elevation as archbishop, and clearly 'knew his stuff'. Prior to this fateful week he had called for a cap on payday loan interest rates and had privately met the head of Wonga,[2] the highest-profile of such lenders, during which Welby had said: 'We're not in the business of trying to legislate you out of existence; we're trying to compete you out of existence.'[3]

On Saturday 26 July 2013 a bombshell dropped. *The Financial Times* discovered that the Church of England had invested in a US venture capital firm, Accel Partners, which had been responsible for much of Wonga's initial fundraising – so parishioners' money had gone directly into the pockets of the very industry the archbishop had pledged to compete out of existence for its sinful practices. The credibility of the archbishop, his Church and the bumbling ethical investment industry was blown. Or was it?

Welby's embarrassment was genuine and sincere; he immediately questioned whether the 25 per cent figure – more a garden riddle than a sieve – was appropriate for usury, and vowed that his plan for the Church to support credit unions was intact.

Although a number of sources reported that the sum of money concerned was only £75,000, no commentator publicly pointed out that this represented only one thousandth of 1 per cent of the Church's total investment portfolio: it was hardly a ringing endorsement of Wonga. Most important of all, Welby had, albeit inadvertently, raised the public profile of ethical investment and stimulated much-needed debate.[4]

Under its ethical policy around 60 per cent of the Church of England's funds are invested in securities, bonds and shares, and over a quarter is in property. A significant amount is loaned to clergy or their spouses at times of need – one of the fund's original purposes – and £100 million is invested in sustainable UK forestry. Of the securities, the biggest beneficiary is UK Treasury bonds and the rest is in

---

2   Around this time the Muslim footballer Papiss Cissé briefly revolted against being required to wear a Wonga logo on his Newcastle United shirt, for similar reasons: http://www.guardian. co.uk/football/2013/jul/25/papiss-cisse-newcastle-wonga-row. He dropped his objection after being photographed in a casino.

3   http://www.bbc.co.uk/news/business-23459932.

4   In February 2014 the Church announced that Sir Hector Sants, former Chief Executive of the Financial Services Authority, would lead the drive to establish credit unions throughout its 12,000 'branches' http://www.theguardian.com/world/2014/feb/23/church-credit-unions-parishes.

large corporates. Interestingly, not all of these have been entirely blemish-free of late – oil companies, mining companies, GSK and a bank are all in the top ten individual investees – though all undoubtedly pass the test of the ethical sieve.[5]

The Church of England's Ethical Investment Advisory Council is chaired by James Featherby. After a career in the City he was growing uncomfortable, cynical about what he was seeing. We didn't learn from the dot.com boom, he says, and the 2007–8 crash was inevitable – although 'greed' is a very lazy analysis of why it happened. At the age of 50, thinking he 'didn't want to die a lawyer', this active Christian decided to work to support his faith. His first publication in his new life was *The White Swan Formula* (Featherby, 2009), a brief, destructive but accessible analysis of the Black-Scholes formula which made derivative trading, that held that morality was the enemy of business, possible. His second book, *Of Markets and Men* (Featherby, 2012) was a plea for human values to permeate and direct investment, part of a wider Tomorrow's Company programme on 'Tomorrow's Finance'.

Featherby holds that social impact investing is too small, too weak and not delivering enough for the Church of England to engage in it yet, but he looks forward to the day when he can recommend it. With so many thousands of pensioners to support, his investment policy has to be 'hard-nosed'.

The ethical investment market, filtering out ethically objectionable causes from portfolios, has trebled in size in the last decade, but isn't changing the world, partly because of the rise of responsible investing (see below) and partly just because it's still small.

In 2012 the charity ShareAction (then called Fair Pensions) reviewed the 20 largest ethical fund providers in Britain to ask how active and engaged they really were.[6] Did they review their ethical criteria from time to time? Did they assess and respond to investors' changing concerns? How transparent were they in their operations? Most of the providers were equity funds which, as joint owners of the companies in which they invested, had a voice and possible influence on the investee: did they use that voice in the interests of their ethical investors? The results were disappointing, to say the least.

Almost half didn't publish a list of companies in which they invested. Only three took active steps to find out their customers' ethical preferences.

---

5   http://www.bbc.co.uk/news/business-23467750.
6   http://fairpensions.org.uk/press/ethicalfunds.

Two thirds didn't try to influence the policies of the companies in which they invested (though perhaps this is a feature of 'responsible' rather than 'ethical' investment), while a quarter didn't regularly review their ethical criteria. The traditional 'sins' were well represented in the ethical screens (84 per cent wouldn't invest in pornography, 74 per cent eschewed gambling), but newer concerns were poorly represented: only 11 per cent wouldn't invest in a company utilising child labour, and just a fifth would avoid companies with a record of fraud or corruption.

Of the 20 surveyed, five leaders stood out with scores of more than 80 per cent on ShareAction's chart: F&C Investments, Standard Life, WHEB Asset Management, The Co-operative Investments and Jupiter Asset Management. The charity accused some other providers of ethical investment products of applying a tick-box mentality based on outdated screening criteria in order 'to have an ethically-badged product as part of their range'.[7]

Ethical investment policies should allow disinvestment when an investee changes the nature of its business or an investor changes its ethical criteria. The Campaign Against the Arms Trade (CAAT) has long campaigned for public bodies to disinvest from armaments in general, and from BAe (formerly British Aerospace), 95 per cent of whose work is military technology, in particular. In July 2007 CAAT revealed that 75 local authority pension funds had invested in arms companies, arguing that fund members would be unaware of this and would generally disapprove. Some councils and universities have heeded the call to disinvest from the arms trade: Liverpool City Council has, for one, but an attempt by the Scottish Green Party to persuade Edinburgh City Council to disinvest was defeated.

An early British disinvestment campaign was waged by individual shareholders of the Midland Bank (now part of HSBC) calling for withdrawal from companies operating in apartheid South Africa in 1977, when the United Nations arms sales embargo was imposed. They soon discovered that the voice of the individual, while it may literally be heard at the shareholders' annual meeting, is drowned out by either the noise or the silence of institutional shareholders with millions of pounds of investment to protect.

Aware of the impact of disinvestment on South Africa, in 2006 the Sudan Divestment Task Force was set up to encourage disinvestment in that country

---

7   http://fairpensions.org.uk/sites/default/files/uploaded_files/researchpublications/EthicalFund ReportII.pdf.

following the genocide at Darfur. This initiative was specifically supported by the American government through its Sudan Accountability and Divestment Act of 2007.

In 2010 the Church of England disinvested from Vendata Resources, a mining company, because of concerns over the company's approach to community matters in developing countries. Piqued by the damage the disinvestment did to its reputation, the company commissioned an independent examination of environmental and social issues in its operations with a view to negotiating the terms for reinstatement of the Church's investment and the status that goes with it. Not so Rupert Murdoch's News International, from which the Church disinvested as a protest against daily 'page three' topless women in *The Sun* newspaper; the pinprick caused by that disinvestment can barely have been noticed.

Responsible Investment

Every corporate scandal – Polly Peck, Maxwell, Enron, WorldCom, Madoff's $60 billion Ponzi scheme and Allen Stanford's double life – generates another official inquiry, yet while there's widespread condemnation of the scale of pay inequalities and bonuses rewarding failure that typify the finance industry, nothing ever seems to be done. Every inquiry suggests the same cures: more transparency and accountability, better regulation and longer-term thinking.

One step up the ladder from ethical investment is responsible investment. Moving on from the passive filter of ethical investment, responsible investors will actively choose areas of business in which to invest and seek to positively influence the corporate behaviour of those in whom they invest. Pursuing what's sometimes called sustainable and responsible investment (SRI), the public service pension scheme of California, CalPERS (California Public Employees' Retirement System), gradually became the first 'responsible investor' across its whole portfolio in the 1980s; prior to that, even 25 years earlier, American labour unions had used pension fund assets to invest in medical facilities, social housing and other services from which their members would benefit. In Britain in 1999, the Universities' Superannuation Scheme (USS) bowed to members' pressure to become 'responsible' in all of its financial transactions.

USS's responsible investment doesn't involve simple 'in/out' screening; legal advice is that such could jeopardise its fiduciary duties to maximise the benefits to its 400 member organisations and quarter of a million pensioners. Instead, it aims:[8]

> *to work with investee companies and assets and fund managers to encourage responsible corporate behaviour based upon the belief that:*
>
> 1. *Management of such issues is good for long-term corporate performance*
> 2. *Better management of these issues protects and enhances the value of the fund's investments.*

It goes on:

> *If a company systematically mishandles environmental, ethical, governance or human capital issues, this can be an early indicator of wider management or financial problems which may not yet have come to light. There is also good evidence that poor corporate governance decisions affect the interests of long-term investors. USS exists to safeguard the long-term interests of our participating institutions and individual members and pensioners. Part of our fiduciary duty, therefore, is to take appropriate action if there are concerns about corporate governance issues or mis-management of other extra financial risks including environmental and social factors.*

This describes an approach of monitoring to detect and anticipate ESG issues, and intervening with the company to have them addressed.

Joan Bavaria founded Trillium Asset Management, the first American SRI advisory service, in the 1980s. Throughout the 1990s the environmental wing of SRI came to prominence as climate change climbed the political agenda. Although the first specific brokerage for SRI lasted only a year – in Brazil, home of the Amazonian rain forest, in 2001 – the idea caught on through Jupiter Asset Management in London and ABN AMRO bank's operation in Brazil (subsequently taken over by Santander). The movement continued to grow, and by 2010 the global SRI market had reached $3 trillion – up 34 per cent in five years (13 per cent over three years compared to an increase of 1 per cent in the wider share market). The US market for SRI is thought to be double that of Europe.

---

8   http://www.uss.co.uk/UssInvestments/Responsibleinvestment/BackgroundRationale/Pages/default.aspx.

The UK telecommunications giant BT can trace its history back to the telegraph pioneers of the mid-nineteenth century. Its predecessor, formed from the merger of several companies, was incorporated into the Post Office after the Second World War. It remained there for thirty-five years until it became the first of the high-profile privatisations of the early 1980s, when it became British Telecommunications plc. Its logo then was the winged god of communication, Hermes. British Telecom later split to create O2 (the mobile telephone company, now part of the Spanish Telefonica group) and the BT Group. The BT pension fund is one of the country's largest occupational pension schemes, and the canniest of investors.

At the time of privatisation internal pension funds appeared to work better than open ones, so Alistair Ross-Goobey, BT's pension fund chair, established a wholly owned investment company, called Hermes, to manage its assets. Hermes knew that 'beating the market' wasn't good enough. It would invest in companies where share price was identified as depressed and help them to thrive by investing the skills and experience of its advisory team at senior management or board level, without assuming ownership. It wouldn't behave as some investors do, in the colourful phrase of David Pitt-Watson, 'like a dentist waiting for teeth to rot'.[9]

Today Hermes is a diverse group of companies with an ever-extending influence, typified by EOS, the Hermes Equity Ownership Service,[10] which Pitt-Watson co-founded in 2004. Colin Melvin is its current Chief Executive. It's a global not-for-profit organisation helping institutional share owners meet their fiduciary responsibilities as asset owners by influencing public and private companies. It styles itself a stewardship scheme, and with £20 billion of assets under management – a quarter of all global stewardship funds – it's the largest umbrella fund manager in the world. Hermes believes that companies with informed and involved shareholders are more likely to manage risk effectively and achieve superior long-term performance than those without.

'If you asked a trustee in 2001 about their risk budget, they wouldn't have known what you were talking about,' Lord Myners, arch-reformer of the investment world, told *The Financial Times* in 2011. 'Hermes was the only organisation taking ownership of investee companies seriously.' He reported

---

9   Personal communication.
10 http://www.hermes.co.uk/eos and http://www.sri-connect.com/index.php?option=com_comp rofiler&task=userProfile&user=1001407&Itemid=4.

that the role of pension fund trustee was sometimes likened to 'community service, not dissimilar to being a scoutmaster or churchwarden'.[11]

The world could do with more like Hermes EOS, as David Pitt-Watson argues eloquently in *The New Capitalists* (Davis et al., 2006).

While Hermes may be unique, the market in which it works is growing.

In recognition of this growth, in 2005 United Nations Secretary General Kofi Annan invited 20 experts to establish a London-based body called UN Principles of Responsible Investment (UNPRI), to which all institutional investors and their agents were invited to subscribe. The committee tasked with drawing up the principles was chaired by Colin Melvin,[12] and it was announced at the New York Stock Exchange in April 2006. The 70 founders included USS, BT's pension scheme and CalPERS.

The six voluntary principles cover engagement, disclosure, promotion, implementation and reporting of ESG matters by investors as 'active owners' of assets.[13] The outcome of such a policy is responsible business: aware, engaged, ethical, open, inclusive – but not yet changing the world.

Melvin was worried that the growing interest in responsible investment evident at that time would be put at risk by the global financial crisis in 2007–8:

> *I was so concerned about a potential decline that I spent much more time than usual with print and broadcast journalists, at home and abroad, explaining and exploring the connections between the financial crisis and short-term thinking and behaviour by investors and companies, and particularly their agents and advisers, presenting the crisis as one of ownership, accountability and governance.*

He needn't have worried. As Figure 5.1 shows, today it's thought that over US$30 trillion, or 20 per cent of the investment market, is under 'responsible investment'. However, some wonder whether the UN definition is tight enough: perhaps UNPRI should rank its members as gold, silver and bronze standard according to their commitment in practice?

---

11 http://www.ft.com/cms/s/0/af0358a0-782c-11e0-b90e-00144feabdc0.html#axzz2c1LJ4FRa.

12 Colin Melvin gave a lecture on 'Tomorrow's Finance' for Tomorrow's Company on 11 July 2013: http://www.tomorrowscompany.com/168/News/253. I'm grateful for his permission to quote extensively from it.

13 http://www.unpri.org/about-pri/the-six-principles/.

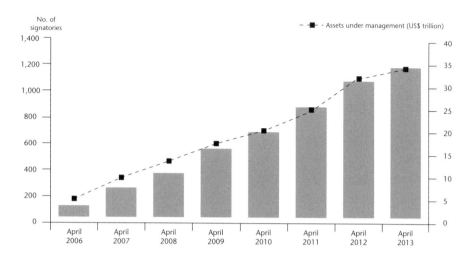

Figure 5.1   Growth of the UNPRI initiative since inception

Source: Adapted from United Nations Principles for Responsible Investment:
http://www.unpri.org/about-pri/about-pri/. © United Nations.

Melvin went on:

> *Indeed, considering the very many post-crisis enquiries, reviews and*
> *regulations hard and soft, on governance, stewardship and tackling short-*
> *termism, the PRI initiative now seems prescient. Those of us involved in*
> *the PRI expert and investor working groups in 2005 and those who drew*
> *up the principles, and the initial group of asset owner and asset manager*
> *signatories, were sufficiently concerned about the dysfunctionality of the*
> *investment process and the relationship between investors and the entities*
> *in which they invested that we were prepared to spend countless hours in*
> *the underground bunkers at the UN Headquarters in New York arguing*
> *over each word of the later drafts, over whether the principles should be*
> *voluntary and aspirational, which they were, and whether or not we*
> *should reference behavioural norms and standards, which we didn't.*

UNPRI wasn't the first to promote longer-term thinking by businesses and their
investors 'in the interests of the broader economy, society and the public good',
as Melvin put it. However, it was the first to bring international recognition, a
proactive approach and a seal of approval to responsible investing.

In some ways UNPRI poses more questions than it answers, as around the
world different financial arrangements raise questions of compatibility and

understanding, but these are being overcome. 'Fiduciary duty', for example –
the duty of the fund manager to uphold the client's best interests – is bound
by (and limited to) contracts in some countries, but more widely interpreted
as creating an ethical environment in others. UNPRI acknowledges that
investment in a company which works to mitigate climate change, for example,
must by its very nature be long-term as its impact may only be felt a generation
after the investment is made.

Some remain concerned that social criteria are a diversion from the main
purpose of investment: to secure and enhance capital wealth. It would be a
mistake to see fiduciary duty and social criteria as alternatives, says Rob Lake
of UNPRI.[14] Successful, long-term investment institutions have to consider the
factors that affect value and performance over the long term:

> *It is absolutely relevant to your fiduciary duty to be very interested
> indeed in climate change, the social consequences of globalisation,
> corporate governance and indeed the long-term functioning and health
> and stability of financial markets themselves, and all these things are
> embraced by the concept of responsible investment.*

UNPRI's aim is to narrow the gap between investor interest and public interest.
Now that this process is under way, we can anticipate a greater contribution by
mainstream investors to tackling some of our planet's most intractable problems.

There's nothing wrong with ambition.

Social Investment

Social investment is a commercial investment in which a lower than otherwise
expected rate of financial return is offset by the generation of positive
social change.

The patron saint of social investment is Amy Domini. In 1990 in the USA she
founded Domini Social Investments, which sells a number of social investment
portfolio products to the public. Her Domini 400 Social Index (also known as the
FTSE KLD400) is composed of the 400 most socially positive companies listed
in the USA. It's determined, in April of each year, by applying an ethical screen
to the top 500 best-performing stocks on the open stock market and topping

---

14 http://www.responsible-investor.com/home/article/lake_diff/.

it up to 400 by adding other known companies with some social purpose to produce a ratio of 360 large, 36 medium and 4 (exceptionally performing) small companies. If you had invested $100 in the Domini fund at its inception, by 2005 you would have made $439 compared to just $382 if you had invested in the top 500 companies on the general index. This shows that suffering a lower rate of return through social investing compared to the mainstream isn't inevitable, at least over the longer term.[15]

Yet if you trawl the websites, magazines and publications aimed at the amateur or small-scale investor, you will find scant mention of social investment. Pursuit of quick profit is what sells magazines to potential investors, apparently.

When in 2000 Britain's then Chancellor of the Exchequer Gordon Brown asked the millionaire philanthropist and founder of Bridges Ventures Sir Ronald Cohen to chair a Social Innovation Task Force, he may not have known what he was creating. While the term 'social innovation' hardly trips off the tongue of every social entrepreneur, social investor or activist, it did much to create an environment in which the potential of social investment – powered, of course, by social finance – can inspire social change and create positive social impact.

Its 2000 report proposed five key policies (SITF, 2000):

1. introduce Community Investment Tax Relief;

2. provide matching finance to establish a community development venture capital fund;

3. require additional disclosure by banks of their lending activities;

4. promote legislative and regulatory changes to allow and encourage charitable trusts and foundations to invest in community development finance;

5. create the Community Development Finance Association (CDFA) to support community development finance institutions (CDFIs).

Since then social finance in the UK has developed a momentum of its own. Table 5.2 shows that most of the Task Force's ambitions were achieved within the decade.

---

15 http://www.socialfunds.com/news/article.cgi/1703.html.

Table 5.2   A social investment timeline

Year	Events
2001	UnLtd launched using Millennium Lottery Funds, CAF Venturesome established Community Investment Tax Relief announced Charity Commission's social investment guidelines published
2002	Charity Bank and CDFA set up Bridges £40 million Community Development Venture Fund (CDV1) established
2003	First CDFIs set up, with DTI funding 63 local ones by year end
2004	Legal basis of Community Interest Companies established, Financial Inclusion Task Force and Investing for Good advisory service First Skoll World Forum on Social Entrepreneurship in Oxford
2005	Big Issue Invest initiative launched
2006	UK government sets up Office of the Third Sector (OTS)
2007	Bridges Ventures CDV2 Fund set up without need for government support Commission on Unclaimed Assets recommends their use for social investment Department of Health announces £100 million Social Enterprise Fund Social Finance Ltd established as a potential social investment bank
2008	Global financial crisis has no effect on social investment market (though may make private sector investors more wary) Bridges Ventures and Triodos Bank launch social enterprise investment funds Dormant Bank and Building Society Accounts Act supports creation of a government social investment wholesaler Esmée Fairbairn Trust and CAF Venturesome launch social investment fund
2009	Several new community and social investment funds announced Social Finance proposes Social Impact Bonds to deliver intervention on social issues Global Impact Investing Network (GIIN) launched by Rockefeller Foundation in USA OTS prepares to launch a social investment wholesale bank
2010	Change of UK government – 'Big Society' describes new Prime Minister's ambitions Office of Third Sector becomes Office of Civil Society (OCS) Social Finance launches SIB to reduce reoffending at Peterborough jail
2011	Wholesale social investment hub launched as Big Society Bank, owned 60 per cent by Big Society Trust and 40 per cent by high street banks
2012	Big Society Bank starts work as Big Society Capital with £600 million, mostly from dormant accounts; BSC is chaired by Sir Ronald Cohen
2013	UK government provides funds to help smaller social enterprises and charities prepare contract for bidding to win work from organisations such as Ministry of Justice Allia launches first SIB funded from public subscription to support vulnerable children; later withdrawn due to lack of investors

Source: Based on SITF, *Social Investment Ten Years On*, HM Treasury, 2010, with additions.

Nick O'Donoghue, CEO of Big Society Capital, clarifies the slightly ambiguous purpose of his organisation (not helped by the authorities' ruling that his organisation couldn't legally be called Big Society Bank), writing in its 2013 annual report:[16]

---

16 http://www.bigsocietycapital.com/sites/default/files/pdf/BSC_AR_AW_forwebsite.pdf.

Big Society Capital's mandate is not to supply capital directly to frontline organisations. Our mandate is to grow a network of specialised and sustainable social lenders and social investment funds that will do that – across a range of different social issues, around the UK and employing a variety of different forms of investment capital.

In 2010 Cohen's valedictory report from the Task Force (SITF, 2010) spelt out three new aims, two of which made progress in the following three years.

I. ESTABLISHING THE INFRASTRUCTURE NECESSARY TO CREATE A DYNAMIC MARKET IN SOCIAL INVESTMENT THROUGH INITIATIVES SUCH AS THE SOCIAL INVESTMENT BANK

The mechanism for social investment banking now well and truly exists, built on a solid foundation of government, bank, charitable foundation and philanthropic cash, with the added bonus of the proceeds of bank accounts that had been dormant for fifteen years.[17] Nevertheless, the market is thought unlikely to be capable of growing sufficiently large sufficiently quickly for social enterprise – its principal beneficiary – to take advantage of all the opportunities being presented. These opportunities are mostly in local service delivery, either because of deliberate government outsourcing policies or due to gaps being created in the market due to central and local government cuts. Secondly, social entrepreneurism depends – as does its private sector equivalent – on the right people with the right skills, energy, passion and leadership qualities being in the right place at the right time. Entrepreneurs can't be manufactured, and many communities, especially those upon which CDFIs focus, lack that sort of capacity or an existing business base. The final restraint is that the planned growth of social finance is based on the model being shown to work (let's assume that it does), thus proving itself attractive to private sector investors to enter the market on social investment terms. This has certainly not happened to any great degree yet, and with corporate charitable giving reported in 2013 as being down one fifth compared to 2012, it seems unlikely that it will happen any time soon (Walker, 2013).

2. CREATING NEW TOOLS TO DELIVER SOCIAL CHANGE THROUGH FINANCIAL INSTRUMENTS SUCH AS THE SOCIAL IMPACT BOND

The reducing reoffending Social Impact Bond at Peterborough jail[18] is still the principal UK example, and the largest financial investment of the 14

---

17 As a Member of Parliament I sat on the committee that legislated for the Dormant Accounts Bill.
18 http://www.socialfinance.org.uk/sites/default/files/SF_Peterborough_SIB.pdf.

functioning UK SIBs (as of September 2013). The return to the investor is dependent on there being a readily measurable criterion of success achieved by the delivery body over a manageable period, thus generating a cash saving to the taxpayer which can then be shared with the investor(s). In Peterborough a consortium of charities led by the St Giles Trust was contracted to ensure that the cohort of male prisoners leaving prison after less than a year in custody exhibited a reduced reoffending rate in the following year compared to their peers leaving the prison population nationwide. The greater the reduction in reoffending relative to the norm, the more the taxpayer saves (across a wide range of budgets) and the more the group of 17 social investors shepherded by Social Finance will receive in a cash return, according to an agreed scale.

Many social issues don't have simple input–outcome ratios, and some are very complex. Others require a timescale (such as the eleven years of a school career) which is not feasible for such investments, and even in the Peterborough case the outcome could be damaged by a statistical fluke or by changes to related policies. However, serious consideration is being given to the use of SIBs throughout the Western world, and some progress is being made: The Center for American Progress championed them from 2011,[19] and Social Ventures Australia raised A$7 million in 2013 for that country's first Social Benefit Bond, aimed at reducing the number of children needing to be taken into care in New South Wales over seven years.[20] The New Zealand Ministry of Health has announced that its first Social Bond will be launched in 2014.[21]

A report issued by the Social Market Foundation in August 2013 suggested that to succeed as a way of financing service improvements, Social Impact Bonds would need to either increase the social impact sought (to ensure that the commissioner wasn't paying for that statistical fluke) or mitigate the risk to the investor (by paying a higher return). The market was still a long way from attracting commercial investors, it said.[22]

19 http://www.americanprogress.org/issues/2011/02/pdf/social_impact_bonds.pdf.
20 http://www.treasury.nsw.gov.au/site_plan/social_benefit_bonds/social_benefit_bonds_trial_in_nsw_FAQs.
21 http://www.health.govt.nz/our-work/preventative-health-wellness/social-bonds-project.
22 http://www.smf.co.uk/media/news/big-hurdles-be-overcome-if-social-impact-bonds-move-margins-public-services-says-think-tank/.

3. ENGAGING THE FINANCIAL SECTOR TO INVEST IN DISADVANTAGED AREAS THROUGH A COMMUNITY REINVESTMENT ACT

In the third challenge remaining, there's less progress to report. The American Community Reinvestment Act of 1977 acknowledges that deprived communities receive less direct investment, loans and credit facilities than they need. Without access to finance in such areas, individuals and community groups can't invest in social infrastructure, social capital or everyday needs. Examples might include a community group wanting to employ a debt advice worker, a group of women wanting to establish a community food co-operative, capital needed to underwrite a credit union, the desire of even the poorest family to make their home secure or a carer needing a holiday.

While some of these issues might be addressed by the CDFIs that have been established in Britain and have been able to secure third-party funding from some banks (mostly the somewhat unconventional Triodos, Co-operative and Unity Trust Banks), at the heart of the matter is the availability of personal loans. These are not within CDFIs' remit, and in any case CDFIs' own capital is very limited compared to a bank. Whereas in USA the Community Reinvestment Act has been strengthened over the years – to ensure that poor students can access student loans, for example – banks in Britain still treat deprived communities as no-go areas:

- Poor people without a credit rating often can't set up a bank account.

- Although some banks provide a basic bank account, some don't allow users free use of other banks' ATMs (blatantly encouraging them to move their accounts elsewhere).

- Fee-charging ATMs are more likely to be found in deprived areas (and where there are captive audiences, such as motorway service stations).

- Basic bank accounts don't allow direct debits, depriving users of benefits such as a reduced Council Tax bill for those who pay by direct debit.

- The lack of online banking on basic accounts means no direct access to the savings of online shopping.

These circumstances have led to a massive increase in the activities of pawnbrokers and payday loan companies, often the only source of credit available to the poorest families even though they provide the most expensive access to finance.

Community investment in the USA grew by more than 60 per cent during 2007–10. Assets held and invested locally by American CDFIs totalled $41.7 billion at the start of 2010, up from $25 billion in 2007.

Sir Ronald Cohen was right to demand that commercial banks step up to the mark and to say 'enough is enough', by calling for a Community Reinvestment Act in Britain. The sub-prime mortgage crisis in America which precipitated the 2007–8 crash was the result not simply of excessive unsecured lending to deprived communities, but of the banking system's complete failure to deal with a problem when it arose, other than by lying about the nature of the toxic assets that were subsequently sold. It wasn't caused by banks implementing sensitive, appropriate, customer-friendly and growth-encouraging measures.

In 2009 President Obama established the Office of Social Innovation and Civic Participation with a threefold mission to improve opportunities for volunteering, partnership and social investment. This was his aim for social investment:

> We will work with Federal agencies to create tools, such as innovation funds, prizes and other social capital market structures to drive resources toward community solutions that are demonstrating success. We will also work across government and with non-government partners to promote better mechanisms to measure and evaluate programs and improve outcomes, to create knowledge about what works, and to disseminate why it works. And we will work to create a more effective government by breaking down barriers to innovation.[23]

Impact Investment

If social investment is the soft edge of using investment tools to generate social change, then impact investment is the hard-nosed business end. Typically it involves private equity or venture capital (perhaps as patient capital or social venture capital), but almost any class of capital can be used: equity, debt,

---

23 http://www.whitehouse.gov/administration/eop/sicp.

loan guarantee, whatever. It's normally carried out by institutional investors, although some opportunities for individuals to support impact investment funds exist. Impact investment is larger and has a longer timescale than crowdfunding, to which smaller public impact funds might otherwise be comparable. Its goal is to create measurable social and environmental impact and a worthwhile financial return. Recipients of impact investment can be of any type – including private-sector – but they will have a social purpose and are unlikely to include those not intended to make a surplus. They could therefore include a Benefit Corporation (see Chapter 6), but probably not a not-for-profit social enterprise.

Impact investment acknowledges that mainstream capitalist investment processes can be used selectively to create public benefit; doing good doesn't require new structures and processes to be created.

In 2007 the Rockefeller Institute invited 40 financial and other experts ('philanthrocapitalists', as dubbed by Matthew Bishop, co-author of that eponymous work by Bishop and Green, 2008[24]) to discuss the needs of the emerging impact investment sector. In 2009, at the conference of the Clinton Global Initiative, that group was formally constituted as GIIN: the Global Impact Investing Network. Its role was to facilitate networking between impact investors, develop a standard framework of social and environmental assessment criteria and establish a working party to focus on sustainable agriculture in Sub-Saharan Africa. GIIN's directors represent a blend of process and purpose; they include financiers, bankers and large foundations such as Rockefeller and Omidyar. The two non-Americans on the board are an Indian serial entrepreneur and Nick O'Donoghue, Chief Executive of Big Society Capital in UK.

GIIN reports that despite the negative global economic climate, impact investment isn't becalmed. Indeed, the global supply of private equity funds available to businesses that provide a variety of social services such as education, healthcare and housing for the poorest people is growing while private foundations and pension funds, even clients of banks, are increasingly looking for impact investment options. A global market assessed at $50 billion in 2009 could be worth ten times that by 2019.

Yet there are restraints on the impact investment marketplace: a general confusion in terminology from country to country makes common

---

24 Matthew Bishop, speaking at a 'Tomorrow's Finance' event for Tomorrow's Company in December 2012.

understandings and co-working difficult across borders, leading to inefficiencies; countries where the need for impact investment is greatest – the poorest countries – lack the financial infrastructure and benchmarking which investment on this scale requires, and often also lack the professional skills to manage it themselves.

In 2012, reported J.P. Morgan in its Impact Investor Survey,[25] $8 billion was committed to impact investment, with $9 billion planned for 2013. Two thirds of impact investors were seeking market rates of return (this is the 'hard edge'), and 96 per cent actively measured the social and environmental impacts of their investments. While 83 per cent of investors were based in Europe or North America, the most popular areas for investment were sub-Saharan Africa and South America. A third of investors would invest in their home countries, too. Unsurprisingly, the most popular sectors for investment were food and agriculture, healthcare, financial services, microfinance, education, housing, energy and water/sanitation; 70 per cent of all investees were in the growth phase of their business cycle, and private equity and private debt were by far the most popular investment instruments used.

The year 2013 was a milestone for impact investing, for two reasons. First, David Cameron raised its profile by placing it firmly on the agenda of the G8 meeting of world leaders in Northern Ireland and through a dedicated Social Impact Investment Forum in London immediately preceding it. Secondly, a month later, 30 delegates from 15 countries met for a two-day conference at the Skoll Centre for Social Entrepreneurship in Oxford to agree the London Principles – the essential elements of a strategy for government participation in impact investing. On day three I witnessed a wider group convening at the ancient London Guildhall for the launch of those principles with backing from the British government, the Corporation of the City of London and senior representatives of the business, investment and voluntary sectors. The London Principles are effectively preconditions for partnership. They are:

- clarity of purpose;

- stakeholder (and public) engagement;

- market stewardship (which recognises that policies to increase the supply of impact investing capital must be balanced by others to strengthen social enterprises and other capital recipients);

25 http://www.thegiin.org/cgi-bin/iowa/download?row=489&field=gated_download_1.

- institutional capacity (providing for the appropriate expertise, resources, and durability within government to ensure successful policy implementation);

- universal transparency.[26]

Speaking at the forum prior to the G8, the Prime Minister said:

> We've got a great idea here that can transform our societies, by using the power of finance to tackle the most difficult social problems. Problems that have frustrated government after government, country after country, generation after generation. Issues like drug abuse, youth unemployment, homelessness and even global poverty. The potential for social investment is that big. So I want to make it a success in Britain and I want to sell it all over the world.
>
> ... And here government needs to help. Government needs to be more creative and innovative – saying to social entrepreneurs: 'if you can solve the problem we'll give you money.' As soon as government says that, social entrepreneurs can go out and raise capital.

Cameron went on to announce a new Social Impact Bond on adoption: successful local voluntary schemes would be scaled up through access to private finance such that up to 2,000 more children could be found permanent caring homes with families while the taxpayer saved up to £1.5 billion in fostering fees, some of which would be used to repay the investors their costs and a return. If it didn't work, he said, the taxpayer would pay nothing.

Ben Thornley of Pacific Community Ventures, a co-convenor of Impact Investing Policy Collaborative, one of the Oxford/London conference sponsors, pointed out that the G8 initiative, while universally welcomed, was the product of ten years' work by politicians, investors and service providers. As if to emphasise this continuity, Cameron announced that Sir Ronald Cohen, who had chaired Gordon Brown's Social Investment Task Force, would lead the next phase of development on behalf of the G8. He said he was looking at plans for tax breaks for social investors, reported that the first Social Stock Exchange was up and running, and announced that Big Society Capital and the Big Lottery Fund would be providing up to £300 million over 10 years to help conserve local social assets through community ownership.

---

26 http://iipcollaborative.org/london-principles/.

Thornley said:[27] 'Impact investing has emerged as one the most important new instruments for creating social value at the disposal of governments, through and in partnership with private markets.' This is a crucial point. Left to its own devices, we know that philanthropy often reflects the passion of the donor, and not necessarily the public priorities for investment as determined by objective assessment. An isolated responsible, social or impact investor may be in the same position: only government (or local government) has the resources, information and overview necessary to identify priorities effectively. Electorates judge politicians on their priorities and their delivery; if they are not setting the priorities, they will be judged as though they are; and if priorities are not clear, then they will be judged on the basis of the confusion. But more importantly, despite the season of austerity, government still has significant resources. Working in complementary partnerships with financiers will maximise the impact of both.

The Omidyar Network[28] has a director on the GIIN. Established by eBay founder Pierre Omidyar and his wife Pam, the Omidyar Network describes itself as a philanthropic investor. It invests in small companies and local finance institutions that work largely, but not exclusively, in developing countries and emerging markets on projects that will broaden consumer use of the Internet and mobile technology, boost entrepreneurship, promote financial inclusion and government transparency and develop property rights, with an emphasis on people at 'the bottom of the pyramid'. Its investment since 2004 has totalled $270 million.

Working in the UK, the Impetus Trust, recently merged with the Private Equity Foundation, is a leading venture philanthropy organisation with a slightly different outlook, summed up in its 2012 annual report: 'Venture philanthropy gives social innovators the money, skills and support they need to crack some of our most intractable problems .... And it has the potential to transform public services by taking the most effective solutions to scale.' Impetus works with charities within Britain. In 2011–12 its income was £7.6 million, it had 50 charities in its portfolio, about 30 actively so at any time, and over half a million individuals gained some benefit from its work. Its focus is on young people and reducing reoffending. Key to its work is that it doesn't just hand over a loan and walk away to await a return: trained experts work directly with and within the recipient charities to grow their operations: in 2012, 400 expert

---

27 http://www.huffingtonpost.com/ben-thornley/impact-investing-the-london-principles_
    b_3594304.html.
28 http://www.omidyar.com.

volunteers from 50 companies gave over 21,000 hours of pro bono business support. They are business people, accountants and managers who use their skills to build sustainability and growth in the beneficiary organisations.[29]

Impetus's investees must be scaleable, will have an inspirational leader, some track record (perhaps three to five years of operation) and be of an appropriate size (at least £250,000 turnover). The investments go to organisations rather than projects, and they can include core as well as activity costs. The voluntary sector is generally 'rich in potential but woeful in capacity', says Jenny North, Impetus's Director of Policy and Strategy, which is why the investment of time and skills, and not just cash, is so important.[30]

One of the small charities which has received investment and skills transfer from Impetus is Working Chance.[31] In 2012 its small staff helped 61 female ex-prisoners into regular voluntary positions and 64 into paid employment – which is surely the best way for these women, almost a fifth of whom are graduates, to become productive, reliable and fulfilled members of society.

The women Working Chance supports, largely from Holloway prison, are either near the end of a custodial sentence or recently released. For those who entered employment in 2012, the reoffending rate was zero over 12 months; overall it was just 3 per cent – tiny compared to those without such support who might face a 50 per cent risk of returning to jail.

This ought to be something to celebrate – so why do so few employers seem to agree?

Some companies are committed to considering their clients as potential employees, some work with Working Chance to create work experience opportunities, and some start by providing mentoring and interview practice. Even among these partners few are willing to tell the world about their involvement for fear that associating with offenders will alienate their own clients. The charity woos prospective business partners, and recently celebrated the decision of a major corporate to join the programme – after 12 months of negotiation. It's more common for junior corporate representatives to be so impressed by Working Chance that they pledge support, only to be vetoed by their line managers or distant boards, which want nothing to do with criminals.

---

29 http://impetus-pef.org.uk/about/facts/.
30 Personal communication.
31 http://www.workingchance.org.

In 2013 H.M. Treasury, where staff already support Working Chance through mentoring and skill development for clients, hosted a breakfast for the organisation to broadcast its message. An executive from the retail sector told a packed room of the high calibre of applicants his firm had received through Working Chance, then his colleague, a smartly dressed, confident junior manager, disclosed that she had started working for the company while on day release from prison. At first she had hidden her background from colleagues (other than the HR department), and now, although friends knew she had been 'inside', no one asked her why. It was an impressive performance.[32]

Working Chance isn't unique. Charities working with asylum seekers, drug addicts and those suffering from HIV/AIDS all know what it's like to be kept at a distance by those who fear that the previous misfortune of others may tarnish their own image. There often appears to be less public sympathy or understanding for women who have offended than for men.

Working Chance is always looking for employers who will work with them to provide skills, experience and opportunity for the women it serves. But even better would be the chance to work with employer partners who are willing to go public about their involvement and show that it works. Working Chance's success generates significant cost savings for the public purse – and thus for us all – by helping to tackle reoffending and dependency on the state. But as long as there's that stigma of misfortune, then eyes will be averted and success will remain modest and unrecognised.

In this case, as in so many others, impact investing has indeed delivered a real and positive impact on the lives of the less fortunate.

---

32   http://www.workingchance.org/AboutUs/News/tabid/1082/articleType/ArticleView/articleId/ 18/Business_Breakfast_at_HM_Treasury.aspx.

Chapter 6
The Smaller Corporate Citizen

A journey of a thousand miles begins with a single step.
Ancient Chinese proverb[1]

Running a small business is often held up as the pinnacle of self-expression; independence from the boss (or 'the system') is an attractive motivator of entrepreneurial behaviour, and there's no doubt that the community of small and medium-sized enterprises collectively has the power, flexibility, innovatory spirit and potential to fill many market niches. Yet that community can be very conservative, strangely held back by peer pressures while at the same time largely lacking avenues of communication between players.

People go into business for many reasons: an entrepreneurial spirit which just needs to express itself or years spent being groomed to inherit a family concern; an inspired idea or a passion for widgets, for service – or for making money. This was acknowledged by one of the most prolific (and sensible) business regulators in history, Franklin D. Roosevelt, in his inaugural presidential address in 1933: 'Happiness is not in the mere possession of money; it lies in the joy of achievement, in the thrill of creative effort.'

Table 6.1   Breakdown of UK companies by size

	Businesses	%	Employment	%
All businesses	4,794,105		23,893,000	
SMEs (0–249 employees)	4,787,650	99.87	14,130,000	59.14
No employees	3,557,255	74.20	3,902,000	16.33
1–9 employees	1,022,695	21.33	3,471,000	14.53
10–49 employees	177,950	3.71	3,848,000	16.11
50–249 employees	29,750	0.62	2,909,000	12.18
250+ employees	6,455	0.13	9,763,000	40.86

1   Lao-tzu (d. 531 BC): http://www.quotationspage.com/quote/24004.html.

Half of all corporate wealth generated in Britain is created not by big international corporates, but by small businesses. This isn't surprising: 60 per cent of all private sector employees work for a business with fewer than 250 employees (the EU definition of an SME),[2] and excluding self-employed people and companies with no employees, there are 1.25 million SMEs in the UK (see Table 6.1).[3]

Although the working population has been more or less static for some time, the number of small enterprises has grown out of all proportion over the last 50 years. This is partly due to culture change, partly to do with individual confidence or dissatisfaction with the status quo, partly due to the encouragement of the entrepreneurial spirit and the perception that opportunities for success exist now which may not have done previously.

SMEs are a veritable army of business people about whom, bizarrely, little appears to be known compared to their much-studied corporate cousins. They're clearly a power in the land, but one thing's for certain: they don't speak with one voice about anything, and most appear to epitomise that silent majority we hear about but never meet. They are traders, service providers, manufacturers, exporters, importers, advisers, consultants, retailers, suppliers, franchisees – all of human life is there.

No discussion of business behaviour and social responsibility can exclude the businesses which employ over half of the private sector workforce. Nevertheless, let's remove from our study those who are self-employed or companies with no employees: in these categories we can't distinguish business strategy from personal behaviour, morality or actions. No research of which I am aware has looked at the relationship between self-employment and responsible capitalism. Henceforth, we'll focus on companies with one or more employees.

When I was writing my 2012 book *Partners for Good*, I sought examples of smaller businesses and charities working together. I found plenty: most relationships were non-strategic, organic, temporary or superficial, but amongst them I found a few golden nuggets. One of the most impressive was the Dragon's Apprentice in St Albans: an annual scheme in which schools, local businesses (through the Chamber of Commerce) and local charities (through the Council for Voluntary Services) support teams of schoolchildren as each team turns £100 into £1,000 for a local charity using business techniques in

---

2   In Australia an SME is defined as under 200 employees, in the USA under 500.
3   http://www.bis.gov.uk/assets/biscore/statistics/docs/b/12-92-bpe-2012-stats-release.pdf.

just a few weeks. It's of high educational value, and the awareness it raises of charities and businesses among the pupils is invaluable.

I visited another area of good practice, Merton in South London, where voluntary organisations and businesses share common training resources, and asked: 'Why is this such a good area for collaboration?' I was told that the image was misleading: within Merton, Wimbledon businesses and charities 'got it' and worked together well, while in Mitcham it didn't happen. I looked at Hertfordshire again, where St Albans and Hemel Hempstead both did well but Stevenage wasn't in the same league, and I thought of other localities in my own experience.

Was it that in more working-class, more deprived communities small businesses engaged less with their community? Were those areas more deprived because business engaged less, or did business engage less because the areas were more deprived? Or was it simply the case, as former Trade Minister Lord Sainsbury suggested later in conversation, that businesses were simply absent from some deprived communities? Some large purpose-built dormitory towns are SME deserts, as are inner-city areas abandoned when businesses that had once employed many in towering Victorian factories migrated to horizontal greenfield sites in the 1960s and 70s. David Sainsbury made the point that in cities such as Leeds and Salford, new technology and new businesses centred around universities had helped to keep the inner city vibrant, whereas in others the unemployment caused by that migration of businesses a generation ago had become endemic, dispiriting and self-perpetuating.

I thought then of Gamesley in Derbyshire, in my former constituency.[4] In 1960 it was created on a greenfield site to house people displaced by a Moss Side slum clearance programme. To this day they are Manchester City supporters, true Mancunians. Gamesley was designed with flat-topped buildings which let in the rain. It has a road around it which acts as a moat, setting it apart from other communities. The streets on the estate barely allow two cars to pass, and the warrens between the housing blocks are renowned for their disorientating effects: it's easy to get lost. A local railway line passes close by, but despite 50 years of campaigning, no train has ever stopped there. Most significantly, while the original design featured two pubs, a community centre and a small row of shops, there was no significant employment within a mile. Even the one small factory in sight of the estate closed a decade ago and stands derelict today.

---

4   I was High Peak's MP from 1997 to 2010.

Today Gamesley remains in the 5 per cent most deprived wards in the country. Its figures for incapacity benefits, unemployment benefits, disability benefits, housing benefit, skills, educational achievement, car and home ownership, smoking, teenage pregnancy, smoking during pregnancy all remain depressing – in many cases the worst in the county. Abandoned cars, broken windows, graffiti and overgrown gardens can all be found; yet this is a proud community which pulls together. *From Smoke to Grass* (Edgar, 2004) chronicles the transition from inner-city squalor to the glorious Derbyshire countryside through the memories of older residents.

Although earlier regeneration efforts failed, in 2006 the estate experienced a moment of joy: it received a quarter of a million pounds in Lottery funding, to be spent over three years. A host of small projects made Gamesley more fun, brought new skills into the community and celebrated what was good about life there. One was an award ceremony in which each year for three years I invited a junior government minister to hand out certificates to acknowledge real achievements. These might have been in tackling disability, excellence in the Brownies or, in one memorable case, a 24-year-old mother who was publicly praised for breastfeeding her new baby, not having done so for her first four.

Looking back, Gamesley was designed as a dormitory and not a community. It was never intended to stimulate imagination, enterprise or success. It was 'out of sight, out of mind' for the planners who created it, without even adequate transport links to make it easy to work elsewhere. Whatever income comes into the estate from benefits or low-skilled, often part-time or temporary employment goes straight out again. Young people with talent leave as soon as they can and don't return. There is nothing on the estate designed to keep capital there or to make it grow and thus to create a sustainable and viable local economy – no SMEs to retain skills and wealth in the community or play the role of corporate citizens. Adam Smith would have been appalled.

Surely there are middle-class estates which are equally bereft of industry? Indeed there are – but they are rich in social capital, sharp elbows, skills and confidence, not to mention disposable wealth and access to transport. They have the capacity to create social structures, community identity and pooled resources, and while they may be boring to look at (one can only tolerate so much wisteria), they could hardly be described as deprived.

Table 6.2   Bradford and York: comparison of economic indicators

Rank order of 64 (2010)	Bradford	York
High-level qualifications in workforce	20.1% (58th)	39.9% (7th)
No formal qualifications	18.3% (61st)	7.2% (6th)
Youth JSA claimant count (November 2011)	7.8% (52nd)	2.7% (3rd)
Welfare bill per capita (2009)	£2,806 (34th)	£2,186 (5th)

Source: Centre for Cities, *Cities Outlook 2012*,
http://www.centreforcities.org/research/2012/01/23/cities-outlook-12/.

Bradford and York

Anxious to prove a point, I wanted to test my theory that there was a link between vibrant communities and engaged SMEs, and I secured funding from the Joseph Rowntree Foundation to carry out research in the two cities where it focuses its work: York and Bradford.[5]

Naively, I anticipated my conclusions: York was the smaller city, but felt more active, engaged, capable; Bradford's economy clearly didn't function at the same level. Bradford is more racially diverse, and the trappings of poverty are more evident there. While I was considering my approach, Centre for Cities published a ranking list of Britain's 64 cities, using comprehensive economic criteria which seemed to confirm my impression (see the examples in Table 6.2).[6] The business profiles of the two cities weren't dissimilar, with service industries dominating both economies; Bradford had a slight disposition towards manufacturing.

Both Bradford and York have a significant presence of major national corporates (Nestlé and Aviva in York, Morrisons and the Yorkshire Building Society in Bradford), all too big to include in my survey.

The largest business organisation dedicated to corporate social responsibility in Britain is Business in the Community (BITC), whose 850 members are almost entirely large corporates. Promoting community engagement isn't a core activity of any of the umbrella groups which represent the interests of small business:

---

5   My report is available at http://sector4focus.co.uk/home/smes-in-the-community-my-jrf-report/.
6   http://www.centreforcities.org/research/2012/01/23/cities-outlook-12/.

the British Chambers of Commerce (BCC) represents 104,000 of them,[7] but only local Chambers with over 1,000 members may affiliate to it. This explains why in London there are a handful of Chambers, only one of which (the London Chamber) is affiliated to the BCC. Although the BCC caters in theory for the full gamut of SMEs, the Federation of Small Businesses (FSB) works among smaller ones, typically those with four to five employees, and has 200,000 members. Neither organisation actively advocates community engagement.

In a 2007 survey involving a self-selecting 1 per cent of FSB members the organisation claimed that 97 per cent of its membership behaved in ways which were environmentally and socially responsible.[8] That survey, taken at face value, concludes that SMEs are at the cutting edge of environmental excellence. For example:

> *83 per cent of respondents actively engaged in waste minimisation and recycling and 41 per cent of businesses bought products that were more environmentally friendly. Well over a third (39 per cent) reported that they engaged in energy efficiency measures and 30 per cent changed their core products and services to be more environmentally friendly.*

There would have been no stigma in admitting that the survey was carried out against a background of rising fuel and electricity prices, fears of energy insecurity, legislation obliging local authorities to increase waste recycling massively (including raising the rate of Landfill Tax and the cost of business waste collection services), not to mention a high media profile by government and campaign groups seeking to raise awareness of the dangers of climate change. The survey hardly reflected effort that was entirely voluntary.

Community engagement wasn't considered in detail by the FSB, and the business case for engaging with the community wasn't discussed at all.

All of the arguments for business to engage with the community listed here are valid for SMEs, and they are based upon those given by Business Link[9] when advocating corporate responsibility:

---

7   http://www.britishchambers.org.uk/about-the-bcc/#.UMXA8aXB_zI; 104,000 is about 2 per cent of SMEs.

8   http://www.fsb.org.uk/policy/assets/CSR%20Dec%202008.pdf.

9   List based upon Business Link's archived site: http://webarchive.nationalarchives.gov.uk/2012 0823131012/http://www.businesslink.gov.uk/bdotg/action/detail?itemId=1075408491&r.i=10754 08480&r.l1=1074404796&r.l2=1074446322&r.l3=1075408468&r.s=sc&r.t=RESOURCES& type=RESOURCES.

- A good CSR record feeds a good reputation, which makes it easier to recruit employees and generate customer loyalty.

- Employees stay longer, reducing the costs and disruption of recruitment and retraining, and reducing skills lost through employee turnover.

- Engaged employees are better motivated, more team-conscious and more productive, and speak more highly of their employer.

- Engaged employees enjoy higher levels of self-worth and are less likely to suffer from mental health problems

- Good CSR practice helps to ensure compliance with regulatory requirements.

- Involvement with the local community creates ideal opportunities to generate positive press coverage and brand recognition.

- Good relationships with local authorities make doing business easier.

- Understanding the wider impact of a business can help in the development of new products and services.

- CSR can make companies more competitive and reduce the risk of sudden damage to reputation (and consequent loss of sales). Investors recognise this, and may be more willing to invest.

My plan was to obtain email addresses for as many SMEs as possible – there are 13,500 in Bradford and 7,000 in York – and direct them to a website where I would survey them about their community engagement practices. Meanwhile, I would interview key people in business, local government and the voluntary sector in both cities.

Even before processing my data I was able to make several observations:

- The paucity of available contact data suggests that electronic networking between SMEs and between umbrella organisations and their members isn't well developed.

- Online data about local companies was only available for about 40 per cent of SMEs; most online local business databases don't include email addresses.

- Companies with fewer employees were less likely to publish an email address.

- Franchisees or branches of national retailers were very reluctant to respond, usually referring it 'up to the regional manager', invariably with no reply.

- In Bradford the very low response of Asian businesses in my sample may reflect a lower than average penetration of email, a cultural preference for face-to-face or telephone communication, or a preference for a language other than English.

The first thing that struck me from the responses was that the level of reported payroll giving was roughly double the national level: either Yorkshire is exceptionally generous (belying its stereotypical image) or, more likely, companies which use payroll giving or otherwise engage with communities were more likely to respond positively to a questionnaire like mine than those that did not. Headline findings from the survey include:

- Half of all SMEs had donated raffle prizes to good causes, the most popular type of giving, followed by skills, time and services.

- Larger SMEs had more complex engagement patterns than smaller ones.

- Payroll giving wasn't found in SMEs with under five employees, rising steadily to 50 per cent of companies with 50 employees or more (but see above).

- Employee volunteering was most likely to involve schools' careers events; permission for time off was more likely to be given to an employee volunteering to be a magistrate or a Territorial Army officer than to listen to children reading.

- It was accepted that employee volunteering should be allowed in company time, but in practice little of this happens.

- York businesses were much more likely to purchase fair trade supplies than those in Bradford – the only marked difference between the two cities.

Companies generally felt that businesses were expected to engage with communities (roughly 60 per cent) and that, by and large, they could do more in this respect. Views about the desirability of different types of engagement (cash and kind, time and talent) were mixed, and the business case for using volunteering to help build team spirit – rather than produce a community benefit – had significant support (30 per cent). Half or more of all SMEs hadn't heard of any local or national initiatives to promote community engagement such as BITC, Give & Gain Day and Bradford Cares or York Cares.

York Cares is a 'partnership of the city's leading employers committed to making York a better place through employee volunteering'. Created by Business in the Community as part of its 'Cares' franchise in 2006, it's now an independent group of 32 (mostly large) businesses co-ordinated from the University of York and working with 200 local voluntary organisations. There's a constant and varying supply of volunteering opportunities for employees available throughout the year, and three themed programmes supporting disadvantaged young people. So far over 2,000 business people and 1,000 students have given over 15,000 hours of volunteering. York Cares has won several awards and honourable mentions.

Bradford Cares used to do something similar but, following funding problems, had been in abeyance for three years at the time of my survey – though there were plans to reinstate it. Nevertheless, it was as well known among Bradford's SMEs as York Cares was among York's – which wasn't very much.

I found an interesting relationship between time volunteering and skills volunteering. Time volunteering is unskilled or low-skilled labour (usually by skilled people!) engaged in either fundraising activity or menial work such as digging or litter picking. Skills volunteering or, at its most sophisticated, skills transfer or exchange is when professional skills are deployed to benefit a good cause: this might be an accountant performing an audit for a local charity or a team of business people designing and implementing a marketing strategy with a charity to help it grow capacity. Figure 6.1 shows that time volunteering was only half as likely to be found in the smallest companies compared to skills volunteering, and that while the incidence of both rose with company size to as much as 50 per cent, there was comparatively less skills volunteering in companies with over 20 employees than in smaller companies.

Among those with more than 20 employees, time volunteering grew while skills volunteering actually fell.[10]

There's a place for time volunteering, not least from a team-building point of view, doing good in a way that maximises impact over a short and defined period, or as a small but regular ongoing time commitment like listening to children read in school. But skills volunteering offers a greater opportunity for employees to develop new talents and life experiences, and is likely to generate a greater impact per person-hour volunteered.

Very few businesses claimed a relationship which could be described as a Charity of the Year scheme (this tends to be a feature of bigger companies), although those that did work with a particular charity showed an element of business–charity harmony – for example, a car dealership raising funds for its industry's hardship charity or a dog rehabilitation business working with the RSPCA. Where a charity was chosen, the nominator was usually the owner or manager rather than the workforce.

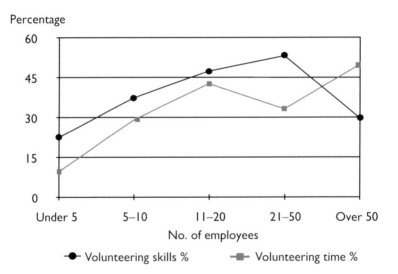

Figure 6.1   Volunteering

Source: T. Levitt, *The Social SME: A Study of Small Businesses and Selected Social Responsibility Issues in Bradford and York* (2013), http://sector4focus.co.uk/files/2013/03/ JRF-Report-FINAL-May-2013.pdf.

---

10 http://sector4focus.co.uk/files/2013/03/JRF-Report-FINAL-May-2013.pdf.

Throughout this story of Bradford and York I have emphasised the business case for community engagement and suggested that it's stronger for some activities than others; if the community engagement case is allowed to push the business case out of the reckoning, this becomes philanthropy – which, while nice, doesn't appeal to SME owners who often feel that their own lives are generally a struggle. However, that business case for engagement – the justification of community activity through the long-term benefits it can bring to a business – is widely under-appreciated. My results in both Bradford and York showed no significant appreciation of the business case for the strategic deployment of resources, human and otherwise, to meet community needs.

In short, SMEs do engage with their communities, but they do so in a way which is not strategic, not organised, not co-ordinated. It's reactive rather than proactive, without consideration of the business case, and is usually well under the radar.

This is a pity: it means that communities are not maximising the benefits of sharing the surplus resources of SMEs (time, skills, goods, services) and that SMEs are by and large not behaving as efficient corporate citizens. It's the view of the European Commission that:

> They may not know and use the term 'CSR', but their close relations with employees, the local community and business partners often mean they have a naturally responsible approach to business. For most SMEs, the process by which they meet their social responsibility is likely to remain informal and intuitive.[11]

A story from the Midlands is taking on the status of an urban myth – but it deserves to be shared.

A rather reclusive elderly lady runs her own jeweller's shop. Every year, because it gives her pleasure and makes her feel that she's 'giving something back', she sends a cheque for £100 to the RSPCA as her contribution to charity. It's suggested that she might consider giving her money to help people in the local community instead of animals – to which she reluctantly agrees, stressing that she still wants to support the RSPCA, but doesn't want to spend more than her £100. Accordingly, one year she gives £25 to the RSPCA and £75 to the local

---

11   http://ec.europa.eu/enterprise/policies/sustainable-business/corporate-social-responsibility/
     sme/index_en.htm.

morris dancing team (there's no accounting for taste). That was several years ago. Today, if you see those morris men perform, you will see a board at every dance bearing the name of their sponsor, the local jeweller, and you will even see the old lady's company name embroidered on their jackets. She watches every event, alive with joy. She now voluntarily gives more than a hundred pounds to the morris men each year to reflect the thrill she gets from watching them and being part of their community.

Underlining this story is the business case: how many more people locally now associate her name with jewellery, recognise her name when they walk past the shop, think of her name first when considering an anniversary present for their spouse? How much would that sort of publicity have cost if she'd had to buy it? And how much has her contribution done to secure the future of this ancient custom locally?

Research by Volunteering England suggests that while seven in ten FTSE100 companies have a formal employee volunteering programme, fewer than a quarter of SMEs do – and these will principally be the larger ones.[12]

Business Connectors

Will Popham was one of 20 in the pilot wave of Business Connectors whose role, promoted and overseen by Business in the Community, is to connect business better with communities.[13] In July 2012 Will had the opportunity to tell Prince Charles about his work, face to face.

The event was at The Oval, home of Surrey Cricket Club and an England test match ground. Will, an aspiring young manager seconded for a year from BT Group, gave an example of his work. There at the Oval, he told the Prince, much of the employment was 'flexible': many staff had temporary or occasional contracts because for most of the year there was little demand for security cover, while for a few days a year it was a priority. This meant that there were few opportunities for staff to undertake professional development and training, and the ground couldn't command their loyalty from one season to another. The lack of continuity meant that a different cohort of security and other staff came through the ground each year. Although it's not a large

12 http://www.theguardian.com/voluntary-sector-network/community-action-blog/2012/apr/04/
    charities-voluntary-organisation-business.
13 http://www.bitc.org.uk/programmes/business-connectors/about-programme.

employer, the Oval is iconic; it would be nice to be able to demonstrate good employment practice against this difficult background.

Popham realised that The Oval couldn't deliver a solution by itself: working with Kennington Jobcentre Plus, he brought nearby Fulham and Chelsea football clubs on board. Working with a local training company, a social enterprise SME, training programmes were created for staff to help establish a more settled routine of working for football clubs in the winter and cricket clubs in the summer. Through bespoke training they could consolidate and build on their experience and become more useful employees, who could in turn demand higher pay than casual unskilled workers could earn. In turn, the employers (who had been reluctant to invest in training for staff who might work with them for a week and then never be seen again) were better disposed towards investing in a pool that was going to be, collectively, more reliable. As an added bonus, priority was given to applicants with a Lambeth address, to help the local community.

That particular spring Will thought to tell the Olympic authorities about the project. Some of the trainees subsequently found work at the London Olympic Games.

Prince Charles clearly appreciated the story: it pressed every button that BITC, a charity he had set up, was designed to press. Better still, his own remarks were followed by Nat Sloan, Chair of the Big Lottery Fund's England committee, who announced a £4.8 million investment to grow the Business Connector programme. By 2017 there will have been three years of Connectors in 200 localities. To cap it all, Lloyds Banking Group, the programme's largest corporate sponsor, announced that it would nominate 60 Connectors and that BITC would have full access to the bank's West Midlands training facilities in order to develop the cadres.

A year later over 70 had gone into or through the system, including the 20 pilots, in 55 communities. The pilots have been comprehensively evaluated by NCVO, and while they clearly identify lessons to be learned (such as needing to be more sensitive to the communications needs – real and virtual – of rural areas), they were happy to give their support to the project's development.[14] Since its launch there have been changes to procedures, with secondments generally being longer than in the pilots (typically now 12 months rather

---

14 http://www.bitc.org.uk/sites/default/files/bitc_business_connectors_pilot_ncvo_evaluation_
    report.pdf.

than six, with two years not unknown); by general consensus, a 12-month secondment is more productive in a particular locality than two six-month ones. Connectors now have three days of training in Solihull and two annual networking events. A Web-based good practice resource of case studies is compiled by the IT company Fujitsu.

The growing number of Business Connector alumni also come together occasionally, and companies now established in the programme are finding volunteers competing for the chance to be nominated, to the extent that BITC now provides guidelines for interviews and practice sessions for potential recruits.

Duncan Tait, CEO of Fujitsu, an early supporter of Business Connectors, is unequivocal about the benefits his company gets from the process:

> *In seconding Business Connectors from Fujitsu, I have been struck by the way our people have developed. That's why I am increasing the number of secondees and including the Business Connectors programme as part of our overall approach to talent development. Previously we may have sent our potential leaders to Harvard or INSEAD, but now, if people want to be a senior leader in Fujitsu, I will be asking, 'Have they been a Business Connector?'*

The pilot period from August 2011 had started shortly after that year's London riots. Thrust into the 'deep end' was Kay Horne, a Sainsbury's supermarket manager from Waltham Cross who became the first Business Connector for Tottenham – a very different area to her workplace and the sparking point of the week-long destructive rioting. The first action of any new Business Connector is to build the contacts and networks they will be relying upon throughout their tenure to bring the right local people and the right local ideas together. After that, Horne says, her main role was going to be brokering support between SMEs and local charities, but she swiftly realised she would need to refocus. 'Most of the SMEs needed as much support as the charities did,' she told *The Guardian*. 'Some still had no front to their shop.'[15]

Business Connectors is unique in the corporate–community interface: it's size- and issue- neutral, relevant to both SMEs and corporates, with action priorities being set by and with communities. It's targeted on areas of most need, unlike most corporate philanthropic giving, which is poorly focused – if at all (Walker, 2013).

---

15 http://www.theguardian.com/society/2012/jul/10/challenging-introduction-post-riots-tottenham.

It feeds back good practice both into the next generation of Connectors and into the corporates themselves, which are keen to learn what level and type of engagement works. Indeed, one supermarket, Sainsbury's, which was investing four Connectors and a million pounds into the programme over three years, has described a 'community arms race' in which large retailers seek to improve their community engagement as part of their strategy of competing with other supermarkets locally.[16]

Ideally, businesses that have things that charities need should be able to talk to those charities directly, and people like Horne and Popham are catalysts, making that happen. But, says Kay Horne, echoing my own frustrations in relation to deprived communities, what happens when the local economy is predominantly, in her words, 'chicken shops, betting shops and nail shops'? To which we might add pawnbrokers, money lenders and minicab offices. They're probably not going to be able to provide the managerial, IT and marketing advice that charities appreciate most, let alone be able to spare the time to volunteer.

Accentuate the Positive

The marketing pitch for the Liverpool-based SME consultancy Coethica includes the words:

> To protect and grow a business of any shape or size, every director, manager and grassroots employee needs to understand how social and environmental issues will affect your profit margin. The intelligent way to financial success is through collaboration, respect, transparency, innovation and communication.

The CEO, David Connor, has been in business since 2006; he also moderates the Linked In group CSR for SMEs and, as @davidcoethica, has over 17,000 followers worldwide on Twitter. He provides bespoke business advice which emphasises how ESG issues should be seen even by the smallest business as opportunities to create competitive advantage, and not as impositions on 'normal' business operations. While he's ploughing a somewhat lonely furrow, it's important that evangelists for business engagement with communities at every level are celebrated.[17]

---

16 http://www.theguardian.com/sustainable-business/companies-emulate-barack-obama.
17 http://www.coethica.com.

Jill Poet, another activist from the Linked In group, is practising what she preaches in Southend, Essex, where her Organisation for Responsible Business (ORB)[18] was launched in 2010. Several hundred have signed up to join the organisation's directory, mostly from south-east England. Her tool for self-assessment, the Responsible Business Questionnaire, encourages introspection. Since 2012 she has published a *Responsible Business Workbook*, and in 2013 she launched a series of 'Double Whammy' events which follow a formula of bringing businesses together to get to know and support a local charity. Everything ORB does is predicated on the business case for being a good corporate citizen, respecting people and planet.

In South London, Merton Connected[19] was launched in March 2012 with £380,000 of government money from the Transforming Local Infrastructure (TLI) pot. The purpose of the TLI fund is to help local infrastructure organisations avoid overlap and duplication, achieve savings and efficiencies, and work more collaboratively with the private sector. Here, Merton Voluntary Services Council brought together Merton Chamber of Commerce and Enterprise, Merton Unity Network (of black, Asian and minority communities) and Volunteer Centre Merton.

Ray Kinsella, recruited from a business background to keep the project lubricated, claims that Connected has encouraged ever greater collaboration between Merton Voluntary Services Council and the Chamber of Commerce. The two had already been sharing training programmes, recognising that the training needs of small organisations – business planning, marketing, human resource management, finance – were similar whichever sector they came from.

Connected is working with businesses, public and voluntary sectors on common public health messages under a 'Responsibility Deal'. Once partnership brokerage had taken place, charities and businesses proved capable of talking to each other and doing their own negotiation, often being agreeably surprised to have found a partner and found them interested.

Merton Connected has witnessed an increase in business people interested in becoming charity trustees and so is stepping up the recruitment and training of trustees. Archetypal stories of the business trustee thinking 'If I ran my business like they run this charity it would never survive,'

---

18 http://www.orbuk.org.uk.
19 http://www.mertonconnected.com/tli-launch.

and the charity trustee thinking 'We appointed X because of his business skills: why doesn't he use them?' had both come to light. Trustee boards were often seen as out of touch and a barrier to progress, so the partnership planned to put greater than usual emphasis on utilising national Trustees' Week to the full.

Local charities had found it frustrating that business people were aware of larger national charities, but not of smaller ones in their own communities; businesses were frustrated to find that even in a single locality there were 'too many' charities, duplicating functions, often lacking individual capacity while missing out on generating it collectively and making it difficult to decide with which charity partner to work.

A lot of misunderstandings had been unearthed: not only did businesses and charities not appreciate how each other operated, but there were also unhelpful myths: 'We're a charity, employment law doesn't apply to us.' One business person observed, 'I was surprised how much support exists out there for charities – far more than for start-up businesses.' Voluntary sector management was seen to be at least as good as SMEs on managing change, but of a lower calibre on day-to-day affairs.

Young professionals are regarded by some charities as an under-utilised asset; where such networks exist they tend to be engaged, active and skilled – legal, financial, IT and so on. Several such groups exist in York, for example (though they didn't show up in the survey described above), and they undoubtedly add to the image of competence and engagement in that city. Such young professional networks are usually absent where their need is regarded as greatest, such as in the Merton suburb of Mitcham.

In the year that Merton Connected had been operating at the time of writing, a phenomenon had been sweeping Britain. A 170 per cent increase in demand on food banks nationwide had been met by a 76 per cent increase in the number of Trussell Trust food banks in just one year. In Merton the trust had little problem collecting food through its networks of churches, voluntary groups and, latterly, Tesco supermarkets, but the logistics of storage and distribution had been problematic. Applying the principles discussed earlier in this chapter, one might predict that the supply of both food and volunteers would come mostly from the Wimbledon part of Merton, and that demand would come almost exclusively from Mitcham – and so they did.

The American Way

While the American company the Marriott Group can hardly be described as an SME, most of its hotels are. The York Marriott overlooks the famous historic racecourse. When I met the manager, Mark Leyland, we exchanged querulous looks before we realised that I had taught him at a Derbyshire comprehensive school twenty years previously.

'Spirit to Serve' is the CSR programme of the 3,600 hotels of the global group. The York Marriott has 100 staff who completed 400 hours of in-work volunteering in 2012, as recorded by the HR department. One scheme, listening to local schoolchildren read, involves six employees for an hour a week throughout each school term. Payroll giving is actively promoted through the company intranet.

The manager's an active volunteer himself, as the company expects its local leaders to be, and serves on the board of York Cares. Through one of the York Cares programmes the hotel recently recruited an employee from a disrupted background, while school students come to the hotel for a week's work experience throughout the school year. Employees have helped a local charity clear ditches and footpaths, and volunteers have also spontaneously organised sponsored events to support a multiple sclerosis charity.

In 2011 the hotel's Charity of the Year was Macmillan. As a cancer charity, this was an easier cause to 'sell' to employees and potential sponsors than the challenging 2012 choice of Fairbridge, which supports disadvantaged teenagers with multiple needs – but employees have nevertheless pulled together and made each year a success.

York Marriott receives up to a dozen requests for support from local charities every week and tries to respond to all, generally offering raffle prizes which cost the hotel little or nothing – such as a week's free use of the hotel's fitness suite.

When a new cohort of managers is appointed to Marriott Hotels anywhere in the world they have three days of induction in California. One day will be spent working as a team with other novice managers on a physically and emotionally demanding social programme in a deprived area – and California has many. Again, it builds the team spirit – but it also says to managers: 'You are privileged; with privilege goes responsibility. Whatever you do, you are still part of a community. What you see today could have been you had things been different.'

As the Marriott example suggests, business engagement with communities is better established in the USA than in the UK. In the USA a quarter of people have no health insurance, and thus no guarantee of healthcare when they need it. A quarter of pupils don't finish their statutory years at high school, and only one adult in three is deemed 'healthy'. In places like the Lower East Side of New York four children in five qualify for free school meals, 28 per cent live in poverty and four in ten don't have English as their first language. Society values and community capacities are being challenged.

United Way[20] is the world's largest privately funded non-profit organisation, and is the major player on the business–community interface in the USA. Its management is dominated by business people committed to values of corporate citizenship whose motivation isn't simply philanthropic: it's the duty of business to respond to human need, successful people are 'paying for their fortunes', says Mike Durkin, President of its Massachusetts Bay operation.[21] In the starkest terms, 60,000 donors gave to his Boston office last year, including 5,000 companies donating over $1,000 each and 15 companies giving over $100,000; nationally, United Way has raised over $1 billion every year since 1974, as much as $3 billion in a good year. It's the biggest collector and distributor of payroll giving to good causes. Among its corporate supporters, banking, professional services and retail companies are most engaged, with pharmaceuticals and high-tech businesses markedly less so.

United Way has 125 years of history and 1,800 branches, mostly in the USA, but in over 40 countries overall. American government support for specific social programmes can't be taken for granted, so the organisation – with its emphasis on health, education and financial security – intends to help halve the high school drop-out rate in this decade. At the same time it wants to reduce the number of financially unstable families by half, and increase the number of young people who are healthy and avoiding high-risk behaviour. It does this by directing the money it raises towards community and voluntary groups as well as its own huge network of volunteers – largely employee volunteers – matching employee skills to local needs wherever possible.

In Britain voluntary organisations have long been seen as 'progressive' on social issues while business complies with the law but rarely engages in politics. In the USA by comparison, some United Way employers have pulled support away from big voluntary organisations for being, for example, 'anti-gay'.

---

20 http://www.unitedway.org/pages/about-united-way-worldwide/.
21 Personal communication.

In areas like Boston and New York United Way's corporate supporters are seen as very pro-immigrant, reflecting the area's history.

In an interesting contrast with the voluntary sector in Britain, United Way was founded in Detroit, a manufacturing hub throughout the twentieth century, and a hotbed of trade unionism. Trade unions have been essential in the development and operation of United Way, and have seats on its national board, despite the fact that in the 1970s it wasn't unusual to hear employers describe the union presence in the organisation as a 'first step towards communism'. It's perhaps noteworthy that in 1960 half of all American private sector employees were union members; today it's just 12 per cent. Communism in America has been averted. In Britain the development of trade unions – not legally 'charitable' because they support their members rather than 'public benefit' – has largely been independent of other forms of voluntary work, with traditional unions often being suspicious of the volunteering philosophy in the workplace.

Benefit Corporations and B Corps

The Benefit Corporation is a new concept in American law which recognises the power of business to tackle social and environmental problems – in short, to redefine what 'success' means in the business vocabulary. Already the status is recognised in 20 US states, and the decision of Delaware to acknowledge it in July 2013 was significant – as half of all publicly traded US companies and two thirds of the Fortune 500 are registered in that state. A Delaware public benefit corporation is entitled to seek access to venture capital, private equity and public capital markets. Broadly speaking:

- Their corporate purpose is to act in a responsible and sustainable manner in the interests of society while creating value for stockholders (shareholders).

- The fiduciary duty of their directors includes long-term triple bottom line goals.

- They are accountable on ESG issues through integrated reporting.

The legal status of the Benefit Corporation shouldn't be (but will be) confused with certified B Corp status, which is to sustainable and ethical business what fair trade certification is to trade justice. As of February 2014 there are nearly 1,000 Certified B Corps in 32 countries, mostly in the USA, almost all SMEs.

Australia's first B Corp was Small Giants, an organisation which finds, supports and develops other social enterprises. B Corp status means that they have been approved by the independent B Lab organisation against a set of community, environmental, accountability and transparency standards (in that order of priority). Certification isn't necessary to acquire the legal status, although it does bring access to support and other services from B Lab, which legal status alone does not. Certification is rigorous, requiring a company to score at least 80 of 200 available marks. Etsy, the online artisan marketplace, qualified with a bare 80 in 2012, but has used the experience to set an agenda for improvement prior to the certification's biennial renewal.

A newly certified B Corp is invited to sign up to a 'Declaration of Interdependence' which draws on the American Constitution, Gandhi and others for its inspiration:

> *We envision a new sector of the economy which harnesses the power of private enterprise to create public benefit. This sector is comprised of a new type of corporation – the B Corporation – which is purpose-driven, and creates benefit for all stakeholders, not just shareholders*
>
> *As members of this emerging sector and as entrepreneurs and investors in B Corporations, we hold these truths to be self-evident:*
>
> *That we must be the change we seek in the world*
>
> *That all business ought to be conducted as if people and place mattered*
>
> *That, through their products, practices and profits, businesses should aspire to do no harm and benefit all*
>
> *To do so requires that we act with the understanding that we are each dependent upon another and thus responsible for each other and future generations.*

The vision is coherent and concise:

> *Government and the nonprofit sector are necessary but insufficient to address society's greatest challenges. Business, the most powerful man-made force on the planet, must create value for society, not just shareholders. Systemic challenges require systemic solutions and the B Corp movement offers a concrete, market-based and scalable solution.*

In August 2012 Ben & Jerry's achieved Certified B Corp status – the largest company to do so, and the first wholly owned subsidiary of a major corporation. The Yonkers-based Greyston Bakery has supplied Ben & Jerry's with chocolate fudge brownies for its ice cream since 1988. Greyston is a social enterprise and both a B Corp (the first in New York State, scoring an impressive 128) and legally a Benefit Corporation.

Greyston is the answer to every sceptic on responsible business. An SME with around 70 employees, it has survived for 30 years on strong Buddhist principles: the 'Mandala' describes the community of stakeholders of which Greyston is the hub, and the 'Pathway' is the company's mission. Established by a Jewish Buddhist teacher, Bernard Glasman, to create employment for his meditation group of six ex-offenders in 1982, the heart of the business is its approach to recruitment and employment. In short, Greyston employs people others will not. Its 'open hiring' philosophy is simple: 'We don't employ people to make brownies; we make brownies to employ people'.

Recruitment to vacancies on the 60-strong shop floor is on a first come, first served, 'no questions asked' basis from a list of 'hard to employ' volunteers. These are ex-offenders, people in rehab, homeless or at risk of offending. Every few weeks at a hiring session a batch of candidates will receive two days' training: one generic, valuable in future whether the candidate will work for the bakery or not, and one specific to Greyston. Apprenticeships last a year, subject to assessment every two weeks: working here is no holiday camp. Fifteen people will be 'on call' for casual or seasonal employment at short notice at any time. Up to 20 people a day apply for a job at the bakery, knowing that if they are successful the job will give them health insurance, a credit history, skills, experience, union membership and references which may not be readily available elsewhere. Some employees have been with the company 15 years; the number who drop out is tiny, as almost all of those who leave go to other jobs.

Each employee is allowed eight hours per year paid leave for volunteering; half of the workforce take part in a twice-yearly environmental clean-up operation in Yonkers, as Ben & Jerry's-sponsored Community Days.

Although the majority of Greyston's 12 tons of product per day goes to Ben & Jerry's, it makes other cakes and biscuits, including its own brand, for 200 supermarkets, including one for the Whole Planet Foundation, a company which finances micro-credit loans in developing countries. It also produces six gourmet products for dessert bars.

As any visitor can see, Greyston is undoubtedly a growing business (with a $10 million turnover) and isn't a charity, but it's owned by the Greyston

Foundation, which is. In turn the Foundation provides 100 units of low-rent housing locally (spending $50 million to date), 100 childcare places, after-school programmes, HIV care and tenant services to 2,200 direct beneficiaries each year – as well as six community gardens for all in the poorest parts of Westchester County to enjoy.[22]

Where are SMEs Going?

During the 2011 riots in London a number of images were seared onto the public consciousness. This wasn't just because they were endlessly repeated on 24-hour news programmes, and again on the first anniversary, and again on the second, but because they were genuinely remarkable: a burning furniture store in Croydon, a woman jumping for her life from a burning flat, youths in hoodies helping themselves to flat-screen televisions and a disabled man being robbed in broad daylight. But another image will also pervade: in the days after the riots, armies of civilian volunteers, armed with sweeping brushes, dustpans and black plastic bags, mounted a clean-up operation which dwarfed anything the local authorities could deliver alone.

The civilian army consisted not just of traditional community activists, but of ordinary people, possibly 'volunteering' for the first time, motivated by civic consciousness and co-ordinated by Twitter. This ubiquitous icon of our decade enabled the tools, the workers and the purpose all to be in the right place at the same time. This was a type of citizen mobilisation that's likely to become more common in future as the tools of focused but disintermediated engagement grow in both quality and quantity. The same phenomenon has also led to crowdfunding of 'good' projects in the arts, culture, business, aid and the environment, as well as high-skill volunteering networks like Good People.[23]

When riots, floods and other catastrophes occur it's said to 'bring out the best' in British citizens, recalling the Dunkirk spirit of hordes of little people taking on a leviathan enemy against the odds. But why wait for disaster? What does this portend for our biggest group of corporate citizens, the SMEs?

---

22 http://greyston.com/wp-content/uploads/2013/11/Financial-Data-2012-Annual-Report.pdf. Also Kiser and Leipzig, 2014.
23 http://about.goodpeople.co.uk.

My research has shown that in Bradford and York the visible, public profile of SME engagement in communities is low, but not absent. Employee fundraising for good causes is widespread even among the smallest companies. We saw earlier how time volunteering and skills volunteering grow as we move our focus from the smallest to those with 10–20 employees, above which size time volunteering continues to grow and skilled volunteering falls off. While time volunteering is welcomed by small voluntary organisations – especially if focused, ongoing and not being carried out to tick a CSR box or simply provide a day out for staff – focused skills volunteering is appreciated so much more in terms of its positive impact.

Common and potent drivers of SME engagement include personal interest and fulfilment, enhancing employee morale and motivation and 'giving something back to the local community'. Less common are 'business reputation' or a desire to implement 'good practice'. A 2008 survey by the International Institute for Sustainable Development (IISD) found that half of all SMEs believed that social responsibility was a matter of *ethics and intuition* rather than a business strategy. The FSB research previously quoted suggests that no fewer than 90 per cent of SME community engagement strategies were motivated by their owner or manager's personal values – half described them as 'altruistic', with just one in three saying it was business-led. It's likely that most SME community engagement activity starts with someone asking a business to get involved rather than resulting from a positive community engagement policy.

Smaller SMEs generally lack a strategic basis for community engagement because owners and managers don't look for a business justification for it; without evidence of a business case for doing so, a strategy isn't deemed a priority. There are fears that the net costs of such commitments are high in time and resources, although these are probably exaggerated; and SMEs feel that having a CSR strategy is more applicable to larger companies, not recognising that they already do things which could be described as community engagement.

This is reflected in the types of engagement I found, informed by a theory I put forward in *Partners for Good* (Levitt, 2012), which appears to be withstanding the test of time. It is that corporate community engagement happens at three levels (ad hoc, organised and strategic) and in three categories: Cash and Kind, Time and Talent and Head and Heart (see Tables 6.3–6.5 below). Engagement tends to start in the bottom left-hand corner of Table 6.4 (ad hoc/cash and kind, typically employees collecting cash for a good cause) and progress in a generally 'north-easterly' direction. However, strategic levels of engagement, informed by and in pursuit of a business case, can't be achieved without management, if not boardroom, levels of engagement. In her excellent work the 2013 *Corporate Giving Almanac*, Dr Catherine Walker of the Directory of Social Change makes the valid point that funds raised by employees and customers may be acknowledged, but shouldn't properly be included in any measure of corporate giving by the company itself (Walker, 2013). This is a message that some companies, especially those involved in large Charity of the Year projects, have yet to take on board.

Table 6.3   Types of CSR activity

Type of community engagement activity	Examples of helping good causes
Cash and Kind	Giving money; supporting employee fundraising and matched funding; payroll giving; giving surplus stock or materials; giving second-hand equipment; allowing rooms and other facilities to be used by community groups; pro bono gifts of services (such as printing)
Time and Talent	Supporting employee time volunteering, including fundraising and direct volunteering; supporting employee skills volunteering; pro bono gifts of skills (such as auditing, Web design or marketing)
Head and Heart	Procurement and supply chain management in support of good causes such as sustainable forestry, social enterprise and fair trade; encouraging work placement and mentoring within the workplace; measuring impact of CSR activity, including benefit to the company; allowing outsiders access to in-house training; supporting employees to be school governors, councillors etc.; working with schools on curriculum matters; social investment of surplus cash into local enterprise

Table 6.4   Categories of corporate community engagement

	Cash and Kind	Time and Talent	Head and Heart
Strategic	Promote payroll giving, top up employee fundraising; complex charity partnership; strategic donation of goods and services	Strategic volunteering menu designed to maximise community benefit while developing employee skills	SROI used to justify cost of programme; deeper commitment such as granting leave for Voluntary Service Overseas; shared value approach
Organised	Employer allows payroll giving and fundraising in company time; adopts Charity of the Year; some goods donated	Employees volunteer in company time; some skill matching and longer-term commitment; pooling of volunteering opportunities	Engagement determined by local need based on consultation; affinity marketing; ethical supply chain
Ad hoc	Employees raise money for charity independently; employer donates raffle prizes or small amounts of cash in response to requests	Occasional employee volunteering in own time; team volunteering not always matched to community need	Employer has ethical procurement policy, e.g. fair trade drinks, good causes linked to some awareness-raising activity

Table 6.5   Mapping of York and Bradford SMEs' engagement activity onto Table 6.4

	Cash and Kind	**Time and Talent**	**Head and Heart**
Strategic	SERVICE DONATION	UNPAID LEAVE >5 DAYS Paid leave – 3–5 days *Paid leave – over 5 days*	WE GIVE MORE THAN MOST A month's unpaid leave
Organised	Surplus goods donation Payroll giving Charity of Year (fundraising partner)	**PAID LEAVE 1–2 DAYS** SKILL MATCHING COMPANY TIME AVAILABLE UNPAID LEAVE 3–5 DAYS Team volunteering/building	**SCHOOLS CAREERS TALKS** 'GIVING BACK' We give our 'fair share'
Ad hoc	**RAFFLE PRIZES DONATED EMPLOYEES FUNDRAISE IN OWN TIME**	**PRESTIGE VOLUNTEERING*** EMPLOYEE TIME Own time volunteering Unpaid leave – 1–2 days *'Fun' volunteering*	**WE GIVE A LITTLE** ETHICAL PURCHASING (BASIC)

Notes: **DOMINANT** (>40%), COMMON (21–40%), Occasional (5–20%), *Insignificant* (<5%).

*   Prestige volunteering is that with a high positive public profile – for example, magistrate, councillor, Territorial Army officer. Volunteering leave is available more in principle than in practice.

Table 6.3 defines the categories of engagement, while Table 6.4 shows how each can operate at different levels of sophistication. Table 6.5 depicts what I found in the SMEs of York and Bradford.

Larger SMEs and companies that are members of business networks – two in three SMEs of 20–250 employees in size, according to BITC/DTI[24] – believe that social responsibility helps create a successful business, while a quarter disagree. This is in line with my own findings, in which around seven in ten SMEs agreed (or agreed strongly) that 'businesses have a responsibility to engage in communities' and six in ten felt that 'our company does what we can in the community'.

The IISD found that leaders of larger SMEs were notably better informed on CSR issues than those of smaller ones, which is consistent with both BITC's work and my own conclusions. While 91 per cent of SMEs said that their business was already 'socially and environmentally responsible', it may be that few smaller SMEs could justify this intuitive claim objectively. Many wouldn't

---

24 http://www.bitc.org.uk/resources/publications/engaging_smes.html (2003).

consider that compiling such evidence was a worthwhile use of their time. It's likely that a lot of smaller companies are doing the 'right thing' without realising that they are doing so; certainly, this is the impression I got.

What triggers community engagement? As one charity told me in Bradford: 'It is easy to ask the corner shop for a voucher or a raffle prize. If you ask a shop from a national chain they will probably pass the request up the management chain before saying 'no' two weeks later.'

Table 6.6 is based on that work carried out by BITC/DTI ten years ago, with my additions. It shows four categories of stimulus.

Missing from any list of current drivers for corporate community engagement are external incentives such as tax breaks or other rewards from government, despite the fact that 76 per cent of respondents to FSB's 2007[25] survey called for them.[26] As the business case is strong, tax incentives shouldn't be needed. There are other difficulties with tax incentives: how to define desired behaviour and how to avoid minimum or cosmetic compliance. It's difficult to justify reducing tax to stimulate public benefit when taxation exists to further public benefit. The same survey also showed, pointedly, a desire for more information (37 per cent) and access to good practice examples (42 per cent). Only a third (35 per cent) wanted to be left to their own devices, which is consistent with my own results.

Table 6.6   Triggers for developing community engagement

Local stimuli	Sector stimuli
Identified by employees, community groups or the local authority Especially critical in more deprived areas, crime and environmental blackspots Some degree of co-prioritisation – e.g. with local authority?	*Informed by sector networks and personal experience in business* Skills development and shortages for business purposes, climate change, education, future recruitment, pro bono work
Business stimuli	**People stimuli**
Day-to-day challenges The image of the company or industry, communication strategy, opportunities and need for innovation, customer expectation Social Value Act 2012, ISO 26000	*Issues of interest to management and staff* Employee engagement and commitment, team spirit, exposing hidden skills, developing new skills for career development

25 http://www.fsb.org.uk/policy/assets/CSR%20Dec%202008.pdf.
26 These are not the same incentives the UK Chancellor promised to consider in the 2014 Budget, which concerned social investment, a strategic manifestation of 'Head and Heart'.

Table 6.6 also mentions the Social Value Act of 2012 and ISO 26000, which is an international standard of social responsibility launched in 2010.[27] Unlike many International and British Standards this is advisory and not compulsory – so compliance isn't an issue, and its force as a driver for community engagement is therefore weak.

Barriers to Community Engagement

Some SMEs are simply not aware of the advantages that community engagement can bring, and a few may have decided against engaging after assessing those benefits – based on sound information or otherwise. Barriers to community engagement often cited include cost and time constraints, neither of which argument is supported by those who have passed through the 'engagement barrier'. Other reasons, some of which are very telling, include lack of guidance, leadership and buy-in from management or other stakeholders, and low levels of knowledge, leading to fear of failure or a feeling that 'CSR is not for us.'

Indeed, time constraints are well known for restricting SMEs' ability to address issues that are beyond immediate operational concerns. 'Discretionary slack' is time larger companies use to plan ahead or innovate without the need to show an immediate return on the use of that time. SMEs typically regard themselves as 'firefighting' and less able to plan beyond the immediate future. The IISD points out that for companies already engaged in social responsibility, lack of time is less important than lack of skill in making the right decision in the business context. Therefore, the constraint isn't really a lack of time, but a lack of expertise in understanding the social responsibility agenda and its benefits, prioritising it within their business, and then allocating the time and resources required to address it.

Perhaps the management structures of SMEs aren't suited to this sort of strategic planning: relationships between smaller SMEs and their employers and customers are often characterised by a high level of informality. Employee relationships may be more family-like, with greater cordiality and social integration. There appears to be less demarcation between the roles of management, ownership and shop floor in SMEs, where roles are more likely to be flexible and multi-disciplinary compared to larger companies. Table 6.7 suggests how these attitudes may progress with growing business size.

---

27 http://www.bsigroup.com/en-GB/ISO-26000-Social-Responsibility/.

Table 6.7   Possible links between SME size and propensity to engage

1–4	5–10	11–20	21–50	50+
Family at work	**Team at work**	**Employees at work**	**Business at work**	**Strategy at work**
Engagement is very local and non-strategic; there are limited opportunities to engage; the major influence on corporate behaviour is the conscience and passion of key individual(s)	Manager dominates business activity and is business-focused; business interest is perceived to outweigh that of community	Employees are more influential collectively than as individuals, so employee initiatives and a focus on employee engagement emerge		Appreciation of business case for community and employee engagement grows,* responsibility may be devolved

*   Concepts like impact measurement and Social Return on Investment are more common on the agendas of larger companies.

Promoting SME Engagement: Holland and Elsewhere

Picture the scene: a vast hall contains six bases where different commodities are bartered, where people in brightly coloured coats facilitate the striking of deals. As the mayor launches proceedings a gong is struck, and for two frantic hours folk mill around, looking for the best bargains. This is no stock exchange: no shares, bonds or money changes hands, yet over ninety deals are struck, roughly the number expected.

In the regional government's main hall in Utrecht 80 voluntary organisations and 50 local businesses, mostly SMEs, are taking part in a Beursvloer,[28] of which there are 75 across Holland each year. The movement has grown every year since the first events ten years ago. 'Beursvloer' literally means 'trading floor', but 'social marketplace' is the preferred translation.

Prior to the event Utrecht's local voluntary sector umbrella body invited charities to say what they needed (pleas for cash aren't allowed) and to publicise the event. Businesses – from the giant Rabobank, whose HQ is nearby, to tiny consultancy or accountancy practices – register what they can offer.

Armed with only a spreadsheet listing offers and needs, the charity representatives (orange name badges) and businesses (blue) circulate to find not just any match, but through negotiation, the best available match;

---

28 http://www.beursvloer.com/english.

this 'speed dating' element is part of the fun. Each new partnership is registered and rewarded with a sticker, every deal listed on a giant screen.

The regions of the hall are labelled 'Coaching, Expertise and Research', 'Communications and Marketing', 'Legal and Financial Advice', 'Materials and Facilities', 'Volunteering' and 'Strategy, Organisational and IT Advice'. At one point the public address system begs, 'Is there a graphic designer in the house?' Tea and coffee are freely available and there's a glass of wine for all afterwards.

Such trading is in its infancy in Britain, but a founder of the Beursvloer, Esther Schoustra-Hofstede, says that once started in Holland it acquired a momentum of its own. Depending on the city, experience and sophistication, an event can cost the organisers anything from €2,500 to €55,000 plus up to 300 hours of preparation, much of the cost being met by gifts in kind like free use of the hall or commercial sponsorship, typically from a big bank or insurance company.

As the final gong sounds there are cheers: most go home happy to have taken part in the 'new sharing economy', as Dutch academic Jan Jonker calls it.[29] A health charity has obtained a host for a conference in exchange for a day's first aid training; an amateur theatre group has recruited backstage volunteers, and take-up for a small training provider's free workshop on 'How to Lead Volunteers' has been good, the market exposure welcome.

The beauty of the Beursvloer, and the key to its success, is the personal contact. The event is modelled on a traditional stock exchange floor, and it works – with the important proviso that the purpose isn't to find just a match between supply and demand, but to find the *best* match, the most 'profitable', in a values sense, to both parties. The outcomes are that charities gain business support, businesses are engaging with communities, skills are being transferred, the economic sustainability of each party is enhanced, profiles are being raised, networks are being grown and quite a lot of fun is being had.

I'm not aware of businesses and charities coming together on this scale anywhere in Britain, but the potential certainly exists: again, the Internet provides the opportunity.

Tameside 4 Good[30] is an initiative to encourage local businesses, SMEs in particular, to share resources with local charities and voluntary organisations.

---

29 http://www.nieuwebusinessmodellen.info/nl/onderzoek/.
30 http://tameside4good.org.uk.

As with the Beursvloer, the secret is to create a market in which participants can gain mutual benefit on the basis of being members of a shared community.

In 2011 the Council for Voluntary Action Tameside (CVAT) carried out local research which showed that while businesses were willing to help out local good causes where they could, they didn't know how to engage with them. When a charity approached them it was usually for cash or a raffle prize, neither of which necessarily felt appropriate, while few members of the public could name any local charities with confidence. When Chief Executive Tony Okotie heard of the Cabinet Office funding scheme Transforming Local Infrastructure, he saw an opportunity. CVAT already worked with 150 local voluntary organisations, so there was no problem with the demand side of the market he was seeking to create. Through the medium of the Tameside 4 Good website, supported by generous and ongoing coverage in the local press, CVAT publicised:

- the business case for behaviour linked to corporate social responsibility;

- opportunities for employer-supported volunteering and payroll giving;

- matching supply and demand of non-cash contributions in kind;

- a central fundraising initiative to support local good causes and brokering and advice for employers seeking to raise money for a specific cause.

In June 2013 I attended the second face-to-face event to promote Tameside 4 Good, at which it was announced that a further strand was about to be added to the 'offer':

- Talent Pool, an online way to match skilled volunteers with the skill needs of organisations within the community.

Talent Pool is provided within the Tameside 4 Good website by Good People, a social enterprise specialising in skill matching in volunteering and employment.[31] It uses sophisticated 'dating' technology to match supply and demand, and does so to good effect for BT and Help for Heroes (a job site for

---

31 http://about.goodpeople.co.uk.

former service people called Transition Force), the Foyer Federation (pop-up employment shops linking mentors to young people excluded from the jobs market), UnLtd (matching social investors with initiatives) and London's Shard (recruiting staff from and engaging them with the local community).

At the forum, also attended by the new Business Connector for Tameside, we heard that in its early months Tameside 4 Good had recruited 60 local businesses, raised £6,000 for its central funding pot (thanks in part to a sponsored headshave by a former *Coronation Street* actress) and utilised over £30,000 of non-cash resources donated by businesses which had been taken up by over 30 local organisations.

A local garage proprietor told us how he added £1 to every customer invoice, which he donated to the CVAT 'pot', and that some of the free tickets for motor racing events he regularly received would be donated to charities as raffle prizes in future. A family baker told us that 10 per cent of her takings on certain products during Valentine's Day week had been donated to a women's refuge. The owner of a very small bespoke steel stockholder said she knew that she couldn't afford to encourage employee volunteering or cash donations to charity, but through Tameside 4 Good had donated and erected a steel fence at a youth club utilising surplus stock. 'Things that are small and easy for us to do have made a big difference for others,' she observed.

Quite. The creation and utilisation of markets in this way can only be a good thing; it matches surplus with need, supply with demand, capacity with cause, and these are concepts SMEs can understand. It creates personal and professional fulfilment, and enhances the reputations of the businesses concerned.

This must be the future for small businesses.

Chapter 7

Market Forces

I believe the distinction between a good company and a great one is this: a good company delivers excellent products and services; a great company does all this and strives to make the world a better place.
William Clay Ford Jr, Executive Chairman, Ford Motor Company[1]

The market is the most fundamental of all of the tools in the capitalist toolkit. The principle's simple: I have something that you want. We arrive at a price you are willing to pay for it and that I am willing to accept. If the commodity is in short supply, or if I have a monopoly, I can charge the highest possible price; if the market is flooded, the price is forced down. In some situations I might be willing to sell for less than the market price (or even less than it cost me to make the product, at least for a while) if I thought it made sense to do so in the long run, perhaps to tempt you into loyalty towards my brand. In the long term the price I charge must cover all of my costs – labour, materials, transport, maintenance, taxes – as well as an element of profit. The profit can be used to reinvest in the company, to give to a good cause or to reward myself or my fellow shareholders.

Where the supply and demand sides of the market are in balance, the market is predictable and prices are likely to be stable; stable prices reduce pressures that could lead to higher labour costs – often a significant element of overall costs – and a tendency towards inflation. It's regarded as healthy for national inflation to be low, stable and predictable, at perhaps 2 per cent. Deflation – the reduction of costs and prices year by year – is generally held to be unhealthy because something in the chain isn't holding its value and other costs, such as labour costs, are politically difficult to cut.

If what I am selling is made of different elements combined together, then each constituent and each phase of the manufacturing process goes through the procedure outlined above; every transaction in the supply chain is capable of yielding profit, and of course, I am always keen to find ways of minimising

---

1 Ford was urging school students to support the USA's National Parks in April 2003; quoted at http://sloanreview.mit.edu/article/the-high-impact-of-collaborative-social-initiatives/.

my costs in order to boost profit while keeping the price of my product competitive. Cost savings can come from new ways of sourcing materials, greater productivity on the production line, business growth to achieve economy of scale, keeping wage costs low and minimising 'interference': the imposition of external factors that increase costs in the marketplace.

And that, in a nutshell, is the market.

There's nothing inherently good or bad about the process; the system's value-free, although the players within it are not. The history of capitalism is that those determined to maximise profits at any cost have been able to thrive, and at its extreme it has given rise to the philosophy of 'greed is good', epitomised by the character of Gordon Gekko in the 1987 film *Wall Street*. In 2013 *The Wolf of Wall Street,* based on the story of stockbroker Jordan Belfort, reprised the theme. Certainly some countries have been blighted by cold, capitalist exploitation: the infrastructure of Africa, constructed during the nineteenth century, shows how minerals, slaves and other commodities could be readily removed out of the continent with nothing going back in and with no capacity created for developing an intra-continental market.

As far as the UK, Europe, Australasia and the USA are concerned, capitalism has become, without doubt, the most successful economic system ever known; for the most part, it has delivered wealth that can be more or less equitably shared within a nation (how much it's shared comes down to political decisions rather than a function of the market, thus becoming inexorably tied into the governance of modern democracies in the 'marriage' identified by Al Gore).[2] Alongside it runs another system, the state, which provides those services where (by popular consensus) market failure (or even market prices) would be unacceptable: most people would agree that the cheapest way of running a school is unlikely to be the best. Where it's legitimate for the market to determine the relationship between supply and demand, it's rarely good for the customer for a monopoly supplier to exist (Handy, 1998).

Only a generation ago the market was held to be the answer to everything. Margaret Thatcher and Ronald Reagan believed that market forces and the 'free market' were infinitely preferable to the Soviet command economy, and constantly reminded us of its virtues, symbols of freedom and democracy. Clearly Mikhail Gorbachev had sympathy with this idea, and went some way to putting his ideas into practice. Thatcher, meanwhile, saw the European Union's 'single market' as

---

2   See Chapter 1.

its greatest attribute, not just as a free trade area, but a pro-trade area, capable of lifting weaker European partners out of poverty by creating and sharing affluence. Her enthusiasm for the European single market – and her logic, on this policy at least, was impeccable – is today a matter of some embarrassment for her staunchest supporters. As the Thatcher era passed, the 'Third Way', essentially the Blair–Clinton debate on how to get the balance right between the powers and responsibilities of the market and the state, followed naturally.[3]

The market is therefore a tool. It can be manipulated insidiously by strong players within it or externally, and more openly by governments – and nowadays by governments acting in concert. The world is full of overlapping free trade areas such as the European Single Market, European Free Trade Association, North American Free Trade Agreement and Association of Southeast Asian Nations, as well as global agreements such as the General Agreement on Tariffs and Trade. No market is free from outside pressure, and history lists many examples of governments having to step in to prevent them collapsing. It's legitimate for governments, if they are prepared to intervene to save markets from catastrophe, to be allowed to intervene in good times too, to bend the market towards delivering social goals agreed through democratic processes. While capitalist purists decry this as 'interference' or 'meddling', public opinion is overwhelmingly in favour of the imposition of certain standards of behaviour within the market.

Let's explore how markets can be used for good and how they can be regulated effectively to make them deliver even more in terms of public benefit.

Using the Marketplace for Good

Let us turn from the broad concept of 'the market' to the narrower one of 'the marketplace'. The marketplace is the epitome of small-scale trade, the place where smallholders and stallholders come together and earn their living by selling to the public. As with other traditional bailiwicks of capitalism, the marketplace can also be a force for good.

Really Useful Stuff[4] is the brainchild of Kay Allen, one of the most energetic and inspiring women in the world of responsible business. Kay made her

---

3   In 2002, well into his retirement, Mikhail Gorbachev told me of his interest in 'the Third Way'. We were in the back of a car; I was co-hosting his visit to London.

4   http://www.reallyusefulstuff.co.

name 20 years ago when at the Kingfisher Group, where she was responsible for the policy under which the DIY store B&Q actively recruited older and/or disabled people to work in its stores. This led to a parallel career as an Equalities Commissioner and the award of an OBE; she took her magic to BSkyB and then the Post Office before finding her department disbanded in the latter's preparation for privatisation. She became an adviser to the Cabinet Office during the establishment of BITC's Business Connector programme, and in 2013 she set up Really Useful Stuff.

Really Useful Stuff is a marketplace – nothing else. Kay's ageing mother was frustrated because the things she needed for independent living as a person with disabilities were expensive, medicalised and not much fun. Where was the tool to help her fasten her own bracelet when she needed it? The self-stirring cup? The one-handed egg cracker? The talking watch? More to the point, how could Kay help her access the tools that she needed?

Kay knew from past experience that such exciting products were available on the market, but that anyone who wanted to shop around for the best product would need to invest in shoe leather or gain Internet skills and develop the patience of a saint – or settle for second best. Two or three chance conversations led her to the revelation that a marketplace could be created almost instantaneously.

It's generally accepted that the private sector can often make decisions on a much shorter timescale than voluntary or (perhaps especially) public sector bodies. Once she had stumbled upon her website provider, Kay's project was up and running within weeks. She set up a company and easily recruited half a dozen suppliers of aids for disabled people, allowing her to hit the ground running. As we know, Internet selling entails fewer overheads than running a shop, so the goods could be competitively priced; as of February 2014, just six months after inception, the site carried over 500 products from 100 suppliers, and numbers were still rising. Her business model involves a low profit margin (commission on each sale), but a large volume.

Volume necessitates marketing, for which she had no budget. So she recruited three national disability charities to be beneficiaries of Really Useful Stuff: at the end of each purchase the customer is asked to which cause 'Stuff' should make a donation of 1 per cent of the order price: 25p from the price of a floating bath thermometer (which flashes if the water is too hot) might not be a lot, but if 50 such purchases are made in a week it starts to add up – and it gives the charities an incentive to market Stuff for her through their own networks.

Perhaps Allen based her idea on Etsy,[5] an American website which has been likened to a cross between Amazon, eBay and 'your grandmother's attic', partly inspired by Schumacher's 'small is beautiful' philosophy of people-centred economics. Etsy is a marketplace for art, craft and artisan practitioners, as individuals or small companies, to sell their products and the materials needed to make them, or vintage (over 20 years old) craft products. Etsy creates nothing but opportunity, and having built up a turnover of over $10 million a month from zero in 2006, it has clearly done well: the company, which was registered in 2012 as a B Corp, works on the basis of charging 20 cents per item listed on its site plus 3.5 per cent commission on sales (which makes it far cheaper to sell than on Amazon). Etsy hasn't been without controversy, with some vendors accused of giving misleading information about their sources, and despite its success it has been performing below projected levels of turnover. In 2012 it took on a further $40 million of venture capital. Yet it has remained true to its ideals of encouraging artists, craftsmanship, ethnic and fair trade goods which are environmentally sound, and the site now has a 'support your local economy' filter.

Rockford, Illinois was once identified as the USA's third most miserable city. When the mayor of Rockford heard of Etsy through Twitter, he got in touch. Through Etsy he contacted his local arts and crafts community, leading to the establishment of arts and entrepreneurship training courses aimed at low-income communities to help address that unemployment-related misery.[6]

On a larger scale, the charity Oxfam recently carried out a global survey to establish which were the most sustainable global food companies. The results from the 'Behind the Brands' campaign surprised some and disappointed others, which is no bad thing.[7] Clearly the purpose of the research and subsequent campaigning has been to bring influence to bear not just on the ten largest such companies, but on the whole global food market.

Companies were assessed on their policies and practices relating to smallholders and suppliers on several criteria, based on publicly available information.

No doubt Nestlé, the world's largest food company, was relieved to have ranked number one following years of outdated criticism of its marketing of baby

---

5   http://www.etsy.com.

6   Recounted by Etsy's Chief Technology Officer Chad Dickerson at RSA, London in June 2013.

7   http://www.oxfam.org.uk/get-involved/campaign-with-us/our-campaigns/behind-the-brands.

milk substitutes. Unilever would have been frustrated to have come second –
it's high profile in its chosen role as a power for good in developing countries,
particularly through its Lifebuoy campaign on personal hygiene.[8] Seeing Coca-
Cola in third place will surprise many, but this no doubt reflects its change of
direction a few years ago, focusing on issues such as water conservation with
the Worldwide Fund for Nature and supply chain sustainability more generally
(Miller and Parker, 2013). These three, scoring 51, 49 and 41 per cent respectively
on the Oxfam measure, were head and shoulders above the rest, but even these
scores suggest there's still considerable room for improvement. Pepsico, Mars,
Danone and Mondelez (which includes both Kraft and Cadbury) form the next
cohort, with General Mills, Kelloggs and Associated British Food (13 per cent)
bringing up the rear. The top ten rankings roughly correlate with size, suggesting
that either responsible behaviour has helped them to grow or that large
companies which can call upon consistent and uniform practices throughout the
organisation have more leeway to act responsibly than those that do not.

So far, so good: this is Oxfam's observation. It's now trying to influence the
market by encouraging all of those listed to do better, based on objective evidence.

There's no room for any to be complacent:

> the scorecard also clearly shows that all of the Big 10 – including those
> which score the highest – have neglected to use their enormous power
> to help create a more just food system. In fact, in some cases these
> companies undermine food security and economic opportunity for the
> poorest people in the world, making hungry people even hungrier.[9]

No doubt Oxfam is also attempting to influence the purchasing power of the
consumer in the marketplace, building on strong evidence that a company's
ethical record (as opposed to simply its stance) can influence purchasing
practices – especially where two comparable products are on the market at the
same price and one company has a stronger brand reputation than the other.
Some consumers are prepared to pay a premium for 'good' – witness how,
for many years, the market for organic vegetables grew despite a significant
price differential. The Ecover range of cleaning products is now established
as a growing mainstream brand despite years of higher prices, built on a very
strong marketing line of environmental responsibility.

---

8   http://community.businessfightspoverty.org/profiles/blogs/samir-singh-the-business-of-
     saving-lives?xg_source=msg_mes_network.
9   http://www.behindthebrands.org/en//~/media/Download-files/bp166-behind-brands-260213-
     en.ashx.

Nestlé was the target of a massive lobbying campaign by Greenpeace in 2010. After just eight weeks of campaigning (involving a spoof Kit Kat advert, seen online by 1.5 million people, and 200,000 emails) the food company promised a zero deforestation policy in its palm oil supply chain. Greenpeace said: 'We didn't expect Nestlé to come up with this policy so quickly'.[10]

Although consumer boycotts are a traditional way of influencing the behaviour of a player in a market, this doesn't appear to be on Oxfam's agenda at the moment. According to the Ethical Consumer website there are around 60 current boycott campaigns in Britain, some targeting countries, but mostly companies, though it's some years since there was last an entry on the 'successful boycotts' page.[11] In 2012–13 a number of companies were in the public spotlight for engaging in massive, if legal, acts of avoidance of UK tax: Starbucks, Google, Amazon, Barclays and the French-owned Thames Water. It's highly likely that Starbucks' initial response – to make a payment in lieu of tax – and its subsequent decision to restructure so that it would pay UK Corporation Tax in future was prompted by the reputational damage the issue threatened rather than any formal boycott. However, a boycott was declared by UK Uncut, which held demonstrations outside several Starbucks outlets, and by the Coalition Treasury Minister, Liberal Democrat Danny Alexander. It's difficult to tell how effective the boycott was, although in December 2012 – the month when the issue arose – sales at rival Costa Coffee rose by 7 per cent.

Michael Sandel worries that everything today has become the subject of a market: surrogate parenthood, insurance companies incentivising weight loss, professional queuing to lobby US Congressmen, some prisons even allowing prisoners to pay to upgrade their cells. He argues that after the era of absolute faith that markets alone could deliver prosperity and freedom, in the Thatcher–Reagan era, and the Blair–Clinton belief that markets and the state together in dynamic flux were the best way of doing so, the ascendency of the market in politics is over:

> *Today, that faith is in doubt. The era of market triumphalism has come to an end. The financial crisis did more than cast doubt on the ability of markets to allocate risk efficiently. It also prompted a widespread sense that markets have become detached from morals and that we need somehow to reconnect them.*
>
> (Sandel, 2012)

---

10 http://www.ethicalconsumer.org/boycotts/successfulboycotts.aspx.
11 http://www.ethicalconsumer.org/boycotts/boycottslist.aspx (August 2013).

Promoting a Market for Good

We have seen elsewhere that 'responsible investors' have aped their mainstream counterparts by producing a share index by which the ESG market can judge them. The mainstream market has done the same: as with the Domini 400 Share Index, companies listed in FTSE4Good have also outperformed the market as a whole over the last decade with a 52.3 per cent ROI since 2001.

Using simple criteria, FTSE4Good companies need to show acceptable performance on all three ESG fronts: Environment (environmental management and climate change), Social (human and labour rights, supply chain labour standards) and Governance (countering bribery, corporate governance). An ethical sieve is applied (excluding tobacco and weapons, originally but no longer also excluding nuclear power, uranium mining and baby milk substitutes); over the years 288 companies have been removed from the index for non-compliance. There are currently around 900 companies on this global index, and around 1,000 more are engaged with the process and/or working towards recognition.[12]

Not only can the reputational premium of FTSE4Good membership assist a player in the market, but it's almost as though there's a market – a supply and demand relationship – within the field of corporate responsibility itself.

Business has rarely welcomed 'intervention' by government in what many, especially smaller companies, regard as their own, private, affairs. We've seen how after a century of regulating the market there are many rules which few would now want to remove. Actions to enhance consumer rights, environmental measures and anti-discrimination legislation have all in turn been lobbied against and dismissed as harbingers of doom for small business in particular, as it protests that it's already drowning in red tape and can't cope with more legislation. Invariably Armageddon hasn't happened, laws have generally been observed and 'progress' has been accepted as 'normal'.

No one today would seriously argue that the Americans with Disabilities Act or the 1995 UK Disability Discrimination Act, now embedded in the 2010 Equalities Act, had no positive effect on society – they even created market opportunities for companies that manufacture or market aids to help disabled people. Few would seriously argue that the Acts should be repealed on the grounds that they intrude upon the rights of businesses to manage their

---

12 http://www.ftse.co.uk/Indices/FTSE4Good_Index_Series/Downloads/FTSE4Good_10_Year_
    Report.pdf.

own affairs. The same will already be true of legislation aimed at combating corruption in developing economies; in enacting a United Nations convention, this has helped to establish worldwide standards of transparency and accountability to which no conscientious business person could object.

Twenty years of environmental legislation, not least through International Standards like ISO 14000, has imposed new burdens on business, and this too was resented when it was introduced. Today, not only have whole swathes of SMEs emerged to take advantage of opportunities presented by the fight against and the mitigation of climate change on the back of the accompanying legislation, but mainstream companies have developed and recognised the business case for serious investment in environmental measures too. The Co-operative Group and Marks & Spencer, not least through the latter's innovative and highly successful 'Plan A', have led the way in championing the tackling of climate change in the commercial world while proving beyond doubt that a business case exists for doing so. In the north of Scotland, where shops are few and distances are large, the pharmacy chain Boots, the stationers WHSmith, the clothes retailer Next and the high street chain Poundland share each others' delivery vehicles to economise on transport costs and carbon emissions, saving around £1 million per year between them.

Where does an initiative prompted by market intervention end and an identical action informed by the business case for protecting the environment begin?

Essential Regulation

While of course it's possible to over-regulate a market, or regulate it badly, good regulation is undoubtedly a force for good. Such regulation encourages the market itself to deliver 'public good', not least by limiting the damage it can cause.

Lord David Sainsbury, a business leader in his time who served for eight years as Trade Minister in Tony Blair's Labour government, is very clear: 'If we use the term "free market" to describe a market free of government regulations and social control, no such thing exists' (Sainsbury, 2013).

The message of his book is that although no such thing as a totally free market *should* exist, the state should support the market to function as effectively as possible, to establish level playing fields and to minimise abuse:

Sainsbury calls this the 'enabling state'. He lists four fundamental areas in which institutions properly support the operation of markets, by restricting:

- **Who can participate** – children under a certain age won't be allowed to participate in the labour market; a stock market listing necessarily excludes some companies.

- **What can be traded** – it's illegal to create a market in hard drugs, wrong to create one in human organs, and lethal weaponry is universally regulated (in theory).

- **Rights and obligations** – the most basic environmental and health and safety considerations are no longer controversial.

- **The conduct of trade and exchange** – it's taken as read that fraud and breach of contract shouldn't be tolerated, and that in some cases a customer should be able to claim compensation.

Perhaps 150 years ago there wouldn't have been agreement even on these basic tenets of acceptable market behaviour; yet even Adam Smith recognised that, left to its own devices, 'the market' couldn't be relied upon to be a force for good. Nothing annoys an upright business person more than seeing a competitor 'getting away' with a practice which is unfair, outside the rules or anti-competitive; the same sensibility is reflected in the widespread British perception that within the European Union some countries (the UK) 'play by the rules' more than others.

The business world remains divided on the role and value of regulation; as Sir Mark Moody Stuart (former Chairman of both Shell and Anglo American) says, catalytic converters on cars would never have existed if their development relied on market forces alone:

> *There's a big role for government and a big role for regulation. I make myself quite unpopular by saying we need sound regulation. Sensible regulation.*
>
> *Too often, regulators tell you exactly what you have to do, what you need to put in the catalyst, or how you have to build the building, which can take out the flexibility. What we need is a combination of a regulatory framework and a market which can work out how best to do it.*
>
> *(quoted in Gitsham and Wackrill, 2012)*

Sainsbury ends his book with an eloquent plea:

> *Capitalism is not a form of spontaneous order or the embodiment of a*
> *structure of basic human rights, but one of the greatest constructs of*
> *the human mind. It is a set of institutions which must be justified by its*
> *contribution to the well-being of society, and as such should be perpetually*
> *open to reform. There is no one best set of institutions which all countries*
> *should adopt, and a country's institutions need to be reformed constantly*
> *to meet the challenges of a changing world. Capitalism should not be*
> *seen, therefore, as a static concept but as a perpetual work in progress.*
>
> (Sainsbury, 2013)

Everything that happened during the crisis of 2007–8 – from toxic assets to bonuses for failure, from Fred Goodwin's pension to the farce of Lehman Brothers' governance – served to undermine faith in the market. As in a marriage, total and utter loss of confidence takes a long time to restore, if indeed it can ever be regained.

At the end of the First World War there was a widespread view that lasting global peace could only be achieved through social justice supported by the operation of the capitalist economy and its foremost tool – the market. So, in 1919, representatives of governments, employers and workers of nine countries – Belgium, Cuba, Czechoslovakia, France, Italy, Japan, Poland, the United Kingdom and the United States – met in Washington to draw up what became the International Labour Organization (ILO) conventions. These recognised that social justice was generally lacking from the working and living conditions of working people, and that the presence of 'injustice, hardship and privation' were such that they could generate 'unrest so great that the peace and harmony of the world are imperilled'. No doubt the events of 1917 in Russia were at the back of their collective mind.

The ILO called for:

- regulation of the hours of work including the establishment of a maximum working day and week;

- regulation of labour supply, prevention of unemployment, and provision of an adequate living wage;

- protection of workers against sickness, disease and injury arising out of their employment;

- protection of children, young persons and women;

- provision for old age and injury, protection of the interests of workers when employed in countries other than their own;

- recognition of the principle of equal remuneration for work of equal value;

- recognition of the principle of freedom of association;

- organisation of vocational and technical education, and other measures.[13]

Within two years 16 conventions and 18 recommendations had been agreed as the passion for workers' rights, originally called for by the Welshman Robert Owen over 100 years earlier, exploded onto paper – at which point the ILO was tactfully requested to slow down in its fervour. In the years immediately after the Second World War the ILO grew to over forty member nations, approved Convention 87 on freedom of association (crucial to its later support for Solidarność in Poland) and became part of the newly formed United Nations. In 1969 the ILO won the Nobel Peace Prize to mark its fiftieth birthday. Today it has 185 members, though 192 countries have established a minimum wage (first legislated for in New Zealand in 1894).[14]

If ever there was a completely free market in labour, there is not one now. Regulation has obliged capitalism to be a force for good – potentially, at least.

Frances Perkins: A Hero of Regulation

How did the United States respond to the idea of regulating market behaviour?

Frances Coralie Perkins was born in Massachusetts in April 1880 to an upper-middle-class family.[15] She would become the first woman to sit in the US Cabinet, as Labor Secretary, the sixth most important post in the government,

---

13 http://www.ilo.org/global/about-the-ilo/history/lang--en/index.htm.

14 In 2013 there were 736 UK employers in breach of minimum wage regulations, affecting 26,000 workers (BBC News, 23 August 2013).

15 Sources for Frances Perkins include: http://www.ssa.gov/history/fperkins.html, http://www. francesperkinscenter.org, http://www.aflcio.org/About/Our-History/Key-People-in-Labor-History/ Frances-Perkins-1880-1965 and von Drehle (2003).

for the entire twelve years of Franklin D. Roosevelt's presidency – longer than any other incumbent.[16]

A redoubtable feminist and liberal, she was aware of the changes that would lead to women's emancipation in the USA from an early age. She opted to be called Frances rather than 'Fannie' some time between joining the Episcopal Church, aged five, and leaving home to live in the adult world at 25. However, she retained her family surname when she married in 1913, and always kept her daughter Susanna and her ailing husband, Paul Wilson, out of the limelight. Indeed, for much of her married life public duties led her to see little of Susanna, who was brought up by a governess.

While a student (1904–1906) she visited many factories and became passionate in support of the working poor. She received a master's degree in Political Science from Columbia University in 1910. In 1911, as a Sociology Professor and working for a consumers' organisation in New York, she lobbied for a maximum working week of 54 hours for women and children in sweatshops and factories, confronting the Democratic Party's Manhattan Tammany Hall establishment. On 25 March that year she watched as the Triangle Shirtwaist Factory fire killed 146 people in little more then ten minutes, mostly Jewish and Italian immigrant girls – the largest workplace tragedy in US history until 2001. That fire and ensuing trial ushered many changes in the USA: a new generation of Democratic leadership, the mainstreaming of trade unionism and votes for women (von Drehle, 2003).

Perkins organised and mobilised women in many causes, her lobbying experience winning her a role on the Factory Commission which followed the Triangle fire. She worked as an aide to New York State Governor Al Smith, who would later run unsuccessfully for president in 1928. It was said at Smith's funeral that he owed his campaigning zeal to 'a book – called Frances Perkins'.

The next state governor was Franklin D. Roosevelt, who, coming into office in 1929, asked Perkins to be the State Industrial Commissioner, in which post she advocated insurance against unemployment and, following a study visit to Britain, state old age pensions too.

When Roosevelt won the 1932 presidential election he brought Perkins with him as Labor Secretary: as Chair of the President's Committee on Economic

---

16 In 1987 a second female appointment was made, since when six of the eight incumbents have been women.

Security, she wrote the 1935 Social Security Act. It included unemployment and old age insurance, but not health insurance – 'We couldn't deal with health in the time available,' she later admitted. This time Smith's contemporary in the transitionary Tammany Hall establishment, Robert F. Wagner, now Democratic leader in the Senate, saw the legislation through. On the day the Act was passed, Perkins's husband went missing in New York. She attended the Washington White House photo and newsreel call before dashing off to search for him. Several hours later she found him wandering the city in a daze, probably caused by bipolar disorder.

Roosevelt came to power with a mandate to move on from the Great Depression through 'the three Rs': Relief for the unemployed and poor, Recovery of the economy to normal levels and Reform of the financial system to prevent a repeat depression. Together these constituted the 'New Deal': its goals and principles were to dominate the Democratic Party's domestic agenda for three decades and return a Democratic president for seven of the next nine terms – not least by dividing Republican opinion. People who believe in a free market are usually very happy for the state to intervene when their industry is in trouble; in the first New Deal phase there was massive state intervention – both regulatory and financial – to rescue the banking, railway and agricultural industries. The second was more controversial: promoting the rights of labour unions, migrants and tenant farmers.

Frances Perkins did not believe in a free market, although she never set out to change the basic tenets of capitalism: it was the lifeblood of the American nation, despite what had happened in the Depression. But she had seen for herself that the 'free market' led to exploitation of women and children, to working hours so long that family life was impossible to contemplate, to illness without treatment, old age without security, employment without escaping poverty. It scarred the joy of childhood, and even took it away. A century of US capitalism had failed to address any of these issues, and she was determined to use what privileges she possessed – education, a forceful character and access to power – to tame and control it, direct it and make it a cause for – perhaps she was not so optimistic as to see it as a cause for good, but she believed it could be something other than a force of exploitation, inequality and suffering. So, under her jurisdiction, the USA enthusiastically signed the International Labour Organization Convention in 1934.

Even as a senior member of the government she could be found in politically dangerous situations, literally out in the street reminding demonstrating trade unionists of their rights to free speech and collective action. She persuaded Roosevelt not to bend to public pressure by using military force to quell a general strike in San Francisco; instead she helped to negotiate a peaceful resolution.

Under her intellectual leadership, the USA brought in the Wagner Act, giving workers the right to organise unions and bargain collectively, and other ground-breaking legislation. Unfortunately, much of the 1935 Social Security Act, passed in the House and Senate, was thwarted by the Supreme Court. It was only when Roosevelt was re-elected in 1936 with a larger majority that he felt strong enough to replace dissident judges. One new judge was Harry Black, an active supporter of workers' rights and an advocate of a 30-hour maximum working week. Roosevelt told Perkins she had free rein: the Fair Labor Standards Act of 1938 followed.

That Act brought in a maximum 44-hour working week for all, to be made up of five eight-hour days plus up to four hours overtime at time-and-a-half. It banned under-18s from working in some industries and prevented any child under 16 being employed during school hours. Around 700,000 workers benefited from the new laws, and Roosevelt later said that this and the 1935 Act were the two high points of the New Deal. They had been achieved through the guiding hand of Frances Perkins, the muscle of Robert Wagner and the leadership skills of FDR himself.

Perkins remained a controversial figure: in 1939 the House Un-American Activities Committee tried to impeach her after she refused to deport a trade union leader, Harry Bridges. The impeachment proceedings were eventually dropped for lack of evidence, and Bridges won his case against deportation.

Historian Arthur Schlesinger Jr described Perkins thus:

> *Brisk and articulate, with vivid dark eyes, a broad forehead and a pointed chin, usually wearing a felt tricorn hat, she remained a Brahmin reformer, proud of her New England background ... and intent on beating sense into the heads of those foolish people who resisted progress. She had pungency of character, a dry wit, an inner gaiety, an instinct for practicality, a profound vein of religious feeling and a compulsion to instruct ....*

Others described her as aloof, good at gaining the respect of her colleagues, but rarely their affection. Roosevelt was clearly a team player, a fair man, and probably a feminist; how could he not be, with Perkins at his side for 16 years? She said of him, in her 1946 book *The Roosevelt I Knew*: 'He didn't like concentrated responsibility. Agreement with other people who he thought were good, right minded, and trying to do the right thing by the world was almost as necessary to him as air to breathe.'

She resigned as Labor Secretary on Roosevelt's death in 1945. President Truman appointed her to the Civil Service Commission, on which she sat until 1952 when her husband died, at which point she left Federal service.

Perkins continued to be active as an academic and feminist until 14 May 1965. She is buried in New Castle, Maine. Her legacy lives on: the US Department of Labor building in Washington is named after her, and the day of her death is remembered each year in the Episcopal Church calendar. Each year 140 women are admitted to Mount Holyoke College on Frances Perkins Bursaries which support older women to study. In 2011 the Republican governor of Maine, where both of Perkins's parents were born, caused a public outcry when he had a mural removed from the State House depicting her, among others, because he deemed it 'anti-business'.

In 1911, at the time of the Triangle fire, many industries in the USA and elsewhere regarded workers literally as 'disposable': deaths in the workplace or through diseases of poverty were the price of progress. Then, as at every turn since, 'restraints' on free trade were resisted by some business leaders while being championed by the minority. After each step, those who might have wished to turn the clock back kept quiet while those who advocated positive corporate citizenship, like Frances, gradually grew in strength.

Reporting

A modern 'restraint' on the free market is the requirement to report. We don't say to businesses, 'You can report what you want, when you want, to whom you want'; we have long accepted that financial reporting should be on a statutory basis to allow investors, traders and prospective purchasers to know how sound, prepared or resilient a company is. But there's a debate about how much further reporting requirements ought to go.

Information is the lifeblood of business, politics, society, science, research, education and finance. Like blood, it brings nutrition, oxygen and potential to the organs it reaches. Cut off its flow to a limb, and the risk is that it will atrophy and die. So would it not be a good idea if we could know what the ESG status of every company was every year?

The Global Reporting Initiative (GRI)[17] is a non-profit organisation dedicated to making it standard practice for all organisations to make reporting on their sustainability (ESG or triple bottom line) as routine as financial reporting. It emerged from the American non-profit Ceres and the UN Environment Programme in 1997. While the use of GRI standards is voluntary (and has been criticised for not being policed sufficiently toughly), its aim is to make such reporting universal. The question should be, the GRI says, 'Why should you not report?' rather than 'Why should you report?'

Currently 4,000 organisations across 60 countries choose GRI standards as their benchmarks.

A broader requirement to report would, of course, be another example of a demand or restraint on the market – an imposition, an interference. But it would be a demand justified by public calls for transparency and the planet's need for sustainable economic activity.

The fourth iteration of the GRI came into being in 2013, bringing the principles closer to those of other measures such as the UN Global Compact, putting greater emphasis on the impact of supply chains on ESG issues, and making it easier to distinguish between quality of behaviour and quality of reporting. G4, as it has become known, has been criticised for being more complex than its predecessors, reflecting the apparent impossibility of making reporting more useful and simpler at the same time.[18]

A significant change took place in Britain in 2006 with the passage of the Companies Act:

Clause 172: Duty to promote the success of the company

1. *A director of a company must act in the way he considers, in good faith, would be most likely to promote the success of the company for the benefit of its members as a whole, and in doing so have regard (amongst other matters) to –*

---

17 https://www.globalreporting.org.
18 http://www.kpmg.com/Global/en/IssuesAndInsights/ArticlesPublications/Documents/g4-the-impact-on-reporting-v2.pdf.

a.   *the likely consequences of any decision in the long term,*

b.   *the interests of the company's employees,*

c.   *the need to foster the company's business relationships with suppliers, customers and others,*

d.   *the impact of the company's operations on the community and the environment,*

e.   *the desirability of the company maintaining a reputation for high standards of business conduct, and*

f.   *the need to act fairly as between members of the company.*

Clause 172 governs the behaviour of directors of companies and it applies to every company in the UK. Sub-clause (1) deals with broad areas of what we recognise as 'corporate responsibility' with (a) indicating a move away from the short-termism which, as we have seen, is recognised by consensus as unsustainable, while (c) and (d) in particular put social responsibility right at the heart of what the company is for.

Traditionally the legal minimum basis of company reports is that the company should report on its financial affairs quarterly to its shareholders. Clause 417 of the Companies Act changed this, so it now includes:

5.   *In the case of a quoted company the business review must, to the extent necessary for an understanding of the development, performance or position of the company's business, include -*

a.   *the main trends and factors likely to affect the future development, performance and position of the company's business; and*

b.   *information about –*

i.   *environmental matters (including the impact of the company's business on the environment),*

ii.   *the company's employees, and*

iii.   *social and community issues, including information about any policies of the company in relation to those matters and the effectiveness of those policies*

Unlike Clause 172, Clause 417 doesn't apply to all companies, but only to those UK-incorporated companies whose shares are traded on a UK- or EU-regulated market or on the New York Stock Exchange or Nasdaq, according to Clause 385. This number fluctuates, but is around 1,000. It doesn't include privately owned companies such as Virgin or John Lewis, although such companies could adopt the same principles (witness Virgin Group's social responsibility arm, Virgin Unite). It's likely that, following consultation, the government will add 'human rights' to the list of information required, and following EU regulation, the 'environmental matters' will have to include specific reporting on greenhouse gas emissions.

Some, such as South Africa's Professor Mervyn King, would go further, balancing the 'business doesn't need any more red tape' argument with 'increasingly complex situations with multiple variables require complex reporting if we are to understand them':

> *Traditional accounting which follows the international financial reporting standards emphasises discrete assets. These are presented as additive. In the new economy, human resource, financial, capital, information technology, natural capital and society are all critically interdependent and create value. No company in developing its strategy can overlook financial, human, natural, social, manufactured and technological capital aspects.*[19]

Integrated reporting, he implies, shouldn't be a year-end task, but an ongoing interactive process of communication with stakeholders:

> *On a reading of the Integrated Report, which should be the primary report in clear and understandable language, the user should be able to ascertain the material, financial and ESG issues and how the sustainability issues have been built into the long-term strategic planning of the company. The user must be able to make an informed assessment of the sustainability of the business of the company.*

Given that investors will hopefully be more and more interested in integrated data, and ESG data in particular, and that the European Union and others are moving in this direction, King's appears to be a very reasonable demand:

> *From the corporate report, the reader should be able to tell that the company has not profited at the expense of the environment, human rights, a lack of integrity or society; that there are adequate controls in place to monitor and manage material risks and opportunities; that remuneration is linked to overall performance which includes social, environmental and financial, that there is an interactive communication*

---

19 http://tomorrowscompany.com/tomorrows-corporate-reporting-a-critical-system-at-risk-3.

with the stakeholders who are strategic to the company's business and
that the company is conducting a sustainable business.

As for detail, Tomorrow's Company lists 10 national and international consultation exercises on corporate iterated or narrative reporting which were open in the period 2009–11. There must be concerns that too many cooks may spoil the reporting broth by cancelling each other out and providing the global economic establishment with plenty of reasons not to change. But something has to give: the corporate world is full of the unintended consequences of legitimate but contradictory actions causing unexpected, disproportionate or counter-intuitive outcomes based on poor access to information, especially in the environmental and resource management spheres. The good news is that those closest to the front line appear to want to make the running; see the account of Unilever in Chapter 8 and this quote from Samuel Parmisano, President and CEO of IBM until January 2012:

> *We occupy a world that is connected on multiple dimensions, and at*
> *a deep level – a global system of systems. That means, among other*
> *things, that it is subject to systems-level failures, which require*
> *systems-level thinking about the effectiveness of its physical and digital*
> *infrastructures.*[20]

What this means, says Tomorrow's Company, a highly respected thinktank at the cutting edge of debate around responsibility in finance, business and related fields, is that the analytical approach of the past – the two-dimensional spreadsheet, the tickboxes – has to be replaced by a systems-based approach in which data from different sources can be obtained by those such as potential investors and remodelled in ways which can better predict the consequences of interaction.

In 2008 a regulation brought in under the 2006 Act obliged UK companies to report donations to charity if they were over £2,000. This helped charities seek out prospective partners and funders, helped companies demonstrate a practical commitment to partnership working and, according to the Directory for Social Change (DSC), created no additional administrative burden for companies – which would have to show such donations in their accounts in any case. In October 2013 the government – without consultation or notice – announced that the requirement would no longer apply even as it launched a consultation on how to improve the corporate social responsibility activity of

---

20 Ibid.

UK companies. The DSC was aghast: its Director of Policy and Research, Jay Kennedy, said: 'Sadly yet again we see our Government acting in the interests of big business not the public interest. We need more, not less, information in the public domain about what charitable causes companies are supporting and how'.[21]

To date, regulation has determined the nature of reporting, and although elements of the UK Companies Act are welcome, they remain constraining in terms of how data might best be presented. Investors, for example, invest for different reasons and are looking for different outcomes. They require different types of data from other potential investors, or to process it in different ways, or to obtain third-party data – perhaps from a credit ratings agency – about the investee and to integrate that into their analysis. The absence of externalities from calculations of wealth and GDP may render such figures nearly useless: a company which disregards its externalities in its reporting procedures today should not only be regarded as a dinosaur, but should expect a similar fate.

Every company wants to show itself off at its best. If this leads to superficial reporting, it's not helpful, though this trend will continue unless and until there's a common understanding of what reporting is actually supposed to achieve. If it's to make employees and other stakeholders feel part of a happy, successful, perfect team, leave that to the PR or Comms departments. If it's to comply with regulations in a minimal, least intrusive way, to spend as little time as possible on an annual chore, then shame on you. If it's to offer a prospectus to future potential investors, partners, takeover targets and governments, then that's great but, for heaven's sake, tell them what they need to know in accessible language and figures: let them choose which data they want to see. And remember that, like a car's MoT certificate, passing the test on one day doesn't mean that the vehicle is roadworthy the next day or will be in eleven months' time. The Internet allows data to be presented comprehensibly, comprehensively, continually and accessibly, and even in (relative) security. And why on earth did we ever think that quarterly reporting – for too long the financial standard – was right for financial purposes when it's so clearly inappropriate for environmental change?

Nothing influences the market more than regulation involving taxes. No doubt the markets in alcohol and tobacco would be considerably different if they were subject to the same taxation regime as toys or garden furniture.

---

21 http://www.dsc.org.uk/PolicyandResearch/Pressreleases/Undertheradarlegislation.

Petrol too attracts high taxation: the claim that this is a hypothecated tax, intended to improve roads for the motorists who use them, wears thin today; it was only ever true for a dozen years almost a century ago. No one seriously questions the right of government to generate income through a simple purchase or value added tax at the point of sale, nor to use taxation to influence behaviour negatively (as with tobacco) or positively (zero VAT on food and children's clothes).

In India, however, a novel form of hypothecation is being attempted.

A CSR Levy in India

The Indian government is promoting corporate responsibility by obliging larger Indian-domiciled companies to give away the equivalent of 2 per cent of pre-tax profits. To fail to spend the 2 per cent wouldn't be a crime, but to fail to explain how they have spent it or to give an unsatisfactory explanation for not doing so would be punishable with a substantial fine, up to $50,000 (with the responsible officer imprisoned for up to three years or fined up to $9,000) under the 2013 Companies Act. The Act is comprehensive in that it makes changes to governance, takeover, bribery and other company issues, including improving the quality of the influence shareholders have on the remuneration of senior staff. Although ostensibly part of India's drive to align itself with modern international business standards, the measure undoubtedly creates a new debate over the division of responsibility for 'people and planet' between government and business.

India has a somewhat ambiguous approach to its economy which has been unchanged since time immemorial. It has one of the fastest growing economies in the world, with an enviable record of scientific research and university placements, but more people there exist on less than US$1 a day than in any other country. It has a history of weak or poorly enforced regulation which has made it attractive to unscrupulous multinational companies in the past, such as Union Carbide (Bhopal). It has more millionaires than any other country, but the proportion of its population that pays income tax, at about 2 per cent, is one of the lowest in the world and fraud rates are high. It receives huge levels of international aid to help fight poverty, yet has its own space programme, and even nuclear weapons.

It may help to explain the Indian proposal, since if it works, there may be pressure to adopt it elsewhere. The new law applies only to larger Indian-based companies with a minimum level of assets, turnover or profit.[22] A CSR committee is required to be created at board level, CSR activity must be monitored and reported on, and the equivalent of 2 per cent of average net profits over the preceding three years must be spent on designated themes. The 'approved areas' relate to the UN Millennium Development Goals plus employment-enhancing vocational skills, social business projects, contributions to the Prime Minister's National Relief Fund and 'such other matters as may be prescribed'. (When BITC was set up in UK in 1984, its aim was for business to voluntarily spend just 1 per cent equivalent of pre-tax profits on 'good causes' each year – a goal it has never achieved across its membership, perhaps because the business case for doing so has never been made as forcefully and consistently as it needs to be.[23])

It is expected that India's top 500 companies could collectively contribute at least 63 billion rupees (US$1 billion) in this way, though some of the money or equivalent that they are already contributing could count towards the levy criteria. Ernst & Young (EY) has calculated that 3,000 businesses, including social enterprises, public sector companies and others, could be contributing US$2 billion worth of good deeds.[24] As most Indian companies are believed to spend less than 1 per cent of pre-tax profit on CSR today, the levy should at least double what's being spent – or provide a good explanation for why not.[25]

This attractive prospect is fraught with difficulties. The proposed law is silent on what explanations for non-compliance might be approved or on who decides what excuse is acceptable. It's unclear whether the levy applies to profits earned by Indian companies outside India, nor whether the financial value of employee volunteering could be counted – something the lawyers have yet to determine. If it can be counted, then much employee volunteering in India is through 'global action days' which are essentially low-skilled time volunteering. In many ways high-skilled volunteering (which ought to be recognised by being allocated a higher monetary hourly equivalent) is of greater value to communities, but how can the levy encourage this?

If a company is already engaged positively in a community in a way not specified by the Act, does the monetary value of that engagement count?

---

22 $90 million, $180 million and $0.9 million respectively: http://asianphilanthropy.org/?p=3113.
23 When BITC used to publish its members' performance, the average figure never exceeded 0.8 per cent. The DSC (Lillya, 2013) believes that UK companies collectively give about 0.4 per cent. The 100 members of the London Benchmarking Group delivered 1.4 per cent in 2012.
24 http://www.ssireview.org/blog/entry/mandatory_csr_in_india_a_bad_proposal.
25 http://forbesindia.com/blog/business-strategy/challenges-of-the-2-csr-paradigm/.

Or should it divert its attention away from something useful and valuable to something less helpful but more measurable? If an apprenticeship programme were redefined as a community benefit, addressing the 'skills' criterion, could a company meet its target without committing an extra rupee?

Recent research in the UK (Walker, 2013) has shown that company giving is very poorly focused on areas of need, and that companies prefer to engage with communities they know rather than with communities where needs may be greater. If this trend is reflected in India, then huge areas of deprivation, even whole states, could miss out on the benefit of this legislation.

Currently half of all Indian children are malnourished. The levy, claim some on the Indian left, is another example of trickle-down economics which doesn't work. On the right, the plan has been attacked because the 2 per cent levy is effectively a tax, and as such will raise India's main corporate rate to 34 per cent, one of the highest in the world – so much, they say, for making India an attractive country in which to invest. Across the board there is scepticism: in the first three months after the new law was passed no fewer than 6,000 new charitable bodies were registered to qualify as recipients of the new levy. Many of these were foundations attached to specific businesses or established by individual members of parliament anxious, no doubt, to be able to influence the spending of a new source of revenue in their own constituencies at no cost to themselves or the Treasury.

The jury's still out on whether the mandatory levy will work to enhance responsible business in the world's second most populous nation.

Marketing

Where there's a market there will be marketing – the use of persuasion to influence consumers in the marketplace. And if there was no such thing as 'Marketing for Good', then someone would invent it. They have.

Marketing for Good was launched in July 2013 jointly by the Marketing Society, the advertisers' professional body, the Media Trust, which encourages pro bono media work for charities, and Pimp My Cause, an online service which in its first two years has generated £1 million of pro bono marketing support for 700 charities and social enterprises. Through Marketing for Good advertising executives can become mentors to a cause or help out on a simple brief, provide placements for young people on work experience or take part as a team in a Pimp My Cause challenge with the prospect of winning an award.[26]

Good causes themselves are not blind to the power of marketing: celebrity endorsement – whether it be One Direction or Lady Gaga fighting bullying, or Mo Farah and the England football team drawing attention to children with cancer – is keenly sought. Interestingly, whereas research has shown that celebrity endorsement makes women more likely to buy a particular brand of shoes,[27] only one in five young people think more of a charity because their favourite celebrity endorses it.[28] No fewer than 85 per cent of Americans would switch purchases to a company that was associated with a 'good cause'.[29]

But charities also gain great kudos from being associated with trusted brands: Macmillan Cancer Care jointly advertises with Boots, Oxfam with Marks & Spencer – even Andrex toilet paper, with its trademark labrador puppies, has teamed up with Guide Dogs for the Blind. Cause-related marketing (CRM) is well established: research dating back to 2004 shows that 98 per cent of the population were aware of it, and seven out of ten had switched brands because of it.[30] The report, coincidentally part-sponsored by Tesco, concludes:

> *Tesco's popular Computers For Schools programme, where shoppers collect vouchers to donate to schools, is an excellent example of a campaign that gets the rules of CRM right. The programme lets customers link the supermarket with its local community. By allowing the customers to hand over the vouchers themselves it gives them a sense of hands-on impact. It has been an ongoing commitment, having run since 1992. And it rewards shoppers for doing what they already do – shop.*

Computers For Schools is indeed a successful campaign. It attracts both celebrity endorsement and gravitas – as I know from experience – by inviting members of parliament to attend a store for the grand handing over of computer equipment each year. Schools that partake certainly do benefit from the scheme, though whether they are those that need the help most is doubtful: the Lidl, Aldi and Costcutter demographic is more likely to be associated with schools in deprived areas where resources are at a greater premium. Tesco has taken the commercially astute decision to market this clear example of money

---

26 https://www.marketingsociety.co.uk/the-clubroom/marketing-for-good.
27 http://www.bbc.co.uk/news/10615182.
28 http://www.prweek.com/uk/news/1052346/.
29 https://live.profits4purpose.com/why-start.
30 http://www.bitc.org.uk/our-resources/report/brand-benefits-cause-related-marketing.

going into social responsibility among the demographic that shops in Tesco and its direct competitors, rather than addressing areas of greatest need.

Faced with two similar products at a similar price made by two different corporations, 82 per cent of consumers said that their choice of what to buy would be influenced by whether the companies supported charities or were known to engage with communities; 40 per cent said they looked for products which were more environmentally responsible and 47 per cent sought out products from companies associated with charities; 89 per cent said that companies should support charities.[31]

It would be easy to dismiss these figures as mere marketing fodder, and they certainly give a strong message to marketing departments. Yet they are more fundamental than that: they suggest that the public has an appetite for responsible business and is prepared to put its money where its heart is. But people aren't daft: they'll see through superficial marketing based on CSR qualities, and where they can see a natural affinity between the cause and the corporate, they will regard the partnership as more credible; 59 per cent of consumers thought that companies made increased profits as a result of charity partnerships, and they're probably right.

But perhaps they should need to do more to earn it.

---

31 http://www.thirdsector.co.uk/bulletin/third_sector_daily_bulletin/article/1183955/most-consumers-favour-companies-support-charities-says-study/?DCMP=EMC-CONThirdSectorDaily.

Chapter 8
The Good Guys

Without question, the balance of power on the planet today lies in the hands of business. Corporations rival governments in wealth, influence, and power. Indeed, business all too often pulls the strings of government. Competing institutions – religion, the press, even the military – play subordinate roles in much of the world today. If a values-driven approach to business can begin to redirect this vast power toward more constructive ends than the simple accumulation of wealth, the human race and Planet Earth will have a fighting chance.

Ben Cohen, of Ben & Jerry's[1]

This chapter highlights seven companies which have, in my opinion, excelled in their commitment to creating public good while being rooted firmly in the private, for-profit sector. No doubt many more qualify, but we'll focus on the following companies:

- **Boots** – this traditional Victorian chemist integrated caring values into its practices at an early stage and committed itself to good health for those who, pre-NHS, couldn't afford to see a doctor. It has one of the best of all corporate reputations.

- **Barrier Break Technologies** – an SME with global reach in the unlikely setting of Mumbai, it uses the experience that only people with disabilities can bring to provide others with access to twenty-first-century communication.

- **Unilever** – one of the planet's largest companies, it is as committed to working for the poorest people in the world today as it was to Port Sunlight, the Shangri-La it created for its Merseyside employees 150 years ago.

---

1   Ben Cohen and Mal Warwick, *Values-driven Business*, Berret-Koehler, 2006.

- **Wates** – not anointed BITC's Business of the Year 2011 for nothing, the construction company epitomises family values in a changing world, committed to finding the most appropriate ways to help communities.

- **Serco** – through the increasing sophistication of its 'integrator model', the company enables charities to work on a scale they couldn't otherwise contemplate, changing the ground rules for future service delivery.

- **GlaxoSmithKline (GSK)** – no company should be condemned for the unacceptable behaviour of some individuals. GSK and Save the Children bring a new meaning to 'partnership', and together will save millions of African lives.

- **Ben & Jerry's** – ice cream was just the start of two men's journey to social justice and community empowerment. It provides a frustrating 35-year lesson in what business can achieve as a force for good.

These Good Guys have each built a reputation for engaging with communities. Sometimes those communities are stakeholders, sometimes literally neighbours, in yet others they are market segments. Frequently they are communities of the voiceless, the dispossessed and those most lacking in capitalism's potent driver: opportunity.

In every case the company would argue that its actions are supported by a business case which improves its reputation in the marketplace, raises the commitment of employees and the supply chain to the company, innovates, improves efficiency, accesses new markets and even enhances profits.[2]

As such, these are beacons for others to follow.

Boots – Health for a Shilling

Alliance Boots formed in 2006 through the merger of the country's two biggest pharmacy chains: Boots the Chemist and Alliance Unichem. The latter was created by a group of pharmacies in 1938 and briefly functioned as a mutual

---

2   There is an excellent discussion of the business case in Miller and Parker (2013).

(1969–90) before becoming a Plc. But the origins of Boots itself were much, much earlier.

John Boot opened his herbalist shop in Nottingham in 1849, selling home-made preparations to those who couldn't afford to see a doctor. He died in 1860, and his wife Mary took over. Jesse, Boot's son, was then only 10, but took full control in 1877, committing Boots to providing cheap medicines for the masses under the slogan 'Health for a Shilling'. The Boots were not Quakers, like several business contemporaries, but Jesse was an entrepreneur with a conscience. He devised the re-sealable and reusable bottle to cut costs and boost distribution, grew the business and, by 1884, had three stores and his first qualified pharmacist.

By the end of the nineteenth century Boots had factories, warehouses, laboratories and offices to support the growing empire.

Jesse took the enlightened view that employees were most productive when healthy and happy, and he described his workers as 'comrades', for whom vocational education, a free medical surgery on works premises and a social programme were provided. The latter included days out to the seaside, where chaperones would protect younger female workers from the evils of drink, or to Jesse's Trent-side home.

As the company expanded, Boot designed a new factory utilising natural light, creating Britain's largest (Grade 1-listed) glass roof. Boots was the first major company to employ a women's officer, in 1911, recognising that most of its retail employees were women, as are 83 per cent of its customers. Boots had a combined heat and power plant, and electric vehicles were introduced on site as early as 1915.

Approaching 70 and crippled with arthritis, Jesse sold the company in 1920. It continued to thrive, opening its thousandth store in 1933 – the year the company came back into Boots family ownership through Jesse's son, John, a financier. It launched its own brands, Soltan and Number 7. John reduced working hours and introduced occupational pensions for all employees.

With this tradition it's no surprise that social responsibility is hard-wired into every department and system. Today the company has almost 3,000 stores, 64,000 employees and a hundred years of values-led heritage.

In 2010 Boots calculated that it came into contact with one in every three people diagnosed with cancer each year: 100,000 of 290,000. Through an innovative partnership with the charity Macmillan Cancer Care, present in every major Boots store, this proportion doubled by 2013; Macmillan has trained 1,000 Boots staff to provide practical and emotional support to patients. The company's main customer-facing website features Macmillan and cancer advice prominently, and Macmillan's site reciprocates. In the first three years of this partnership, Boots staff and customers donated £6 million to Macmillan, and employees are encouraged to engage with the charity in a wide variety of ways: talking to schools, e-campaigning, sitting on hospital bodies, talking to others about their personal family experiences. Look Good, Feel Better is a charity which Boots supports by providing volunteer beauty advisers and make-up to help female cancer sufferers feel better.[3]

Other initiatives, such as requiring every senior manager to spend three days a year working in a shop and allowing every member of staff three days' leave a year to volunteer for a good cause, have led to high levels of employee satisfaction and retention: one member of staff in three has been with the company for ten years or more, and the company has a Top 25 ranking in *The Sunday Times* 'Best Big Company to Work For' list. Even the CEO, Alex Gourley, joined the company as a 'Saturday boy'. Customer satisfaction is also excellent, explaining Boots' consistently high ranking on UK surveys of brand reputation and consumer trust.[4]

Community engagement is a key element in the employee journey at Boots: from the team-building project in preparation for opening a new branch to supporting voluntary work with Macmillan, to considering how more volunteering can assist employees with the transition to retirement, the business case for such activity is taken as read.

Boots doesn't have a CSR department as such, but unlike many other corporates, it didn't reduce spending on responsibility issues during the recession. There's a lesson to be learned here: one man, Richard Ellis, reports regularly on CSR at board level while working with departments to implement long-term sustainable decisions. The departments retain the benefits from decisions such as sharing rural delivery routes in Scotland with other retailers to reduce carbon emissions and transport costs. Boots is a champion of BITC's 'Ban the Box' campaign to reduce prejudice against recruiting ex-offenders

---

3   http://www.boots-uk.com/corporate_social_responsibility/community/volunteering.aspx
4   http://www.bestcompanies.co.uk/Lists/ListedCompanies.aspx?Survey=133&Size=352.

into the workforce: the aim is to remove the 'previous convictions' checkbox from job applications. Three out of four UK employers currently weed out prospective employees in this way, even though one male adult in six has a conviction more serious than a driving offence.[5]

Investment in long-term responsibility and engagement produces employee and customer satisfaction, a solid and positive reputation and commercial success.

Breaking the Barriers to Success

It's not just that most of the 50 employees of Barrier Break Technologies in Mumbai, India have disabilities that makes it an unusual private sector company.[6] Since 1995 it has used a tried and tested, conventional for-profit business model in which enterprise, customer need and innovation come together to achieve what none before has done. Put simply, the company is improving the lives of people with disabilities all over the world, of whom there are over 120 million in India alone. It does this by making websites accessible to those with physical, sensory and learning disabilities, on the sound principle that someone with a specific disability is best equipped to determine what disabled consumers actually need and, with the aid of technology, to address this.

While India is a signatory to the UN Convention on the Rights of People with Disabilities, the state's commitment is measured not in deeds, but in mere words. There's no workplace support available for those who can't walk, see or hear, no obligation to make services accessible, and precious little awareness of the true scale of the problem. Indeed, Barrier Break has very few Indian clients; Shilpi Kapoor, the company's founding CEO, claims that 'practically all Indian websites' are inaccessible to people with disabilities. She even pointed to an Indian website providing information and support on sexuality to women with disabilities which wasn't itself accessible.[7]

The Bank of India paid developers to produce an attractive website that opens to reveal two panes of moving text accompanied by a catchy tune. It couldn't have made it more difficult for a person with limited eyesight to access if it had tried. As a blind employee showed us, off-the-peg software normally

5   http://www.bitc.org.uk/banthebox.
6   http://www.barrierbreak.com.
7   http://www.thehindu.com/sci-tech/internet/article3367118.ece.

allows those with poor vision to move their mouse pointer over text and have the computer read it aloud to them. That can't be done if the text is moving or playing a tune. In response to Kapoor's pressure, the bank has introduced an alternative website for people with visual impairments without such distractions – but with very limited functionality. Clearly the bank believes that people whose eyesight is poor don't deserve the same right to control their accounts as their normally sighted cousins.

Most of Barrier Break's work is international. It monitors English websites for Western governments to ensure compliance with local accessibility laws; other units re-type books and papers into formats that can be read online by visually impaired people, and there's even the beginning of a Skype-like online sign language translation service. Yet the more Shilpi and her team do, the more, it seems, remains to be done.

Much of the Web monitoring and website building is carried out by 18 profoundly deaf sign language users seated around a huge table: my sign language was sufficient to tell them a couple of stories. Many of the deaf workers didn't grow up with English as their family language, but they know it well enough in written form. Some of the few with limited hearing don't understand speech; lipreading doesn't help them. In another, silent, room young men with autistic spectrum disorders carry out challenging but crucial code editing tasks to address the shortcomings others have detected in clients' websites, with absolute accuracy.

The company has all of its employees on permanent contracts as a matter of principle. It's very rare for people with significant disabilities to be so fortunate in India.

Twenty years ago Kapoor, already an entrepreneur, had her vision. She mulled over her options. She considered but rejected the idea of launching the project as a charity or a not-for-profit venture, and when the time came, found that she didn't need all of the investment made available from the Aavishkaar Venture Capital Fund. She chose the for-profit, private sector option because it was the world she knew and she wanted to be taken seriously by both government and market. She has no regrets, though Barrier Break Technologies has yet to show a net annual profit – every time she might have cash to spare she takes on another project, such as supplying Braille text to a university at 2 per cent of the market price, or producing a website to explain simple money-handling principles in a manner friendly to people with learning difficulties.

She has turned down takeover attempts, including the opportunity to become a subsidiary of one of her biggest customers, a global software giant, so robustly does she maintain her independence.

A team of Shilpi's people, mostly with physical disabilities, has become a major asset through developing digital talking books for people with impaired sight. From a standing start she provided this service initially in seven languages, rising to 18 almost overnight; the workload is impressive by any standards. In 2012 Barrier Break took on the Indian franchise for an American technology that enables people with paraplegia to control a computer screen through movement of their eyes alone.

She agrees that the biggest barriers to disabled people accessing what's rightfully theirs aren't physical, such as stairs or potholes, nor India's complete lack of disabled toilets, lifts or induction loops in public places, nor even money to back up governmental good intentions – of which there's none. As ever, the most potent barriers are generated by the ignorance, naivety and shortsightedness of that temporarily non-disabled majority which dominates government, business, families and society.

Shilpi Kapoor's company, her brainchild, her passion, is undoubtedly a social business as defined by the guru of the inclusive economy, Mohammed Yunus. Despite the absence of significant net profit in its first 20 years, though one is there for the taking, the enterprise is sustainable, growable and franchise-friendly. She's an entrepreneur who has used a private sector model to generate services which exclusively serve the public good. Shilpi describes herself as an evangelist for her cause, and she certainly practises what she preaches.

Taming the Giant – Unilever

There are challenges in being one of the world's largest companies. Knowing what's happening on the ground, at the customer- and employee-facing edges of your industry, is one thing; enforcing standards of ethical behaviour, applying them across dozens of countries, businesses and supply chains, is another. Delivering coherent change is possibly the most difficult of all.

Unilever is the world's third largest consumer goods company, with 400 brands, 150 million customers, $50 billion in annual revenue. Under its Sustainable Living Plan it aims to double its turnover over ten years while reducing its environmental footprint and increasing its positive social impact.

In September 2012 the Dow Jones Sustainability Index ranked Unilever top of its food categories for the fourteenth successive year.[8] Oxfam's view is that Unilever is the world's second most sustainable global food company.[9] The company sounds a little nonplussed about the way the NGO, a long-term partner, handled its research and presentation:

> Unilever has worked with Oxfam on a number of activities over a number of years now, including the GROW campaign that calls for more equitable and sustainable use of scarce resources. Unilever feels that the report has missed an opportunity to look at the full range of organisations that need to come together on this. Change of this nature requires wide partnerships and needs to stretch beyond looking at the role of branded food companies.[10]

In the nineteenth century Lever Brothers of Warrington was Britain's largest soap maker. When a new factory was needed to turn palm oil into Sunlight Soap and a suitable site on the Mersey estuary became available in 1888, it pounced. The plot was big enough to build a village for the workers too, so 30 architects, influenced by William Morris and the Arts and Craft Movement, were employed. They designed a community to provide dignified living standards as well as for people's spiritual, cultural and educational needs. Who wouldn't wish to live in such a charming place as Port Sunlight? Today there are still 900 Grade 2-listed buildings there – the largest number in any one place in the world – with 1,400 residents (3,500 at its height).[11]

William Lever's aims in constructing Port Sunlight were: 'to socialise and Christianise business relations and get back to that close family brotherhood that existed in the good old days of hand labour'. He claimed that Port Sunlight was a profit-sharing exercise, though rather than share cash with his workers he invested the profits in the village. He said, in the spirit of old-fashioned paternalism:

> It would not do you much good if you send [the profit] down your throats in the form of bottles of whisky, bags of sweets or fat geese at

---

8   http://www.unilever.com/sustainable-living/news/news/September2012UnileverleadsDJSI sectorsfor2012.aspx.

9   http://www.behindthebrands.org/en/company-scorecard.

10 http://www.foodnavigator.com/Financial-Industry/Unilever-Nestle-tell-Oxfam-to-bring-other-stakeholders-to-food-ethics-table.

11 The Beatles performed in Port Sunlight in 1962, with Ringo Starr playing drums for them in public for the first time.

Christmas. On the other hand, if you leave the money with me, I shall use it to provide for you everything that makes life pleasant – nice houses, comfortable homes and healthy recreation.[12]

The original 'corporate mission' of Lever Brothers was to: 'Make cleanliness commonplace; to lessen work for women; to foster health and contribute to personal attractiveness, that life may be more enjoyable and rewarding for the people who use our products'. Today it is: 'Working to create a better future every day with brands that help people look good, feel good and get more out of life'.

By 1894 public demand for hygiene products led to Lifebuoy soap, central today to the company's fight against communicable disease in developing countries. In 1926 Lever Brothers launched its 'Clean Hands' campaign as part of a child health policy, to educate children about dirt and germs and encourage regular hand washing. The campaign also sold soap. In 1935 vitamins were added to its margarine products to levels comparable to butter.

In 1930 Lever Brothers and the Dutch margarine Unie, sharing a common interest in palm oil, merged to create Unilever. This was followed by a period of more mergers, expansion and diversification. For a period the company was among Britain's biggest users of whale oil. During the Second World War Lifebuoy vans carrying free soap and showers were sent to help bombed communities (alongside Cadbury's hot chocolate vans, no doubt). After the war Unilever pioneered frozen foods in Britain through acquiring Birds Eye.

From the mid-1990s the company's ethical base has grown firmer:

- It unilaterally removed trans-fats from foods because of a likely link with high blood cholesterol.

- It iodised salt in India, with an immediate effect on iodine deficiency illnesses.

- It established nutrition research centres, and later health research centres.

- It created a sustainable agriculture programme.

---

12 http://www.weekendnotes.co.uk/port-sunlight-village/.

- It was a founder member of the Ethical Tea Partnership (Unilever buys 12 per cent of the world's black tea), aiming for 100 per cent Rainforest Alliance-certified sustainable and ethical tea by 2015.

Progress continues, earning Unilever the World's Most Ethical Company award in 2009. In 2007 the Carbon Disclosure Project considered Unilever best in its class on climate change transparency. In 2007 Patrick Cescau, then chief executive, was honoured with an award for representing the highest standards of ethical conduct. Cescau responded:

> Social responsibility and sustainable development are no longer fringe activities, but are central to our business. And just as this has become core to business, so it should also become core to management education. It must be moved to the heart of the curriculum.[13]

It was no surprise when, in 2009, Unilever recruited someone with senior experience at both Nestlé and Proctor & Gamble as its new chief executive: Paul Polman. Since then he has been *Investor* magazine's CEO of the Year three times and has won several other awards, including Business Leader of the World. In 2012 UN Secretary General Ban Ki-Moon invited Polman to join a panel to advise on implementation of the Millennium (now Sustainable) Development Goals after 2015.[14] Polman called for greater emphasis on how to deliver development in an article for the Business Fights Poverty network in April 2013.[15]

Today Unilever donates surplus cleaning and hygiene products to In Kind Direct, one of the Prince of Wales's suite of business-orientated charities, which supports homeless people and hostels for victims of domestic violence. Another of the Prince's initiatives is the Corporate Leaders' Group on Climate Change. Unilever has helped the Consumer Goods Forum, consisting of senior managers from 400 companies across 70 countries, to reach a common position on deforestation and the use of natural refrigerants.

Unilever's 2010 Sustainable Living Plan is a ten-year programme of action, a manifesto for responsible business, a blueprint for a green and pleasant world,

---

13 http://bizgovsocfive.wordpress.com/2012/11/23/unilever-an-ethical-company/.
14 Several quotes here are from Joe Confino's article for The Guardian Professional Network, 24 April 2012: http://www.theguardian.com/sustainable-business/paul-polman-unilever-sustainable-living-plan.
15 http://community.businessfightspoverty.org/profiles/blogs/paul-polman-ceo-unilever-ending-poverty-through-partnership.

a symbol of what capitalism can achieve when it's focused on doing good. In it Polman writes:

> *Put simply, we cannot thrive as a business in a world where too many people are still excluded, marginalised or penalised through global economic activity; where nearly 1 billion go to bed hungry every night, 2.8 billion are short of water and increasing numbers of people are excluded from the opportunity to work.*
>
> *We remain convinced that businesses that address both the direct concerns of citizens and the needs of the environment will prosper over the long term. We need to build new business models that enable responsible, equitable growth that is decoupled from environmental impact.*[16]

The company's sales in emerging markets, he reported, grew 11 per cent in 2012 and now represent over half of Unilever's trade. All its American operations are powered by renewable energy, its plan to source all agricultural supplies sustainably is on track (at 36 per cent with nine years to go) and all its palm oil is certified sustainable, achieved three years ahead of schedule. It targeted 49 million people with its oral health and hygiene campaign (Signal toothpaste sales rose by 22 per cent in a year), while its target audience for the ongoing handwashing campaign has been raised from 50 million to one billion. In Vietnam it's developing washing powders that require less water, and labels on its American bathroom products remind users to conserve water. It's on course to halve the environmental footprint of the whole business.

In the Sustainable Living Plan's introduction, Polman said: 'The Plan pushes us to think ahead, reducing risk and making the business more resilient for the long term.'

That rejection of short-termism sounds like a business case.

Since he took the brave step of stopping the practice of quarterly reporting to the City, Polman has seen the holding of Unilever shares by hedge funds fall by two thirds in three years, to less than 5 per cent. Dismissing fair-weather friends – a source of uncertainty in the market – has reduced fluctuations in the company's share price. To further discourage the short-term approach, he's actively courting long-term investors to buy Unilever shares. Why?

---

16 http://www.unileverusa.com/Images/USLP-Progress-Report-2012-FI_tcm23-352007.pdf.

I don't think our fiduciary duty is to put shareholders first. I say the opposite. What we firmly believe is that if we focus our company on improving the lives of the world's citizens and come up with genuine sustainable solutions, we are more in synch with consumers and society and ultimately this will result in good shareholder returns.

Why would you invest in a company which is out of synch with the needs of society, that does not take its social compliance in its supply chain seriously, that does not think about the costs of externalities, or of its negative impacts on society?

In an interview to mark the end of year one of the Sustainability Plan Polman calls for new ways of thinking by business leaders, politicians and single-issue NGOs to recognise they can't deal with the world's environmental and social challenges in isolation. Partnerships and teamwork will be essential – but so will a resolve that the rate of progress must not be determined by the speed of the slowest. Unilever is proud to lead the way: 'We are showcasing a different business model that shows how you give to society and the environment rather than just taking from them.'

If the world's eighteenth largest company can adopt this sort of approach – consistent, inclusive, responsible, comprehensive, ground-breaking – then others of a more manageable size can, I'm sure, do likewise.

If that's what they decide to do.

A Family Firm – Wates Family Holdings

'Sustainability is about who we are and not what we do,' says James Wates, Deputy Chairman of Wates Family Holdings, on the company's website, and 'Our core value is respect for people and communities.'

He is of the fourth generation of his family to have run the building company that his great-grandfather Edward founded in 1897. Half of the board of Wates Family Holdings, which owns the company, are called Wates. The family's stated values of integrity, enterprise, unity, sustainability and leadership are all borne out by the company's conduct; they set the organisation's philosophy and framework and how it vets capital spending. Each generation has vowed to pass on to the next something better in terms of wealth than they inherited – and so far, so good.

In its long history Wates has always been where it needed to be: building speculative housing in the 1920s and 1930s and making a major contribution to post-war reconstruction in the 1940s. In the following housing boom it was known for pre-cast or 'system' building, which created 60,000 homes, many of the high-rise variety. Today its 2,000 employees are more likely to be found working on major public sector or niche projects, interior retail refitting and designing new communities.

Family director Tim Wates argues that 'business is a force for good', that regeneration 'is about bringing long-lasting change to a whole community', so he's not content to simply build affordable homes on well-designed estates. The family takes a generational, fifteen- to twenty-year view of their company and its role in society while, in a rebuttal of short-term business thinking, the board is required to observe a three- to five-year horizon. The firm's activities 'blend wealth creation with social responsibility', says Tim Wates.[17]

In 2008 the Wates Family Enterprise Trust set up a charitable programme to make 'a real difference to the communities in which we live, work and build.' Through Wates Giving, £5.3 million has been invested in local initiatives, including redeveloping community centres, reducing anti-social behaviour, prisoner rehabilitation and producing classroom resources for vocational education. A distinctive feature of the Wates approach is that community work is often carried out in partnership with a social enterprise – 36 of them in 2012 – sometimes including secondment of one or more members of staff for a significant period. Wates has sourced goods and services from social enterprises to the value of £4 million to date (£500,000 from 10 social enterprises in 2012), demonstrating that social responsibility and sustainability are mainstream activities, and not add-ons. As its website says:

> *Trading with the private sector gives social enterprises a revenue stream and experience in how to scale up and tender competitively for larger scale contracts. It opens out new supply chains, attracts business funding and enhances credibility.*

Employees are encouraged to volunteer, having 16 hours a year paid leave to do so, as well as matched funding of up to £250 per year for their personal giving to charity. On the annual Wates Community Day over a thousand employees, customers and supply chain staff give 10,000 hours to dozens of community projects and raise a quarter of a million pounds for charity.

---

17   Tim Wates, speaking at a Tomorrow's Company seminar in March 2011.

'The local community' to which the business is committed includes localities which are home to Wates's 16 offices and its major construction sites. The company works regularly with the Construction Sector Skills Council, The Prince's Trust, Shelter, Working Links and Job Centre Plus. It's an active member of BITC and the CBI, where it promotes its values and the good reputation of the construction sector.

Wates created 100 apprenticeships in 2010 through 'Building Futures', of whom a third went into full-time work with the company, while 'Changing Paths' provides opportunities for prisoners nearing the end of their sentences. Clinks restaurant at HMP High Down is a Wates-sponsored charitable training enterprise serving prisoners and ex-prisoners.

A formal employee-led partnership between the company and Shelter produced £165,000 during 2009–11 and Wates' current partnership with Barnardo's aims to raise £65,000 per year. Employee engagement through giving, volunteering and fundraising in Wates is a staggering 73 per cent.

But social responsibility doesn't end there. Wates won the Sustainable Contractor of the Year award in 2008, since when it has directed 98 per cent of site waste away from landfill and the company is working to produce an industry-wide standard for dealing with the annual 100 million tonnes of construction waste that is not yet recycled. Wates was one of the first UK construction companies to introduce a sustainable timber procurement policy, working with Greenpeace, in 2005.

In 2012 it worked with eight schools in BITC's 'Business Class' programme to introduce 400 pupils to the construction industry through workshops and work experience for high-risk pupils and provide female role models in construction. Both pupils and teachers reported positive changes in attitude and aspiration as a result of participation.

BITC gave Wates the top Platinum Plus award for corporate responsibility and Company of the Year in 2011[18] and Platinum Plus again in 2012. *The Sunday Times* listed Wates as one of the 100 best companies to work for, and it has won other awards for its employment, training, green and leadership qualities.

Given the plethora of responsible silverware on the family mantelpiece, what's so special about the Wates commitment?

---

18 http://www.wates.co.uk/news/wates-ranked-amongst-top-uk-companies-726.

Wates demonstrates that active community engagement based on cross-sector partnerships, common understandings, common missions and common sense is highly desirable, cost-effective and mutually beneficial. Here are some of the key decisions which have brought this about:

- Working with existing social enterprises shows confidence in local initiatives and capacity and helps create broader sustainability.

- Investing in sustainability by embedding staff in a social enterprise to develop its business avoids the traditional problem of the benefits of the liaison being lost when the project is completed.

- The high level of staff engagement with the company's mission brings business advantages to the company, as shown by the accolades of awards.

- This scale of involvement of customers and the supply chain alongside employees in community work is rare. It builds a feeling of membership of a wider family.

- It took the bold decision to work with fringe disadvantaged groups, such as offenders.

- The total commitment to corporate citizenship, equivalent to 5 per cent of profits, is very high.

- The high level of recognition that Wates has achieved from its peers has bolstered its image still further, while doing good.

It would be remiss not to also point out that Wates is a substantial sponsor of the Royal Opera House, Covent Garden.

Serco – Really?

In terms of progressive, responsible or sustainable capitalism, most of what Serco's 600 business units do in Britain isn't exceptional. Indeed, most people would struggle to say exactly what the company does do – the etymology of its corporate name, a contraction of 'service company', isn't enlightening. Its reputation is less a firefighter, more an ambulance-chaser; over 20 years it has stepped in to run failing public services such as education authorities, or collected the crumbs from the local and central government outsourcing table.

Many of the staff in this part of the company, including very senior levels, are former public servants; in many cases they earn more than they could working for the state and they enjoy being innovative in ways that the private sector encourages. Life's not without challenges, however: Serco runs so many public services – trains, railways, prisons, health services, bicycle hire, convict tagging, school meals, young offender institutions, prison transport, street lighting, military research, the list's endless – that lapses are inevitable and subsequent press scrutiny is ruthless. In many reported lapses, in my opinion, poor public sector procurement and commissioning practices magnify any contractor shortcomings there may be.

Indeed, in 2013 it emerged that both Serco and G4S had received government funds for administering electronic tags on convicts in the community even when they had returned to prison, left the country or died. This may have been the result of fraud, negligence/incompetence or poor contract design. Serco returned money to the Ministry of Justice and called for a full inquiry, while G4S, suggesting that contract design was at least partly at fault, initially denied being in breach of contract. In the resulting fall-out Serco's senior management was decimated and the company's reorganisation in 2014 was not enough to regenerate sufficient credibility to bid for (let alone win) government probation contracts for which it might earlier have been a shoe-in.[19]

Nevertheless over recent years an extraordinary concept has been developing within Serco. What distinguishes it from any other private sector provider of public services, with just a hint of homage to Arnold Schwarzenegger, is 'The Integrator'. This model enables charities to deliver their historic mission on a scale that they couldn't conceive of delivering alone. It has evolved through Serco's involvement in three outsourced public services: the Work Programme, Reducing Reoffending and the National Citizens Service.

The Work Programme was launched in 2011 following the previous government's (not dissimilar) Welfare to Work scheme. In essence, in each of dozens of localities two providers are contracted to help people into work, referred by local Jobcentres after a threshold period of claiming benefits. For every successful sustained employment achieved, the provider is paid a fee

---

19 http://www.independent.co.uk/news/uk/politics/g4s-and-serco-face-50-million-fraud-
    inquiry-8703245.html.

which relates to the degree of perceived difficulty of the placement and the cost of that client's unemployment to the taxpayer. Thus the fee is higher for a person on Disability Benefits or who is long-term unemployed than it is for a younger, fit claimant who has been unemployed for six months. The prime contractor subcontracts the work to a variety of smaller providers, often charities or social enterprises.

Serco has a history of delivering public services through voluntary sector partners, though it has only two Work Programme contracts, in West Midlands and South Yorkshire. Even the smallest subcontractors appear to have a good understanding of the Integrator model that Serco has made its own, recognising that it is superior to the minimum requirements of the Department for Work and Pensions (DWP).

In 2013 the House of Commons Public Accounts Committee (PAC) published a report on the Work Programme which was broadly critical.[20] BBC reporting of the document and contractual restrictions on participants' ability to comment on the detail of the programme tended to reinforce scepticism about outsourcing. The PAC acknowledged that the report didn't include a full year, that targets had been set against erroneous economic predictions and that set-up procedures had hampered early progress for many front-line providers. For example, prime contractors needed to recruit specialist subcontractors to address the needs of a variety of the more challenging benefit claimants, but the mix of claimants (such as the young or disabled, or those with mental health problems) hadn't emerged as DWP had predicted, so the subcontractor match wasn't ideal. These 'arguments for the defence' generated little airtime in the ensuing debate.

Two issues in particular caused the PAC concerns: mandating the behaviour of benefit recipients and the 'creaming and parking' of clients, in which the prime contractor deals with an unfairly large proportion of 'low-hanging fruit' itself and leaves subcontractors to handle more difficult cases. Neither of these criticisms could be made of the Serco delivery model, which doesn't employ mandation and which devolves responsibility for all clients to subcontractors; unlike some other primes, Serco doesn't compete with its subcontractors to place clients.

Although the PAC didn't attempt to discriminate between different providers of the Work Programme, the indications are that Serco is one of the more effective performers.

---

20 http://www.parliament.uk/business/committees/committees-a-z/commons-select/public-accounts-committee/news/work-programme/.

Charities which are subcontractors to Serco speak highly of the company. It's an active partner, protecting small providers against risk and paying bills promptly; personal relations with Serco staff are good, and it's said to be a better source of timely and accurate information about the Work Programme than even the DWP itself.

The innovation of a contract culture in prisons has stimulated new thinking and brought clarity to the roles of health and education for prisoners, making it easier to engage with voluntary organisation partners.

In 1994 Serco became the first private sector company to run a prison, HMP Doncaster,[21] where a Payment By Results (PBR) contract to reduce reoffending among prison leavers, in partnership with Catch 22, is well established.[22] Catch 22, Serco and Turning Point won the right to design and run a new prison, HMP Thameside, which opened in 2012. Over time both Serco and its charity partners have, in the words of one interviewee, 'grown up'.

The Doncaster PBR scheme is very much led by Catch 22, and it involved the transfer of some senior Serco staff to the charity's employment – a sure sign of concrete commitment to partnership. Defined by agreed goals and procedures, Catch 22's role is simple – to maximise delivery of its own historic mission, within the Doncaster context – while Serco's responsibility is to deliver support as outlined in the contract. Both organisations depend upon each other, and this synergy shows great promise: the confidence and enthusiasm of prisoners approaching their release dates is impressive. Clearly, not only is 'the mission' well established in the psyche of all concerned, but the attraction of personal and group success on reducing reoffending was highly motivating.

The success of the contract is measured by a reduced rate of reoffending in the cohort compared to the national population with the same characteristics over a defined, relatively short, period.[23] This is reasonable; changes equal to or less than improvements which might have occurred without the intervention shouldn't be recognised. One concern is that this is no measure of reoffending at all, but of reconviction. Offending behaviour that may previously have gone unreported, undetected or unpenalised may be addressed through changing

---

21 Ninety per cent of UK prisons remain in the public sector; Serco's share is just 4 per cent.
22 http://www.serco.com/Images/Something_Old_Something_New_tcm3-39703.pdf.
23 In the year to September 2012 refunding rates at Doncaster were 3.2 per cent lower than in 2009 whilst nationally they had risen by 0.8 per cent. In 2012-13 almost all the prison leavers on the programme had a home to go to on release and half entered jobs, education or training. http://www. catch-22.org.uk/programmes-services/hmp-yoi-doncaster-offender-management-resettlement/.

government policies and henceforth be reported, making the reduction of reoffending using current criteria more difficult to achieve.

The experience government gained from outsourcing the Work Programme and Reducing Reoffending fed directly into the establishment of the National Citizens Service (NCS), which provides a residential experience for 16–17-year-olds, including designing and implementing a team community project, followed by a second team project in the young people's home area.[24]

The NCS exhibits one of the most sophisticated business–charity partnerships to date: the holder of six regional contracts to deliver it is not Serco, but NCS Network, a consortium of Serco and four national charities as equal partners: v-Inspired, UK Youth, National Youth Agency and the ubiquitous Catch 22. As the Integrator, Serco's role is to provide a national call centre and website and handle major procurement, financial and risk management and back-office issues; the other partners manage the front-line delivery, which also involves 76 subcontractors. Any consortium depends upon a level of trust and understanding that can't be achieved overnight. No doubt a number of factors have made this possible, including the many years that Serco and Catch 22 have been working together and the input the consortium had into the design of the Cabinet Office contract.

Serco's partners drew my attention to certain positive features:

- the clear delineation between delivery and integrator roles;

- the scalability of the model – none of the charity partners would have had the capacity either to deliver at the required scale or grow at the required rate alone;

- Serco's approach to cash flow management, which generates confidence among those with whom the company hasn't worked previously.

However, NCS Network members are not without concerns: the early management of the project at Cabinet Office level didn't impress, and the level of secrecy around the detail of the project is frustrating. There were also teething problems related to the delayed signing of the contract, but by summer 2013 these had been addressed.

---

24 http://www.ncsyes.co.uk.

Once again, the success of a PBR scheme is highly dependent upon a well-written contract, commitment to the common mission by both corporate and charity partners, and partners' clear and common understanding of and respect for contractual obligations, each others' missions, capacity and competences, together with agreement on how success is defined.

Charities are renowned for their flexibility, cost-effectiveness, and ability to innovate and localise. The vision of delivering a national-scale programme which exhibits these qualities simply by enabling charities to punch so far above their weight is inspired – and the charities involved recognise this. It can only work where there's trust and clarity, and Serco has worked hard to build a reputation among its partner charities to make this possible.

The 'Integrator' model has great potential for the service delivery of the future.

GlaxoSmithKline

In July 2012 the world's fourth largest pharmacy company and the fifth largest on the London Stock Exchange pleaded guilty to charges that it had illegally promoted prescription drugs, failed to report safety data, bribed doctors and promoted medicines for uses for which they weren't licensed. GSK agreed to a settlement of $3 billion, equivalent to several months' profit, in the biggest US healthcare fraud case ever, with the largest penalty ever imposed on any drug company. This was the culmination of years of overtime, stress and, no doubt, self-immolation by the company's legal department since the merger of Glaxo Wellcome and SmithKline Beecham in 2000. Since the turn of the century it has lost a string of legal cases, mostly in the USA, costing the company millions of dollars in fines and compensation for corporate misbehaviour in selling, testing, overcharging and other misdemeanours: '"[We are] very sorry that we have had to deal with the echoes of the past,' said Sir Andrew Witty, the chief executive. 'We're determined this is never going to happen again.'"[25]

In the summer of 2013 further allegations of a massive attempt to bribe Chinese doctors and officials came to light. GSK condemned the practice, promised full co-operation with the investigation and handed over documents

---

25 Quoted in 2013 in the Daily Telegraph: http://www.telegraph.co.uk/finance/comment/kamal-ahmed/10192662/China-GSK-and-dealing-with-toxic-bribery-claims.html.

to the UK Serious Fraud Office. The affair wasn't enough to shake the confidence of the company's fans in the business press:

> *If anyone doubted whether GSK was taking the issue seriously, they can put their mind at rest. Sir Andrew – by showing contrition and a willingness to solve the problem rather than fight the allegations – is doing the right thing. An impressive chief executive, he is a man who has led a fundamental re-think of how the medicines industry should work.*[26]

Contrite and co-operative, perhaps; but how can I justify including a company with this record in a chapter on 'The Good Guys'?

GSK's portfolio is huge. It includes Ribena, Horlicks, toothpaste and NiQuitin, a hugely profitable line of antidepressants, drugs to tackle diabetes, asthma and cold sores – even a flu vaccine – not to mention antiretroviral drugs to combat HIV/AIDS; 45 per cent of its sales are in the USA, but it sells in 70 countries, each with their own regulatory controls and conventions. In 2011 its sales were $44 billion, with $9 billion profit.

As a pharmaceutical company it's highly regulated, and as result there are many ways for it to slip over the line of acceptability. It's huge, with 100,000 employees. The opportunities for individuals, perhaps agents not directly employed by GSK, to over-sell products on commission must be great, especially in less sophisticated markets. Such people are not all saints, guardians of the corporate conscience.

For a company this size, in this field, in this environment, it's inevitable that, without Soviet levels of command and control systems, sins will be committed. I'm not arguing that this is the price we have to pay for cutting-edge, state-of-the-art pharmacy; the highlighted behaviour is wrong. Yet I share the confidence that under Andrew Witty's leadership since 2009 GSK is turning the corner and in future will only be controversial for the right reasons.[27]

I attended an international development conference in February 2009 where Witty announced that GSK was cutting drug prices by 25 per cent in 50 of the world's poorest nations and encouraging new drug development by releasing

---

26 Ibid.
27 In summer 2013 GSK's share price was almost at a record high. The record was when it doubled with the large-scale merger in January 2001.

intellectual property rights relevant to a crop of neglected diseases. It would also invest 20 per cent of its not inconsiderable profits from the least developed countries into local medical infrastructure through its partner NGOs Save the Children, AMREF and Care International.

Not enough.

GSK is currently working with the Gates Foundation to find a new vaccine to fight one of the world's most insidious diseases, which kills 660,000 each year, mostly African children, as part of the Africa Malaria Partnership. This has included promoting treated night-nets as well as preferential pricing of existing anti-malarial drugs in all affected countries – including the whole of Sub-Saharan Africa. Thanks to GSK's 30-year mission, which has reached the stage of pan-African vaccine trials up to 2015, some are starting to dare to hope that the end of malaria on an epidemic scale may be coming into sight.

Not enough.

In May 2013 a unique partnership was announced in Kenya. One of the world's leading international development charities, Save the Children, would be working with GSK with the explicit aim of saving the lives of a million African children. This was to be no 'Charity of the Year', where employees fundraise for a year and then move on. This was to be no corporately philanthropic conscience-soothing gift, no flash in the pan. This was a five-year programme to grant the charity exclusive and unprecedented access to and influence over the research functions of one of the world's largest companies. Save the Children claims on its website that as part of the partnership GSK will be accelerating the development of life-saving new medicines designed especially for children.[28] An early 'win' would be the development of an antiseptic commonly used in mouthwash as a gel for cleaning the umbilical cord stump of newborn babies, possibly preventing thousands of deaths from infection.

Several journalists commented on the 'poacher turned gamekeeper' element of the story:

> That Save the Children, a charity that used to picket GSK's offices over its prices for Aids drugs, now runs partnerships with the pharmaceutical

---

28 http://www.savethechildren.org.uk/about-us/who-we-work-with/corporate-partnerships/our-partners/gsk.

giant on the supply of medicines to Africa shows how far the business has travelled.[29]

This unusual aspect of the partnership also earned a cynical look from BBC Television's *Panorama* team in December 2013, in a programme which made headlines by exposing Comic Relief's investments in companies that appeared to undermine the charity's campaigns in their work – but which failed to uncover anything improper about the relationship between Save the Children and GSK.

The initiative gives Save the Children a seat on the company's new paediatric R&D board, advising on new products for the poorest countries, while GSK will pay for the training of healthcare workers to dispense medicines and help tackle the vaccination shortfall. Together the organisations plan to develop new nutritional products for young children and improve the distribution of pharmaceutical and other aid elements. The five-year plan, initially in Kenya and the Democratic Republic of Congo, will cost the company £15 million, of which £1 million will be raised by GSK employees.

In June 2013 the partnership announced its first award: $1 million to recognise innovations in reducing the death rate amongst children under five years old – good, cost-effective practice which must be sustainable and scaleable.[30]

Justin Forsyth leads Save the Children:

> *Many years ago I used to campaign against GlaxoSmithKline and press them to lower AIDS drugs prices. We gave them quite a hard time, but GlaxoSmithKline has changed enormously and under Andrew's leadership is leading not just the pharmaceutical sector but actually the private sector in terms of setting a standard for how a company moves beyond just corporate responsibility and philanthropy to how its core business can be transformative in terms of children.*[31]

Andrew Witty agrees that this partnership is fundamentally different from any the charity world has seen before on this scale: 'What we're doing differently

---

29 http://www.telegraph.co.uk/finance/comment/kamal-ahmed/10192662/China-GSK-and-dealing-with-toxic-bribery-claims.html.

30 http://www.gsk.com/media/press-releases/2013/gsk-and-save-the-children-launch--1-million-award-to-discover-ne.html.

31 Forsyth and Witty, both quoted in http://www.theguardian.com/business/2013/may/09/save-the-children-teams-up-glaxosmithkline.

here is we're really trying to align the full business model of GSK to an on-the-ground delivery partner.' GSK would line up 'a whole portfolio of resources', he said, whatever was needed to tackle the challenges of child health in the developing world:

> It's a way to really shorten the timeline it takes the world to go from need to figuring out how to solve [a problem], find someone who's prepared to do it, generate an answer and eventually get it deployed.

On the Business Fights Poverty website,[32] Francis West of Save the Children and Priya Madina of GSK wrote:

> [We are not] blind to some of the cynicism that has met the announcement of this partnership, with a number of critics questioning GSK's motives. This scepticism miscalculates the value that Save the Children's child health expertise and knowledge of marginalised communities in the developing world can bring to GSK's understanding of its markets. There is nothing untoward about this. If more businesses want to understand the situation of the most vulnerable children in the world and bring that knowledge to their decision-making processes we are comfortable supporting that.

On Save the Children's website, Sir Andrew said:

> By joining forces with Save the Children, we can amplify these efforts to create a new momentum for change and stop children dying from preventable diseases. I hope this partnership inspires GSK employees and sets a new standard for how companies and NGOs can work together towards a shared goal.

Amen to that.

The two statements imply that the whole would be greater than the sum of its parts – which is exactly what a complementary partnership should be.

GSK is no saint: Andrew Witty is human, a Good Guy. Others should follow his lead. There's nothing about this partnership that's not in the interests of both parties: Save the Children gains the influence it needs to pursue its

---

32 http://community.businessfightspoverty.org/profiles/blogs/gsk-save-the-children-partnership-from-ambition-to-action.

mission with maximum effectiveness, generating tangible results in terms of lives saved and individual futures enhanced in Africa; GSK will be spending money it can afford – this is an investment. Its staff will feel good, and the company will benefit from that. The company's permission to trade (blissfully free of controversy in Africa) will be enhanced, both in Africa and globally. The opportunities for innovation from this partnership are great, and capitalism demands innovation from time to time, especially in a research-led market like health.

On GSK's website it says:[33] 'We strive to behave in an open and honest manner in all that we do.'

Keep striving. It will be worth it.

Ben & Jerry's – the Perfect Fit

In the village of Waterbury, nestling among the Green Mountains of Vermont, lies a 30-year-old factory, decorated with gaudy colours and black and white wooden cows and designed with the visiting public in mind. Fifty yards away is a flavour graveyard where you can pay your respects at tombstones representing tastes whose time has gone (like 'Bovinity Divinity') or those which simply failed to sell. This is where 160,000 pints of Ben & Jerry's ice cream are produced every day.[34]

For Ben Cohen and Jerry Greenfield, graduating from a $5 ice cream-making correspondence course in 1978 was the start of an adventure which has gone from rags to riches. Yet neither the rags – a passion for ice cream, a disused filling station and an old-fashioned VW van – nor the riches are conventional. Ben & Jerry's may be a global brand today, but it's hardly mainstream; it's what a social business can be.

The two met at school in 1966, but when fate reunited them over a decade later, neither had established a career. Seven years after those 1978 queues for their unique combinations of flavours, and unknown outside rural Vermont, the company issued shares to state residents – a move which was economically canny and consistent with their 'local' ethos. In 1986 Ben & Jerry's Foundation

33 http://www.gsk.com.
34 This section is sourced from http://www.benjerry.com, Lager (1994) and personal communications with long-standing Ben & Jerry's employee Rob Michalak, Global Head of Social Mission (USA), and Ed Shepherd of Ben & Jerry's UK.

was established, committing 7.5 per cent of annual profit to catalyse social change in Vermont and elsewhere in the USA by supporting 'thoughtful, strategic and non-violent' grassroots organisations, now spending $1 million each year.

In 1984 the company fought off attempts by ice cream rivals Häagen Dazs to cut its sales in Boston by restricting access to distributors. Using the forceful slogan 'What's the Doughboy afraid of?' it utilised the power of advertising to settle the case more cheaply than by litigation. By 1986, as it doubled production for the fifth year running, Ben and Jerry's own personal hard graft had spread the word across the USA, and in 1988 the duo were summoned to the White House to receive a Small Business Persons of the Year award from President Reagan. The overweight, bearded hippy types owned one suit between them at the time.

Using business to make a point came early in the life of this most unusual corporate. Over the years its campaigns have sought to promote family farms, solar power, young people's voter registration, food labelling and children's rights, while opposing the cloning of cows, the insidious rise of genetically modified foods and, most recently, the power of corporate dollars to influence American politics. 'Free Cone Day', involving a million free ice creams, is an annual event where celebrities and charities come together to raise money for good causes at ice cream-based events in local communities.

Animal husbandry standards have always been important to Ben & Jerry's, which adopted free range eggs and Compassion in World Farming standards for the hormone-free cows in the 500 farms of St Albans Cooperative Creamery in Vermont and also Holland, which together provide all of its milk. Milk prices are guaranteed for suppliers at times of price volatility. The company is carbon-neutral, and investing in environmentally friendly refrigeration techniques, which required a change in US law. By 2006 all its vanilla (from Uganda) and then the cocoa and coffee in its US products were Fairtrade-certified – the first commercial ice cream to achieve this – and by 2013 all of its 200 ingredients complied where appropriate. In 2010 it dropped the label 'All Natural' from its products after a consumer group revealed that it used chemically modified ingredients – a story which is more about how different legislations define 'natural' than it is about sharp practice.

Employees have always been at Ben & Jerry's heart. Consultation was essential in the anarchic early years, and felt natural when the company was small; the company has always paid a living wage rather than a minimum one, and since 1993 its pensions policy has been gender- and status-neutral.

Its highest to lowest pay ratio, once 5:1, was formalised at 7:1 in 1990, and although this slipped and was then abandoned as the company grew further, in order to attract professional managers, the ratio remains relatively low due to the living wage policy. Employee satisfaction and engagement levels are perennially high, as is employee support for the company's stated missions:

- **Product** – to make, distribute and sell the finest quality natural ice cream.

- **Social** – to recognise the central role that business plays in society, innovating ways of improving life in broadly defined communities.

- **Economic** – to operate on a secure financial basis of profitable growth, in the interests of stakeholders.

For most of the company's life the idiosyncratic Ben Cohen has played a significantly larger role than his founding partner, who has rarely been far away. Cohen and Greenfield themselves haven't been directly involved since 1994, and although they had a chance to buy the company back in 2000, they acknowledged that a bid from Unilever was better for all concerned. True to the promise that the Anglo-Dutch giant would continue 'these critical global economic and social missions', the transition to the new owners was seamless, as long-time suppliers Greyston Bakery acknowledge. Indeed, in 2010 Ben & Jerry's new CEO, Jostein Solheim, said:

> *The world needs dramatic change to address the social and environmental challenges we are facing. Values-led businesses can play a critical role in driving that positive change. We need to lead by example and prove to the world that this is the best way to run a business. Historically, this company has been and must continue to be a pioneer to continually challenge how business can be a force for good and address inequities inherent in global business.*

The new owners still allow each employee three pints of free ice cream daily, and Ben & Jerry's still retains an independent board of directors charged with maintaining the company's values within the Unilever framework. The wide range of luxury ice cream, now supplemented with frozen yoghurt products, is available in 35 countries worldwide. In 2013 Ben & Jerry's became the largest company, and also the first wholly owned subsidiary, to become a certified Benefit Corporation in USA (see Chapter 6) – which it describes as 'the next chapter for socially responsible business' and 'fully supported by Unilever'.

Ben & Jerry's practice of political humour has been retained: in 2009, when Barack Obama was first elected US president, a nutty ice cream was temporarily re-labelled 'Yes Pecan!', mimicking his campaign slogan of 'Yes, we can!', and 'Chubby Hubby' was re-marketed as 'Hubby Hubby' locally when Vermont legalised gay marriage. Working with the charity Stonewall, the brand 'Apple-y Ever After' was launched to support that same campaign in Britain, with a website link to a Home Office consultation exercise on the pack. Although this view wasn't popular among the company's Facebook followers, sales of the re-branded product actually rose.

In 2012 'Join our Core', a joint annual programme with Ashoka, was launched. One social business idea which demonstrates social, environmental and financial sustainability, submitted by an 18–34-year-old in each of 9 European countries, is selected to receive £10,000 plus 6 months of mentoring and is featured on an ice cream package. Jerry Greenfield is one of the judges. At the same time, Ben & Jerry's Climate Change College works with the World Wide Fund for Nature to support and promote young people's eco-businesses.

The core activities of the company and its values are as important today as they were on day one. Ben and Jerry chose to put their social, environmental and political commitments into practice through the medium of business, encouraged by a common passion for innovative ice cream flavours. They took their model as far as they could, taking professional help on board when they needed it and working frequently with partners. After twenty years they made the biggest decision of their careers – to get out of the business they loved, which had grown beyond their control. They had realised that the economy of a large company was significantly different from that which they were used to and had grown up with, and – as the Body Shop perhaps also found – that passion and activism were no substitutes for business acumen. Fortunately the dream is still alive: Unilever, as we have seen elsewhere, had the right combination of concern and competence to handle the company's now multi-million-dollar operation, to the extent that most people don't realise that Ben & Jerry's is part of that global corporation – surely a sign of success.

Oh, and the ice cream's pretty cool, too.

Chapter 9
Fine-tuning

What's bad for the planet is bad for the economy. What's good for the planet is good for the economy.

Lush Cosmetics, 2013 catalogue

The change in the time horizon to which business works that has occurred in the last century has something to do with technology, something to do with markets and something to do with ownership. Outside the business arena, advertisements aim at instantaneous communication, Twitter is the ubiquitous and instantly powerful soul of brevity, and political parties worry about new opinion polls not each month, as in the past, but daily.

These days gratification must, it appears, be instant.

The period over which shares are held used to be measured in years. The average duration of an equity holding in the 1960s was five years, in the 1980s two years, in 2000 just over one year, and in 2007 it was just over seven months.[1] Today it's measured in days and minutes – if not seconds: under a regime of 'algorithmic trading' 60 per cent of all share trading was classed as 'high speed, high frequency' in America by 2009 and in Europe by 2012 (Gore, 2013). Some extreme examples of this include:

- trading companies site their supercomputers next to trading floors to minimise the time it takes for data to reach them;

- $0.3 billion is being spent on a new cable to reduce data transmission time between London and New York by 0.0052 seconds;

- a US proposal that all shares must be held for at least one second before they can be sold was rejected because it constituted a 'restraint on trade';

---

1   Introduction to 'Tomorrow's Finance', a series of lectures for Tomorrow's Company, 2013.

- in May 2010 the New York Stock Exchange fell by 1,000 points and then rebounded, all in the space of 16 minutes, for reasons unconnected with any human intervention.

Share owners now have little time to engage with companies and their goals, history and procedures, and no reason to see the certificates in their hands as anything other than a commodity to be traded – if they even see them at all, as so much trade is carried out by intermediaries who judge share ownership on potential to deliver profit and nothing else. Not only can shares now be traded instantaneously and repeatedly, so can derivatives, which don't even feel like ownership tokens in the way that stocks and shares used to – because they're not. Originally conceived as such, 83 per cent of derivatives are now based on betting on interest rates, 11 per cent on foreign currency exchange rates, 6 per cent on credit types and just 1 per cent on the real world of commodities. Some financial instruments are so highly derivative that they stretch empathy with their ultimate owners, such as pension fund members, to breaking point.[2] The volume of derivatives trading has risen by 60 per cent in each of the last three years.

Family ownership of companies might sound like a Victorian concept, but it had much to be said for it. Wates (see Chapter 8) is a good example of a company which has retained family control – of strategic direction, corporate citizenship and long-term values – without involving shareholders. It has blended this with professional organisation and sensible risk management to produce a company which succeeds in the stated aim of (almost) every family firm: to pass on to the next generation of owners a company worth more, and with better prospects, than that inherited by the current generation. A company which works to a generational horizon will behave differently in many respects from one which looks for only short-term returns on its management decisions.

A drawback of family ownership which has caused the demise of so many is that success leads to growth and the skills that are needed to run a fledgling company are different from those needed to run a growing one; to run a large company in particular involves different, often devolved, skills compared to running a small one; and to keep such skills 'in the family' requires a growing group of relatives of similar outlooks, complementary skills and a common determination. Wates was lucky; most families don't have these qualities available in the quantities needed, and can feel, once professional management has been recruited from outside the bosom of the family, that values have

---

2   David Pitt-Watson, London Business School, personal communication.

been lost and that the family is no longer its centre of gravity. Once a father entrepreneur has retired and has no son or daughter to whom he can pass on the tradition of active family responsibility, no one to take forward the family values, the ownership of a going concern will naturally pass out of the family.

As far as markets are concerned, quarterly results are eagerly anticipated, but every day's press can cause fluctuations in share price and consumer confidence. In a survey of business leaders carried out for the Cox Review, shareholder pressure was given by 80 per cent of respondents as the most significant cause of short-termism in UK business (Cox, 2013).[3] As Sir George Cox said:

> short-termism constrains the ambition of UK business, holding back its development and inhibiting economic growth. The research established that the causes include, but go well beyond, the oft-blamed functioning of capital markets.
>
> (Cox, 2013)

Observing that short-termism was detrimental when it worked against the longer-term development of a company, Cox specifically said that it undermined both stability and progress as:

> [it] curtails ambition, inhibits long-term thinking and provides a disincentive to invest in research, new capabilities, products, training, recruitment and skills. It results in drastic cost-cutting and staff-shedding whenever revenue growth fails to keep up with expectation.
>
> (Cox, 2013)

He concluded that short-termism made development of the internationally competitive businesses and industries that are essential to the UK's future economic prosperity more difficult, and that three fifths of senior business leaders agreed with this analysis (as did nine out of ten smaller companies). With such a majority holding such a strong opinion, how did we get into this mess? And why can't these people get us out of it?

The blame for the move towards short-term thinking – according to this same population – appears to be the finance industry, whose needs determine the conditions under which investment is made and which also governs business access to investment capital. John Kay, who recently reviewed equity

---

3   An independent review led by Sir George Cox and commissioned by the Labour Party, February 2013.

markets for the UK Department for Business, Innovation and Skills, tells us that just 3 per cent of the liabilities of the UK financial system are accounted for by lending to 'real, non-financial businesses' – those for whose benefit banks were created.[4] The natural reluctance of governments to think longer-term must also be a contributory factor, as they are subject to regular recall by the electorate. 'We cannot mandate the actions of a future government' is just one of the alternative ways the civil service has of saying 'no' when invited to commit to a good idea that's not its own. How can government expect to convince business to think long-term when it's often reluctant to do so itself?

It's not difficult to conclude that the financial services industry exists to serve the financial services industry and no one else. Cox's list of remedies is long but entirely sensible: abandoning quarterly reporting as Unilever has done is prominent among them, as is the greater use of employee share ownership linked to restrictions on how long such shares must be held before they can be sold.

Prince Charles, long an advocate of environmental sustainability, got in on the financial sustainability act in October 2013 when he told a not unsympathetic audience of the National Association of Pension Funds:

> We are facing what could be described as a perfect storm. The combination of pollution and overconsumption of finite natural resources, the very real and accumulating risk of catastrophic climate change, unprecedented levels of financial indebtedness and a population of seven billion that is rising fast.
>
> With an ageing population and pension fund liabilities that are therefore stretching out for many decades, surely the current focus on quarterly capitalism is becoming increasingly unfit for purpose.[5]

He's right: though commenting on his speech, *The Guardian*'s Economic Editor Larry Elliott wasn't convinced that this is the breakthrough we need: 'In practice, US investors would stamp on any widespread attempt by large companies to abandon quarterly reporting'.

Elliott may be wrong: no one has 'stamped' on Unilever. But his broader point is pertinent:

---

4   Sir John Kay, delivering a Tomorrow's Company lecture on 'Tomorrow's Finance' in January 2013.
5   http://www.cnbc.com/id/101120066; UK reports of the Prince's speech concentrated on the 'sustainable pensions' angle without the environmental and broader economic lessons, though see next note.

As ever, one returns to a key underlying problem: more than half the
UK stock market is now owned abroad and corralling foreign investors
into a debate on UK corporate governance is an uphill task.[6]

Quite. A global response is needed to a global issue.

Speaking to a Tomorrow's Company audience in June 2013, Colin Melvin, Chief Executive of Hermes EOS, said that the realisation that event horizons must be made longer was welcome, growing, but frustrating:

I believe it is no less than a hegemonic shift in the way the public, society,
business leaders and politicians view and understand the relationship
between business, finance and the public good, with an understanding
of the need for sustainability and long-term decision-making. But no
one seems able to do anything to change the current system.

He welcomed the fact that the OECD, the European Commission and the Financial Stability Board all have current initiatives to promote longer-term behaviour and that all UK political parties had expressed the need for 'something to be done'. Alongside the Cox Review, the Kay Review (Kay, 2012), the Parliamentary Commission on Banking Standards and Tomorrow's Company's own work on capital markets all reached similar conclusions. Melvin cited Dominic Barton, Managing Director of McKinseys, who had identified that 'a ten or twenty year horizon is needed to embrace the five forces that are reshaping the global economy'.[7] It doesn't take a genius to work out that these five factors – the rise of the African and Asian economies, the challenge of ageing populations, the rate of change in technology, resource productivity challenges and increasing strains on governments – can't be dealt with overnight; but clearly someone had to say it.

Shareholder Value

As a number of authors have pointed out,[8] the protection and enhancement of shareholder value was never really intended to be the ultimate corporate purpose. Starting as a trend in the 1960s, it became mainstream corporate

---

6   http://www.theguardian.com/uk-news/blog/2013/oct/17/prince-charles-pensions-industry.
7   Dominic Barton, co-author of Focusing Capital on the Long Term, speaking to the Institute of Corporate Directors in May 2013.
8   Cited at http://www.theatlantic.com/magazine/archive/2013/07/stop-spoiling-the-shareholders /309381/.

philosophy in the 1990s in the USA, and while maximising shareholder value isn't something that US companies are legally required to do, the trend is supported by the 2010 Dodd-Frank Act.

Why might it be actually be wrong to prioritise the needs of shareholders?

To do so favours short-termism, not least as the portfolios of today's shareholders are unlikely to contain stocks in the same companies even five years from now and we can't know today what factors will be influencing shareholder value then. Prioritising shareholder value potentially alienates other stakeholders, such as employees and customers.

The rise in the ethos of shareholder value over the last 20 years has been accompanied by a disappointing US stock market performance and a reduced number of publicly traded companies. The UK, where shareholder value is most prevalent, is home to only three of the world's largest 100 companies – suggesting that promoting shareholder value doesn't guarantee growth. 'Shareholder value' has become a euphemism for 'short-term thinking'.

Colin Mayer is the Peter Moores Professor of Management Studies at the Saïd Business School, University of Oxford. In his book *Firm Commitment* (Mayer, 2013) he argues that a successful corporation needs to have commitments, beyond contractual ones, that voluntarily bind it to employees, customers and suppliers as well as shareholders. Shareholders are free, after all, to break their commitments at any time by selling their interest in the company for reasons which may have little to do with the its performance or prospects. If the interests of such people take priority over those of other stakeholders, then the credibility of a company's long-term commitments must always be in question. He acknowledges that no one has yet designed the perfect company, but proposes several measures that would improve things: I like the idea of a 'trust firm' which has a constitution with goals and principles over and above those of profit or share price; the idea of giving some shares a higher voting value if the owner agrees to hold onto them for a number of years is also attractive. He points out that because each US state has different corporate laws, the USA has a very diverse selection of corporate types (the Benefit Corporation is one), and that this diversity is healthy.

'Shareholder value' in the early 2000s was a rallying cry particularly associated with the banking industry, where huge gifts of stocks were frequently part of eye-watering compensation and pension packages.

Even after the crash some industry leaders, such as the CEO of JPMorgan Chase in 2012, were reassuring the markets that their aim was to maximise economic value for shareholders, despite the fact that in the banking industry shareholders provide only a small minority of the capital assets.

The Guardian reported in August 2013, in an article to which we will return: 'The [Diageo] annual report also revealed an unspecified number of senior managers at the company made a total of £56.7 million from cashing in share options during the year.'[9]

These are the harvests of short-termism during the years of fat. Whether this figure represents a handful of directors each taking home £10 million each on top of the salary they are paid for the job they do or a few dozen taking home a million each, this isn't the real world of 99 per cent of the population. Such behaviour forms a tough and formidable barrier of understanding and empathy between business and society that it's in no one's interest to perpetuate.

The trend towards maximising shareholder value will only be halted and will best be reversed by the evolution of a dominant breed of shareholder that agrees that a company's priorities should be elsewhere – or rather, that agrees that long-term shareholder value is best served by downgrading the priority given to short-term considerations. That breed already exists – potentially, although it has yet to assert itself fully, not least because of the actions of short-term-biased intermediaries. The investors most likely to care about their own longer term interests are, of course, pension funds, whose challenges and opportunities we discussed in Chapter 4.

Stewardship

In 2002 the Institutional Shareholders Committee published a report which led, via the Myners Report and review on institutional investors (see Chapter 4), to the 2009 ISC Code. With some amendments, this was taken over by the UK Financial Reporting Council in 2010.[10] Its implementation by institutional shareholders isn't compulsory. The Code's purpose is to assist companies to understand the approach and expectations of their major shareholders by helping those issuing instructions to institutional fund managers to make

---

9   http://www.theguardian.com/business/2013/aug/12/diageo-paul-walsh-pay-bonus.
10 http://www.frc.org.uk/FRC-Documents/FRC/The-UK-Stewardship-Code.aspx.

better-informed choices, thereby enhancing responsibility to end-investors. It's applied on a 'comply or explain' basis, and is intended to complement the UK Corporate Governance Code. To an outsider its requirements feel commonsense and minimal; this version is dated September 2012, in which Principle 2 has been slightly redrafted and Principle 4 has (thankfully, given our earlier discussion) had the words 'as a method of protecting and enhancing shareholder value' removed:

> *Institutional investors should:*
>
> 1. *publicly disclose their policy on how they will discharge their stewardship responsibilities*
> 2. *have a robust policy on managing conflicts of interest in relation to stewardship which should be publicly disclosed*
> 3. *monitor their investee companies*
> 4. *establish clear guidelines on when and how they will escalate their stewardship activities*
> 5. *be willing to act collectively with other investors where appropriate*
> 6. *have a clear policy on voting and disclosure of voting activity*
> 7. *report periodically on their stewardship and voting activities.*

Each principle is backed by guidance, and the Code's launch was welcomed by 48 asset managers, 12 asset owners and eight service providers.[11]

In June 2012, two years after the FRC adopted the Code, David Pitt-Watson told a Tomorrow's Company event that 79 per cent of companies reported that there had been no discernible change in the behaviour of their fund managers as a result of the new Code being adopted. Research by Fair Pensions (now ShareAction), cited in Chapter 5 and published in December 2012, found that of the 20 largest 'ethical investment funds' available to the general public, only four didn't disclose their voting records at shareholder meetings – yet three of these were signatories to the UK Stewardship Code. So, too, were all eight of the providers which didn't publish engagement reports. These omissions appear to be in clear breach of Principles 6 and 7 of the Code.[12]

---

11 The Code requires signatories to publish the details of how they comply (or why not) on their own website. A current list of signatories can be found at http://www.frc.org.uk/Our-Work/ Codes-Standards/Corporate-governance/UK-Stewardship-Code/UK-Stewardship-Code-statements.aspx. All the 'usual suspects' are there.

12 http://fairpensions.org.uk/sites/default/files/uploaded_files/researchpublications/EthicalFund ReportII.pdf.

Government provides the way for society to implement essential checks and balances on company behaviour, through laws and regulation. Left to their own devices, Pitt-Watson says, companies do have ethics – but not necessarily the right ones.[13]

In 2005 KPMG conducted a survey of the state of ethics in the Australian boardroom.[14] It concluded that it was a low priority on board agendas, that it suffered from a lack of clarity and accountability, lacked reporting frameworks, and was most likely to be discussed in the wake of adverse publicity or worrying business trends. In short, it stated: 'Australian business suffers a vacuum in the advocacy and stewardship of business ethics.' It went as far as to say that 'major Australian corporations are failing to meet community expectations in matters of ethical conduct', and noted that surveys consistently showed that two thirds of Australians believe business leaders to be 'untrustworthy', with more than half saying that 'big corporations have no morals and ethics'.

Since 2000, Australian law has required businesses to adopt an 'appropriate culture'. Yet although three quarters of big corporations claimed to have adopted one by 2005, usually following a boardroom directive, five out of every six that had done so were doing nothing to enforce or even monitor performance in this respect. A third of Australian employees claimed to have witnessed unethical or otherwise improper behaviour at work.

But things are improving: Pro Bono Australia reports that between 2008 and 2011 the proportion of managers in Australian businesses who believed that 'corporate social responsibility' added to a company's reputation doubled from 40 to 80 per cent, while the proportion believing that CSR could help save costs rose from 20 to 60 per cent – a strong trend by any measure. However, detailed questioning revealed that in both Australia and New Zealand CSR was most widely understood as meaning community investment and philanthropy rather than strategic engagement backed by a strong business case.[15]

Corporate Social Responsibility

You've almost reached the final chapter of this book before finding a section dedicated to CSR. There are several reasons for this: there are already too many

---

13 Personal communication.
14 http://www.kpmg.com.au/aci/docs/rassas_view-from-the-top200510.pdf.
15 http://www.accsr.com.au/html/stateofcsr.html.

books about it, the term has become increasingly meaningless since being coined around 1953, and it's not the way forward.

The number of books reflects expanding interest in the field, a growing belief that business should be doing more than providing goods, services, jobs and taxation revenue.

As early as the 1960s the ambiguity of CSR was being reported in academic literature:

> *CSR means different things to different people. Depending on who uses the concept, CSR could mean legal responsibility or liability, socially responsible behaviour in the ethical sense, charitable contribution, socially conscious, legitimacy in the context of belonging or being proper or valid, or duty imposing higher standards of behaviour on businesspersons than on citizens at large.*[16]

It's all of these things and more, and there's no universally accepted definition today: one question which divides commentators and practitioners is whether CSR should be essentially philanthropic, or whether it's only meaningful when supported by a business case. One charity chief executive I know, important enough to attract private sector suitors looking for partnership rather than the other way round, won't meet a business representative who comes from the 'CSR Department' or from 'Public Affairs'. Too many CSR staff are based in such departments, adding to the popular belief that CSR is an expression of 'greenwashing' – something designed to give the appearance of corporate wholesomeness which may not be justified. If CSR is to mean anything at all it has to be part of the mainstream operation of a business – which is why it's also wrong for some companies to misappropriate employee initiatives and employee fundraising, instigated independently of, or at best tolerated by, a company, in their company's CSR record (Walker, 2013).

Elaine Cohen, a former Human Resources Director at Unilever, believes that the proper place for CSR activity is the HR Department (Cohen, 2010), and this idea has merit in that employee engagement is one of the business case benefits that a well-managed programme can deliver, leading to reputational and other advantages. The 'Sustainability Department' is a relative newcomer on the scene, often meant in more than the green sense of the word, but even when meant in the green sense sometimes including volunteering as

---

16 http://www.examiner.com/article/definition-and-evolution-of-the-concept-of-csr.

an add-on. The head of one such department said to me once: 'I know our community engagement strategy didn't work but don't blame me, I'm an environmentalist.' At Boots, the Head of CSR, Richard Ellis, has regular input at board level and his influence pervades the whole organisation – an enviable but rare position for a passionate advocate of corporate citizenship to find himself in. In a national poll reported in *Third Sector* magazine only 26 per cent of employees said that their workplace had no CSR programme, but 100 per cent of these thought that it should.[17]

Whatever we mean by CSR or its derivatives, corporate responsibility and social responsibility, community engagement or corporate citizenship (my preferred phrase), its impact can vary from box-ticking meaninglessness to a profound statement about the direction in which a company's philosophy is leading it. Social responsibility is the term used by ISO 26000, the international but uncertifiable 'standard' in this field. It divides such responsibility into six fields, of which four are largely covered by law in the UK, USA and Europe (concerning corporate behaviour towards employees, customers, competitors and suppliers) and so have become matters of compliance. One, the environment, also involves compliance issues, although the business case for going further on green issues is well understood – in some quarters. On the sixth pillar, community engagement and development, the law is largely silent. Although clearly respectful of the Millennium Development Goals in content, best practice in community engagement is an under-populated field.

When I say that CSR is 'not the way forward', I'm not deriding the activities which support it, especially when performed in the context of genuine engagement, skills transfer, long-term commitment and a spirit of citizenship. Ninety-six per cent of company managers quite rightly believe that workplace skills can be gained through volunteering, and 57 per cent believe that the experience can fill gaps in workplace skills.[18] I'm not criticising the companies that donated £622 million in cash and kind to good causes in UK in 2012 (Lillya, 2013). But I recall the words of Michael Porter in Chapter 2, when he said that 'shared value' is when the creation of goods and services, profits, jobs, taxation revenue and acts of sustainability and citizenship are *all* the responsibility of business; they exist in a continuum in which all are important and none should be optional.

---

17 http://www.thirdsector.co.uk/bulletin/third_sector_daily_bulletin/article/1183955/most-consumers-favour-companies-support-charities-says-study/?DCMP=EMC-CONThirdSectorDaily.

18 http://www.theguardian.com/voluntary-sector-network/community-action-blog/2012/apr/04/charities-voluntary-organisation-business.

Table 9.1   What makes social innovation different?

Traditional CSR	Social Innovation
Philanthropic intent	Strategic intent
Money, manpower	R&D, corporate assets
Employee volunteerism	Employee development
Contracted service providers	NGO/government partners
Social and eco-services	Social and eco-innovations
Social good	Sustainable social change

Unfortunately, words are often preferred to actions. The UN Global Compact reports that two thirds of companies have CSR policies, but only one third are implementing them fully, with larger companies and those longer established in their commitment performing best. Half those surveyed carried out environmental risk assessments, but only a quarter assessed corruption risks, and a fifth human rights; 99 companies (3 per cent) were removed from the Compact's list of accredited companies in 2013 for insufficient activity to support their professed goals.[19]

That's the context in which I say that CSR as an idea separate from mainstream business practice (and too often seen as in conflict with it) should be rejected and the spirit should be integrated with all mainstream business activity.

'The stage after CSR' is studied in depth at Babson College for Entrepreneurship in Massachusetts and the move towards social value is documented in a recent publication.[20] That study includes Greyston Bakery, which I too have visited, and whose exemplary story is told in Chapter 6. They compare the 'traditional' view of CSR with an approach of social innovation, the creation of social value, as shown in Table 9.1.

It seems to me that this approach, which basically says 'if CSR does not bring about lasting change for the better it isn't worth doing', is both sound and timely. It must be driven by a 'win-win-win' attitude from which community, company and workforce can benefit. Establishing a social value-led approach, or Corporate Social Innovation, as they call it – though I don't see the acronym

19 http://www.unglobalcompact.org/docs/about_the_gc/Global_Corporate_Sustainability_Report 2013.pdf.
20 C. Kiser and D. Leipziger, *Creating Social Value: A Guide for Leaders and Change Makers*, Greenleaf, 2014.

catching on – involves a change in expectation of what we want from business and a recognition that whatever our size we can contribute to meeting the global challenges of our age through new partnerships and a new employee engagement standard: in short a new, sustainable business model.

The American giant Ford is the only motor manufacturer among the world's 100 most ethical companies,[21] and the only global one that remains family-owned. Like every other motor company, it was hit hard by the global crisis in 2007, and unsurprisingly, its corporate philanthropy suffered: in each year from 2006 its total contributions were (in millions of dollars) 83, 54, 49, 29, 29, 30 – showing a recent stabilisation at 2009 levels.[22] In 2006 Ford had just relaunched its corporate volunteering strategy, and the woman they brought in to run it, Jan Lawson, started work on the day when the struggling Ford 'let go' of 13,000 staff. 'One Ford' is today among the best-supported and most comprehensive community engagement strategies in the world: since 2006 its employee volunteering rates (in thousands of hours) have been 80, 86, 100, 100, 112 and 110. Back in 2006 other US motor manufacturers were cutting back on extraneous costs and activities and 'battening down the hatches'. Ford bucked the trend, and 2012 saw 12,000 of its employees support 315 projects in 45 countries, touching the lives of 1.5 million vulnerable people; 80 per cent of this activity is led by community need (the rest is corporate reputation-led).[23]

Ford has done this with the explicit support of its workforce (not least of the American unions) because it understands the business case for a meaningful commitment to community engagement. Ford was the only major US automotive company which didn't eventually need a government bailout to survive the post-crash period.

This is good CSR, in tune with the ethos of the Chief Executive of the company at the time when 'One Ford' launched, still its Executive Chairman – William Clay Ford Jr, grandson of founder Henry Ford. It's what you would expect from the man who told Ford's executives and investors in 1999 that: 'There are very real conflicts between Ford's current business practices, consumer choices and emerging views of [environmental] sustainability.'

In the ten years that followed, much of that was put right.

---

21 http://www.ford.co.uk/experience-ford/AboutFord/CorporateSocialResponsibility.
22 http://corporate.ford.com/microsites/sustainability-report-2011-12/people-data-engagement.
23 Jan Lawson, addressing a workshop at the IAVE global conference on employee volunteering in London, December 2012.

The Chief Executive

In summer 2009 the debate on the future of London's Heathrow airport was enjoined by a letter to *The Times*, the traditional mouthpiece of important people seeking to make a high-profile comment on a topical issue. The debate then was about whether a third runway should be built, later becoming a wider debate about the future of air transport in general. The third runway was supported by the government, unions, the CBI and Chambers of Commerce. The letter sounded a wary voice: 'Climate change cannot be ignored and our approach to transport must reflect the seriousness with which we take our Climate Act target to cut emissions by 80 per cent by 2050.'[24]

This was the voice not of tree-hugging eco-warriors, but of a group of CEOs, including those of Kingfisher, BSkyB, Sainsbury's and News International, the founder of Carphone Warehouse and a private equity specialist. Of these, Ian Cheshire of Kingfisher is a long-term passionate advocate of corporate responsibility who headed up B&Q before going on to lead its parent company, while few businesses in Britain have a record of environmental commitment as proud as that of satellite broadcaster BSkyB. It wasn't the first time senior executives of household name companies had adopted the moral high ground to express concern or advocate action on environmental and social issues.

Research for the marketing company Weber Shandwick has shown that the CEO's character is an increasingly important factor in the public perception of companies and their reputation in the world of social media: two thirds of consumers say that perceptions of the CEO can influence their opinions of a company and its products. Half of all corporate executives agree. This explains why 81 per cent of CEOs of the world's most reputable companies engage with electronic social media (widely defined) compared to only 66 per cent overall.[25]

We have seen that Paul Polman is known as an ethical, responsible, conscientious but practical leader who embodies corporate citizenship in his activities as CEO of Unilever. Polman was an outsider with experience of Unilever's competitors rather than one suffused with its company values. The appointments committee knew what he represented and what they were looking for. Once appointed, the Chief Executive is a powerful position, and the incumbent can ultimately say, 'Back me or sack me.' Most boards would

24 http://www.marketingweek.co.uk/chief-executives-lead-climate-change-in-csr/3001063.article.
25 http://webershandwick.co.uk/media/doc/thinking_doc_1358266409.pdf.

be very reluctant to dispose of a prominent and competent leader without very good reason.

Peter Brabeck-Letmathe is the Chair of Nestlé, formerly its CEO, an outspoken advocate of Porter's shared value. He knows that companies can be a force for good but don't have all the answers; and while NGOs may have good ideas (we need passionate individuals who are prepared to go off script and push for disruptive change, he's quoted as saying), their small size is a drawback. Small organisations, he says, with some logic, find it harder to see and appreciate the bigger picture. Undoubtedly size – and they don't come much bigger than Nestlé – brings added influence on the global stage, and therefore greater responsibility. Brabeck-Letmathe clearly believes that a good cross-sector partnership is worth more than the sum of its parts; he's worried that partners of an appropriate size aren't available to corporate giants, and advocates that NGOs should collaborate more with each other. Partnerships require special skills, and we should do more to develop them in business, in NGOs, in government and in international agencies, he says.[26] I agree.

In 2007 Marks & Spencer launched 'Plan A', an ambitious environmental programme of 180 targets. In 2013 it reported that over five years 139 targets had been achieved, 31 were on target, five behind schedule, four were struggling and just one had been abandoned.[27] The key targets of zero waste to landfill and carbon neutrality had been achieved, and £135 million had been saved accordingly in 2011–12 alone. 'Plan A' was largely associated with Sir Stuart Rose, who had been with the M&S Group for most of his career and led it as Executive Chairman at the time. His work on 'Plan A' no doubt contributed to his being named world Business Leader of the Year in 2007 and his spell as Chairman of BITC. Although concerns were raised when Mark Bolland took over in 2010, 'Plan A' has remained intact, and if anything become more mainstream – as Rose had no doubt intended.

Announcing BT Group's 'Pathway to Carbon Net Positive' in June 2013, CEO Ian Livingston pledged to reduce the company's net carbon footprint to less than its carbon usage, ostensibly through a massive increase in video-conferencing on an ever higher-capacity service. This wasn't 'old-style CSR', he said, but a cost-saving, sustainable, ethical, pro-customer investment that made business sense.

---

26 http://www.guardian.co.uk/sustainable-business/davos-2013-inter-connected-not-new-partner ships?INTCMP=SRCH.
27 http://planareport.marksandspencer.com/review-of-the-year/.

'Doing good business and business doing good are not alternatives,' he said, 'they must go together.'

Hear, hear to that.[28]

The next day it was announced that Livingston was to leave BT Group, after five years at the top, in order to become a government minister in the House of Lords. His post as CEO went to Gavin Patterson, a BT insider who oversees the group's corporate responsibility programme and represents the company on the CBI's Climate Change Board. Clearly, in terms of ethical, environmental and corporate citizenship concerns, this succession marked 'business as usual'.

There's no mechanism to ensure that a direction adopted by a CEO will outlive him or her, other than the will of the human directors who make up the appointments committee and the board. The life expectancy of CEOs in office is falling: one in seven CEOs of the world's largest 2,500 companies changed job in 2011, compared to only one in nine the previous year.[29] The reducing time frame to which an incoming CEO is prepared to commit can't be helpful to long-term thinking. Although there's evidence that the business case for making your company into a good corporate citizen is gaining traction in the business community, progress on the ground is (shall I be generous?) less marked. The UN Global Compact report for 2013 tells us that: 'While 65 per cent of [UNGC] signatories are committing to sustainability at the CEO level, only 35 per cent are training managers to integrate sustainability into strategy and operations.'[30]

The point behind these stories is that the conscience of a company is usually that of the powerful within it. No corporate with a good reputation for sustained responsible behaviour has achieved that without CEO leadership. The jobs of implementing responsible policies and, almost as important, maintaining high levels of visibility and buy-in within the organisation may, of course, be devolved. Above all, the CEO must be the custodian of the ideas and beliefs, and not just the words: according to its 2000 annual report, the values of the American company Enron were: 'Communication. Respect. Integrity. Excellence.'

---

28 Ian Livingston, speaking at the launch of BT's 'Net Positive' initiative which I attended at the RSA, London on 18 June 2013.
29 http://www.booz.com/global/home/press/article/50560531.
30 http://www.unglobalcompact.org/docs/about_the_gc/Global_Corporate_Sustainability_Report 2013.pdf.

In *Partners for Good* I argued that low-level acts of corporate citizenship were often stimulated by employees in support of a popular 'good cause' such as a charity or a local school, and that taking this activity from an ad hoc to an organised level required management buy-in, such as enabling payroll giving. I also argued that to achieve the highest levels of engagement, concerning the responsible behaviour of the company at a strategic 'head and heart' level, there had to be active leadership from the top in order to align company mission and activity and to maximise the business case for engagement. I now believe that I both underestimated what could be achieved and underplayed the role of good leaders in achieving it.

Between 1999 and 2010 the number of American companies reporting on corporate responsibility rose from 500 to over 3,500, implementation of corporate responsibility policies grew more strategic, with responsibility passing upwards, while both confidence in and cynicism about CSR grew. As far as the procedure for establishing a meaningful, sustainable and effective corporate responsibility mission is concerned, a survey produced best practice models for corporate leaders to peruse, saying that such a strategy should include:[31]

- CEO and top management support, critical in driving CSR programmes;

- a comprehensive reporting structure with a direct link to the CEO;

- CSR responsibilities included in every employee's job description;

- research to measure and evaluate the effect of CSR policies, from both internal and external stakeholders' perspectives;

- CEO and top management being held accountable for the implementation and results of CSR programmes;

- coupling the company's standard measurement tools with a regular evaluation of traditional and social media coverage about the company;

- communicating about the company's CSR efforts regularly through social media and the company website.

---

31 Based on Corporate Social Responsibility: Who's Responsible? (2012): http://www.prsa.org/intelligence/partnerresearch/partners/nyu_scps/corporatesocialresponsibility.pdf.

Uniting the goals of people, planet and profit is at the heart of Sir Richard Branson's latest outrageous plan to save the world: the B Team.[32] I'm not being sarcastic: bringing together 46 prominent people in a standing conference – business leaders like Paul Polman, Mohammed Yunus and Jochen Zeitz, opinion formers like Arianna Huffington, political leaders from Branson's 'Elders', Mary Robinson and Gro Harlem Bruntland (the first politician to proclaim about the climate time bomb), along with advisers of the calibre of Michael Green – has got to be good, and their agenda is precisely that of Sustainable Capitalism, to which we will return later.

It's Branson's process that's interesting: while the B Team has a plethora of ideas and talent, its focus is on 'catalysing and amplifying' the work of others. This means identifying small-scale solutions that could be scaled up to make a real difference in tackling the global challenges that confront us; defining the future (triple) bottom line; incentivising pro-planet, pro-people corporate behaviour, and creating a new generation of business leaders for whom these issues are a priority.

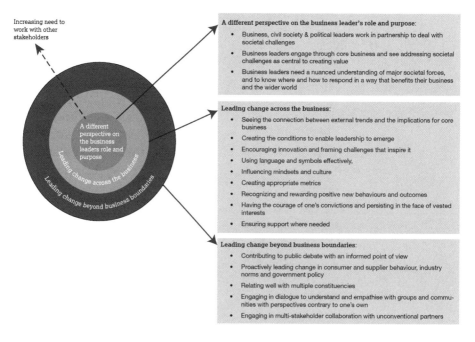

Figure 9.1   The future of business leadership

Source: M. Gitsham and J. Wackrill, *Leadership in a Rapidly Changing World*, International Business Leaders Forum/Ashridge Business School, 2012.

---

32 http://bteam.org/about/vision/.

So who do we need to populate that next generation of business leaders, those who will save us from the legacy of their rapacious and acquisitive forebears? In short, we need citizens: people who recognise not only the power and the responsibility of capitalism, but also their own obligation to use their tools and influence to keep the two in balance, in perpetuity. This is neatly summed up in a graphic from a recent report for the International Business Leaders' Forum and Ashridge Business School (see Figure 9.1).

Matthew Gitsham is Director of Ashridge's Centre for Business and Sustainability. Writing in the Business Fights Poverty blog, specifically about the post-2015 Sustainable (formally Millennium) Development Goals, he argues that CEOs are now much more involved in the debate and the practice of doing good than previously. They acknowledge that they have the power to bring about change, and frustrated that insufficient progress is being made through conventional means, they are ready to take on the responsibility of doing so. Having interviewed many global company CEOs, he concludes:

> *Business leaders see clear value in investing large chunks of their own time and energy into participating in these policy processes, where in the past they might have been happy to send someone from the government affairs or CSR team. While there's a spectrum of starting points, many business leaders have really quite informed and sophisticated points of view on the issues at stake in the Post 2015 agenda. Almost all are coming from a position of wanting to push policymakers to come to a more ambitious agreement, and want to help shape a policy framework that makes it easier for them to contribute. Many often feel out of their depth in participating in policy processes, but are learning on the go and learning fast.*[33]

I welcome the fact that CEOs of companies in international markets are committing their companies to become agents of social change on the global stage and on long-term, fundamental issues. But I remember a senior executive of one of Britain's top companies telling me that he had 'no idea' what went on in the community surrounding his global HQ, so I wish that the welcome commitment Matthew has found could operate at all levels of the business world.

---

[33] http://community.businessfightspoverty.org/profiles/blogs/post-2015-21st-century-leadership-in-action.

The Board Mandate

Here's a good game to play at a cocktail party: ask every business person in the room, on a one-to-one basis, 'What is your company for?' Some will say 'making widgets', others will say 'making money', and very few will say 'making the world a better place'. If you find two people from the same company who answer the question in the same way, unprompted, shout 'Bingo!'

Tomorrow's Company identified a lack of coherence among business leaders as to exactly what their company's role was, both in the economy and in society; it advocates that every company should have a 'board mandate':

> *[A mandate captures] the 'essence' of the 'character' and distinctiveness of the company, in terms of: its essential purpose; its aspirations; the values by which it intends to operate; its attitude to integrity, risk, safety and the environment; its culture; its value proposition to investors; and plans for development.*
>
> *It is a living statement about what the company stands for and how it wishes to be known to all of its stakeholders.*[34]

A mandate isn't the same thing as a mission statement or even a company vision; it defines how the company works, and provides 'tramlines' to operate within and indicate when events take the company 'off the rails'. According to the Tomorrow's Company toolkit, a board mandate should answer six questions:

- Who are we and what do we stand for?

- What values, reputation and culture do we want?

- How do we create a successful and sustainable organisation?

- What relationships do we have with our stakeholders?

- How do we develop our business?

- What is our appetite for risk?

---

34 http://tomorrowscompany.com/the-case-for-the-board-mandate.

Knowing the answers to these questions doesn't guarantee sustainability, reputation or purpose. But agreement at board level on how this company answers these questions at this time is a way of defining the company and its purposes. It will take a lot of the fun out of cocktail parties.

Executive Pay

What more is there to say about executive pay? Although it's a relatively minor beast, it's still an elephant in the room of corporate citizenship. Exorbitantly high levels of remuneration cause the sincerity of companies to be questioned: eyebrows are raised when the CEO's bonus is larger than the entire CSR budget. Earlier we've discussed the link between the bonus culture and short-termism, but here I want to argue that as far as pay's concerned, the moderation of the not-for-profit sector is something from which the for-profit sector can learn.

Dan Pallotta, whom we met earlier, has experience of just what I mean:

> *Business Week did a survey, looked at the compensation packages for MBAs ten years out of business school – and the median compensation for a Stanford MBA with bonus, at the age of 38, was $400,000; meanwhile, the same yearly average salary for the CEO of a five million dollar-plus medical charity in the US was $232,000 and for a hunger charity $84,000.*
>
> *Now there's no way you can get a lot of people with a $400,000 talent to make a $316,000 sacrifice, every year, to become the CEO of a hunger charity.*
>
> *Some people say well, that's because those MBA types are greedy. Not necessarily; they might be smart. It's cheaper for that person to donate $100,000 every year to the hunger charity, save $50,000 on their taxes – so still be roughly $270,000 a year ahead of the game; but now be called a philanthropist because they donated $100,000 to charity, probably sit on the board of the hunger charity – indeed probably supervise the poor SOB who decided to become the CEO of the hunger charity – and have a lifetime of this kind of power and influence and popular praise still ahead of them.*[35]

---

35 http://www.youtube.com/watch?v=bfAzi6D5FpM&feature=youtu.be.

In 2013 Britain's top charities were criticised for paying their chief executives too much. In a story warning of creeping excess ('spiralling executive pay') at Britain's 'hundreds of thousands of charities', *The Daily Telegraph* 'exposed' what charity annual reports have long disclosed: their accounts.[36] The story followed one a week earlier[37] that claimed that the number of people working for international aid charities (including some multi-million-pound charitable businesses) who were paid over £100,000 had leapt by as much as 60 per cent (over three years)! (The actual figure was that in the 14 member organisations of the Disasters Emergency Committee,[38] which includes some of Britain's largest charities, the number of well-paid individuals had risen from 19 to 32). For comparison, a deputy head teacher at a modest London secondary school might also receive this amount. A charity CEO criticised trustees of the 'high-paying' charities for not speaking out to defend their decisions to pay these salaries.[39] Duly outraged, Conservative MPs spoke of public 'shock' and called for charity leaders to remember their voluntary ethos – this is code for 'work for free'.

To balance the story, *Third Sector* magazine revealed that one charity alone employed over thirty people on salaries of £100,000 or more: that was the school for the privileged, Eton College, the alma mater not only of the country's Prime Minister, Charities Minister and London Mayor but also of the Chairman of the Charity Commission who had made the original observation about charity executives' pay. William Shawcross only earns £50,000 per year for his government-appointed post – but then he only works there for two days a week.[40] *The Guardian* reported in the same week[41] that the outgoing Chief Executive of Diageo, the international drinks group, received £15 million in his final year in post (£1.3 million in salary, £1.2 million in bonuses and the rest in 'long-term bonuses'). Although he had already moved to a new, no doubt well-paid, job elsewhere, Diageo would still pay him £400,000 over five years to represent it in the Scottish whisky industry. No doubt he was also enjoying the prospect of his £18 million pension pot.

---

36 http://www.telegraph.co.uk/news/politics/10237808/New-crackdown-on-spiralling-charity-executive-pay.html. In fact, the UK has 160,000 charities, not 'hundreds of thousands'. Most employ no one.

37 http://www.telegraph.co.uk/news/politics/10224104/30-charity-chiefs-paid-more-than-100000.html.

38 http://www.dec.org.uk/about-dec.

39 http://www.thirdsector.co.uk/news/1214522/charities-aid-foundation-head-criticises-trustees-not-defending-senior-pay/.

40 'Third Sector at Large' column, Third Sector magazine, 20 August 2013.

41 http://www.theguardian.com/business/2013/aug/12/diageo-paul-walsh-pay-bonus.

This story shows that it's not just banks – where the 'reward for failure' argument has been even more potent, especially in institutions rescued by taxpayers – which court controversy on this issue of executive pay:

> *Staff in banks who appropriate revenue in ludicrous bonuses which should otherwise go to strengthen the banks' capacity to resist write-offs, panics and bank-runs are in effect stealing from their customers, shareholders and the government.*

So wrote the economist Will Hutton, incredulously, in *The Guardian* in 2009,[42] continuing:

> *The financial community talk of the City being a national asset and a success story; of having to pay football star salaries of necessity; and that any insistence that the banks accept that they have obligations as well as rights to bailouts will be met by an exodus of talented staff to other countries. No other business operates having to allocate as much as half its revenue in bonuses. The reason why financial services is different is that its structure makes it easy for key staff to blackmail managers.*

We have previously met Colin Melvin, Chief Executive of the world's biggest ethical fund manager, Hermes EOS. As the pension funds he represents are significant owners of British business, he talks to people in private business on a daily basis, often those in receipt of bonuses, but his ultimate client is the ordinary person who just wants a decent pension in retirement after a lifetime of hard work. By December 2011, he says, it had become clear that many directors of public companies shared the concerns about executive pay which were being voiced ever more loudly in the press. He told a Tomorrow's Company event in July 2013:

> *[Public company directors] told me that long-term plans had become unclear and complex, which made them inadequate for incentivising directors. CEOs treated a payout of some of these plans like 'winning the jackpot', without knowing what they had done specifically to achieve this outcome. They therefore tended to focus on the shorter term cash bonuses. The remuneration committee chairs felt unable to act alone, owing to apparent competitive and market pressures and some asked for assistance.[43]*

---

42 http://www.theguardian.com/commentisfree/2009/dec/09/tax-bonus-pre-budget-report.
43 Colin Melvin, speaking at a Tomorrow's Company lecture on 'Finance, Business and the Public Good' which I attended on 11 July 2013.

Why didn't fund managers, as agents of the ultimate owners, step in? Because it's those very agents, the intermediaries, who are the problem: 'The basic problem with our capitalist system is its control or capture by agents, rather than principals,' says Melvin. More specifically:

> A major problem with executive pay and a reason for its current dysfunctionality is that its policing has been largely undertaken by fund managers, as agents of the underlying owners of the companies, such as pension funds. A combination of fund managers' disinterestedness, their own often poorly designed incentives and their favouring performance measures which made sense in the context of their own performance targets and metrics has resulted in structures which are wholly unsuited for the companies concerned.

In February 2012 Melvin brought together 44 remuneration committee representatives from FTSE100 companies and an equivalent number of asset owners (pension fund representatives). Over a number of meetings their goal was to draw up guidelines (more guidelines) on remuneration principles for building and reinforcing long-term business success. As of July 2013 the draft principles read:

- Management should make a material long-term investment in shares of the businesses they manage.

- Pay should be aligned to long-term success and the desired corporate culture throughout the organisation.

- Pay schemes should be clear, understandable for both investors and executives, and ensure that rewards reflect long-term returns to shareholders.

- Remuneration committees should use the discretion afforded them by shareholders to ensure that awards properly reflect company performance.

- Investors should commit sufficient resources to enable them to have informed discussions with companies on pay, taking account of their individual circumstances and strategy.

I wish him luck. No one disputes that people who run major companies have a stressful, challenging and difficult life. They take risks and work hard to minimise the chances of loss and disappointment. Getting top pay right is an important part of getting the balance of reward, and therefore the image of the company, right. A charity CEO is likely to be earning £60,000 per year at the peak of his or her career rather than the bloated rates quoted earlier by the *Daily Telegraph*. However, when in dialogue with an opposite number in business, it's hardly a meeting of equals: the corporate CEO would be looking forward to earning at least the charity CEO's salary as a pension just a few years down the road.

Employee Engagement and Ownership

The prime asset of any company is its staff. Employees who see purpose in their work, find it morally acceptable and gain fulfilment, incentive and appropriate recognition from it are more productive and a better advertisement for their company than almost any other aspect of its operation. A century ago Andrew Carnegie spoke of needing to capture the heart of an extremely able man before his brain will do its best. Not for nothing do HR departments monitor and promote employee satisfaction, value team-building efforts and seek to get the best out of every worker. They know that a happy workforce attracts a higher calibre of applicant, encourages people to stay with the firm longer (reducing recruitment and training costs), and that engaged workers are more likely to innovate to the company's benefit than those who are bored and alienated.

They and their marketing colleagues also know that a company's reputation is formed through many channels, including the way the company relates to the community, and that the agent of that relationship is, very often, the workforce.

Before a new branch of Boots opens, the staff spend a week together working on a local community project with a charity or public body. This is an effective team-building exercise which sends out a public message of accessibility, care and competence – and it costs much less than that traditional week of intensive HR training in a windowless room on the sixth floor. Our community, says Boots, is also our customer base.

The Cake Bake, the Three Peaks Cycling Challenge, the sponsored bungee-jump – all have their place in the charity engagement work that goes on inside a corporate or an SME, almost irrespective of the cause it supports. But the marriages made in heaven are those where the match of missions is perfect, the skills of the partners complementary, the outcome tangible and meaningful, and the commitment total. Such is the award-winning national partnership between The Samaritans, Britain's main charity dedicated to the reduction of suicide, and Network Rail, the company responsible for maintaining Britain's railway infrastructure.[44] Two hundred suicides and the same number of failed attempts each year leave rail companies facing an annual bill of £50 million, mostly in fines resulting from delays to services and sick leave for staff, especially drivers unable to work through trauma after witnessing a death. In the first two years of a five-year programme focused on training 4,000 Network Rail staff, more than 50 potential suicides were averted.

Staff speak very highly of that training,[45] and it's clear that the fulfilment felt after successfully dissuading a single person from suicide is profound, irrespective of the benefits to the company. 'At least I tried' is a less traumatic response to a failed intervention than the impotence of 'I did nothing because I didn't know what to do.' Even the responsibility of getting trained, in the hope that the newly acquired skills are never needed, is an act of recognition for the employee which will support engagement with the company. How many of the 4,000 trainees have then volunteered in their own time for the local Samaritans? I suspect some have.

It has been calculated that the cost of employee turnover in the USA is $11 billion per year,[46] that the profit margins of 'engaged' companies are up to three times those of 'disengaged' ones, and that time off through sickness, especially stress-related, is much lower where priority is given to supporting, engaging and trusting employees more. While there are many factors in the sphere of managing employees that impact on engagement levels, access to employee volunteering schemes is recognised as potent: 70 per cent of graduates under 35 years old said that the presence of a volunteering scheme would make them more likely to accept a job offer from a company than if it had none.

While one would expect that (partial) employee share ownership was an effective way of increasing engagement, the jury seems to be out. Employee ownership (not the same thing at all) certainly does seem to prompt more engaged behaviour – witness the cost efficiencies created by the Central Surrey Heath NHS spin-out after becoming an employee-owned mutual – but share ownership, when not total, doesn't seem to work in the same way. Some companies which utilise share ownership as part of their reward package

---

44 http://www.samaritans.org/your-community/reducing-railway-deaths-0/samaritans-and-network-rail-partnership.
45 http://www.samaritans.org/your-community/reducing-railway-deaths.
46 Research by Towers Watson, Deloitte and others: http://secure.microedge.com/rs/microedge/images/Why_Should_You_Care_About_Employee_Engagement.pdf?.

sometimes see this as an HR measure, sometimes as a simple reward option, and in a few cases as a corporate responsibility issue. Following the Nuttall Review,[47] the British government favours promoting employee ownership through share distribution, once it has simplified the taxation rules. In the USA the idea is more widely supported than in the UK. In South Africa the law promotes employee share ownership under black empowerment legislation, but in the former Soviet Union it generates little enthusiasm, no doubt as the offer of shares today in a company that everyone once used to own rings a little hollow.

So employee ownership schemes vary from total to token; the latter is more common and less inspiring. Employee shareholders appear fairly tolerant of sudden falls in share prices, for example, such as happened at Lloyds Banking Group, almost as though it didn't affect them. Is this a recognition that share ownership is seen as a long-term investment?

The Trade Union Congress has clear thoughts about employee share ownership, recognising that it isn't without value, but having opposed privatisations which utilised it in the past. They say that employee share schemes shouldn't replace pay and conditions deals, but should be supplementary to them; that they should involve workers collectively rather than individually, so that the employee interest isn't dissipated by members leaving the company and taking their shares with them, and so that the employee voice is retained; they should be 'substantial', and therefore give employees a voice worth having, and that workforce consultations should continue to involve trade unions as employee representatives rather than employee shareholders[48] – in short, exactly as the share distribution element in the 2013 privatisation of the UK Post Office was not. The demands sound reasonable to me; the transfer of an organisation from the public sector to the private through share distribution has always been more common than from the private sector to its workforce, of which the John Lewis Partnership (see Chapter 3) is a very rare example.

Pilotlight – a Tool for Engaging Business

Pilotlight[49] is a relatively small charity based in London with an outreach office in Scotland. Pilotlight punches considerably above its weight, however, because

---

47 https://www.gov.uk/government/uploads/system/uploads/attachment_data/file/31706/12-933-sharing-success-nuttall-review-employee-ownership.pdf.

48 http://www.esopcentre.com/tuc-principles-for-employee-share-ownership-schemes.

49 http://www.pilotlight.org.uk.

it has a relationship with business which few other charities would dream of – and which many would hesitate to even attempt to build. It's dependent not only on business, but on big business for its survival, though that's because it's highly successful at tapping into what corporates can spare and charities desperately need: business acumen.

Pilotlight helps other charities by creating capacity. A struggling charity will happen upon it and ask for help, and providing it can meet basic sustainability criteria, it will be accepted into the Pilotlight programme. It will have at least one 'responsible' employee, a turnover of at least £100,000 per year, a need to grow, and engaged trustees. It will also have a mission based on social change or alleviating deprivation or disadvantage.

Once chosen and prepared, the charity will work with Pilotlight to create a bespoke business plan. The way this is done is unique and inspired. A team of three 'Pilotlighters' is appointed to work with the charity over 12 months. The Pilotlighters are senior or aspiring (sometimes retired) business people from three different companies who have been chosen because their combined skills and experience are appropriate to the needs of the charity. They are asked to commit to one meeting a month, amounting to up to four hours, plus the occasional email and phone call. Two years after the process is over the charity has typically increased its income by 50 per cent and its impact has improved by 100 per cent. No charity forgets its Pilotlight experience in a hurry!

So far, so good. But how is this paid for? The charities pay nothing. The bulk of Pilotlight's income comes from fees paid either by the Pilotlighters or more often by their companies. It may sound expensive, but it's worth it: every company involved says that the business case is made because the Pilotlighters come back from the experience with enhanced networks, soft (interpersonal) and hard (business-focused) skills, a better understanding of how charities work, and life in society's underbelly. They are empowered through their broadened horizons. Regular supporters of Pilotlight include Bank of America Merrill Lynch, Bank of England, Barclays, BP, Brodies, BT Group – and that's just the Bs. Pilotlight claims to give better value for money than comparable purchases of traditional HR training. In return the Pilotlighters have supported a good cause with skills which – like love – can be given away time after time without ever running out.

Some Pilotlighters repeat the experience, 84 per cent report that Pilotlight has made them feel happier or more fulfilled in their day jobs, 90 per cent have improved their skills or gained new ones, and half are inspired to do more voluntary work in future.

This is the epitome of business relating to communities through charities, and it works in every respect: win for the charities, win for the businesses, win for the beneficiaries, win for the volunteers and win for the community. But how could it be even better?

Our problem, Pilotlight said to me, is that it doesn't know that it's helping the right charities. Which are the best charities to help, with the most relevant missions to the needs of their local communities, and how could Pilotlight identify them? So it developed Pilotlight Connect, in which local councils (starting with a handful of London boroughs) were asked to identify communities, causes and charities which could be offered the Pilotlight process. Progress was slow because it was asking councils questions they hadn't been asked before; however, on a positive note, senior council officers expressed interest in becoming Pilotlighters – an unexpected bonus. Deciding to use Pilotlighters from businesses local to the borough in question was a no-brainer, too, though being spoilt for choice on the south bank of the Thames in Lambeth and Southwark was a luxury that Lewisham, with a paucity of businesses of a significant size, didn't enjoy.

What makes Pilotlight different from other mentoring that charities can obtain from businesses is its thoroughness, the structure it brings, the emphasis on sustainable change, the measurable outcomes and the follow-up. What makes this different from other employee volunteering schemes is its low-volume, high-skill nature and the total commitment to making a sustainable and positive difference for the most vulnerable members of the community.

Chapter 10

Where Next?
Sustainable Capitalism

*In the immediate aftermath of World War II, when the United
States was preparing its visionary plan for nurturing democratic
capitalism abroad, General Omar Bradley said, 'It is time to steer
by the stars, and not by the lights of each passing ship.' Today,
more than 60 years later, that means abandoning short-term
economic thinking for sustainable capitalism.*

Al Gore and David Blood, 'A Manifesto for Sustainable Capitalism',
The Wall Street Journal, 14 December 2011[1]

In Chapter 2 we reviewed a number of different (if largely complementary)
philosophies concerning the direction capitalism should take in discharging
its responsibilities as the world's largest and most powerful economic system.
Towards the end of that chapter I introduced the idea of sustainable capitalism
as the pinnacle of that debate. That laissez-fairism – capitalism red in tooth
and claw – is no longer tenable is, I hope, a given; our wish that the engine
of our economy should assume greater responsibility for its actions feels
fairly uncontroversial, but on whether the necessary changes should or will
be revolutionary or evolutionary, voluntary or regulatory, market-driven or
crisis-driven, the jury's still out and vested interests, as ever, all want their say.
The 'elephants in the room', ever easier to ignore than to tackle, are growth
(and externalities), reward (and its distribution) and timescale. Without major
changes on these fronts, progress – perhaps our very survival – is in jeopardy.

The beauty of the Al Gore model of sustainable capitalism is that it's
couched in language and values that business will understand – although its
values go wider, and they must, as if they didn't, then the change wouldn't be
worth making.

The core argument of sustainable capitalism is that short-term gain is
frequently the enemy of long-term survival; that there's a business case for

---

1   http://online.wsj.com/article/SB10001424052970203430404577092682864215896.html.

lifting one's eyes from the pavement to the horizon, and that liabilities should be viewed on the same timescale as their complementary assets. Generation, the investment fund management firm established by Al Gore and David Blood, has produced a persuasive document which makes the case forcibly, identifying five key steps to create momentum for sustainable capitalism:

1.   identifying and incorporating risks from stranded assets (assets whose value is grossly distorted by the absence of externality costs, such as a true cost for carbon production or a product created through the use of exploitative poverty wages);

2.   making integrated reporting mandatory – requiring all companies to report on their social and environmental impacts in a meaningful and comparable fashion;

3.   ending the default practice of issuing quarterly earnings guidance;

4.   aligning remuneration structures with long-term sustainable performance, removing incentives for excessively short-term activity;

5.   encouraging long-term investing with loyalty-driven securities through reform of employee share ownership rules.[2]

Of course, those final two are complementary, and as Colin Melvin reminds us, the problem they address can be blamed on the intermediaries who emerged as a powerful force towards the end of the twentieth century. Their role appears to be not to facilitate but prevent the ultimate owners of capital directing where they wish their money to go, especially if they want it to do good. At present, by and large, the problem's not so much that the finance industry rewards and incentivises short-term behaviour, but that it fails to take into account the long-term consequences of that short-term behaviour. A finance house can still make a £100,000 end-of-year bonus available to its top team, but if this is paid in shares that can't be sold for five years, then those employees will focus on creating a long-term sustainable rise in share price, and not content themselves with creating a spike (an 'opportunity') that will be a distant memory by the end of the month.

Generation proposes a number of supporting measures, including raising the profile of a broadly defined 'sustainability' in business education and

---

2   Adapted from http://www.generationim.com/media/pdf-generation-sustainable-capitalism-v1.pdf.

as a fiduciary issue, and improving the range, availability and reputation of both sustainable asset management advice and the market for sustainable investment products. The most radical suggestion – and the one with the most inherent practical difficulties – is to either redefine or replace GDP as the principal measure of growth.

'Growth' is the sticking point in any debate about reformatting the economy and our expectations thereof. Traditionally growth has been seen as both the epitome of capitalism and the way in which its success is measured. The need for growth within individual companies isn't seriously challenged, and every measure of growth is welcomed. In the economy as a whole, however, a narrow tightrope is walked between recession (a country experiencing 'negative growth' – falling economic output for two quarters running) and 'overheating' (where growth is out of control). The West looks upon China enviously for its consistently high growth figures over many years, though if apparently sustainable by that country's standards, it may have been dangerously close to overheating by ours. Comparable percentage figures from some African states aren't seen as a competitive threat to the West because the base against which their percentage growth is measured is so abject.

But the real questions are: What does growth measure? And is it the right measure?

In Britain many supporters of the green movement have traditionally condemned the dash for growth outright, yet if government were to incentivise the creation of decently paid jobs in the recycling industry, in low-carbon energy and in environmental protection, this would lead to more recycling, a decrease in carbon emissions and a more sustainable biosphere. It would also generate economic growth, even by our current metrics. 'Growth' itself isn't the problem: its quality is as important as its quantity.

Al Gore, speaking in London in 2013, lamented the fact that our conventional definition of 'growth' includes no measure of the value of investment in the arts, in culture or education, in creating human happiness and a sustainable society; nor, perhaps more critically, does it price the current or future cost of pollution and climate change into the calculation. These items are traditionally regarded by capitalism as 'externalities', but unless they are urgently redefined – internalised – and properly costed, then our measurement of growth, our judgement of success and our long-term viability will all be shown to be awry and the values of Western capitalism will inevitably lead us towards self-destruction.[3]

Gross Domestic Product was developed to measure American income (and hence growth) in the Roosevelt era, and was adopted in 1944 as an international comparator by the same Bretton Woods Conference which established the World Bank and other multinational institutions. Several ways of defining GDP exist, although in theory they should all produce the same result. The simplest is perhaps:

Consumption + Investment + Government spending + (Exports - Imports)

Although a dozen alternatives to the formula already exist, many of which take better account of the externalities which GDP excludes, none has taken root in the way that GDP did. GDP is objective, it allows us to make international comparisons, it can identify trends over relatively short periods, it is (by the standards of these things) relatively straightforward, and any replacement will have to emulate these qualities. But it has significant drawbacks:

- It excludes the economic impact of pollution, carbon emissions and resource depletion.

- It doesn't distinguish between government spending on 'good' (creating future success, such as investment in education) and 'bad' (the current cost of failure, such as unemployment benefit).

- It takes no account of how domestic product is distributed between citizens (surveys suggest that a high level of inequality is a potent source of national unhappiness).

- It takes no account of significant parts of the economy such as voluntary work, open source software, the 'hidden' economy or the value of national assets.

- It's a historical measure, and not a future indication (though often wrongly regarded as such).

---

3   Al Gore, speaking at the launch of ShareAction at London Guildhall on 18 March 2013.

- It has perverse features – following a poor country's devastation by a tsunami or an earthquake, growth levels may appear very high for a long but transient period.

These are all issues which the student of long-term sustainability needs to take into account. A league table of countries by GDP isn't that different from one based on consumption alone, and one can understand why every country has the ambition of climbing that league table. At the same time, no country in the world has an economy today which *both* provides every citizen with an acceptable standard of living *and* produces carbon emissions at or below levels which are consistent with bringing climate change under control.

An early critic of the way GDP has evolved as a catch-all measure of national worth was its own author, Simon Kuznetsk. In 1962, 30 years after his earlier work, he wrote:

> *Distinctions must be kept in mind between quantity and quality of growth, between costs and returns and between the short and long run. Goals for more growth should specify more growth of what and for what.*[4]

Al Gore and others have described climate change and other trends underlying the global economy as 'time bombs': Generation has said that sustainable capitalism needs to be in place by 2020 if these explosions are to be avoided, but that progress towards it has stalled – 'reached a plateau' – in recent years.

Business as Sponsor of Change?

The Social Investment Consultancy (TSIC) provides professional support, from analysis through strategy to implementation, to companies around the world that choose to help bridge the gap between corporate expertise and community need, to 'transform business assets into social progress'.[5] Its key process, TSIC Fuse, is 'open source', positing the idea that each company's development of citizenship values goes through a developmental process that mirrors the development of corporate responsibility itself – from defensive protection against attacks from NGOs (such as the publication of Rachel Carson's

---

4   'How To Judge Quality', *The New Republic*, 20 October 1962.
5   http://www.tsiconsultancy.com/wp-content/uploads/2012/05/TSIC-Fuse-May-2012.pdf.

Silent Spring in 1962 and the activities of Greenpeace's ship *Rainbow Warrior* in the 1980s) to the proactive shared value theory of Michael Porter today:

> *Businesses began their CSR engagement by responding to charity requests for donations, and then progressed to supporting charities that had some connection to their core business. Currently they spend their time seeking charity partners who can make some use of their business. The next iteration will be for businesses to build their own social change platforms to tackle critical challenges and invite charities to participate – with the lead coming from businesses doing what they do best.*

This is ontogeny recapitulating phylogeny, as my university biology teachers taught me. The phylogeny is shown in Figure 10.1.

That 'next iteration' is worth repeating:

> *for businesses to build their own social change platforms to tackle critical challenges and invite charities to participate.*

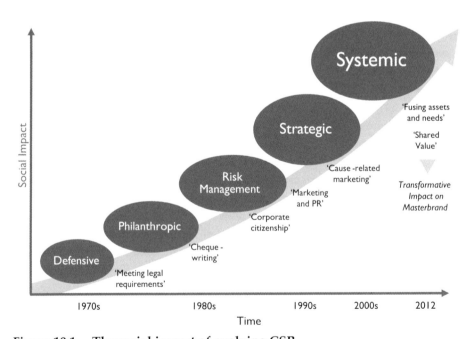

Figure 10.1   The social impact of evolving CSR

Source: © The Social Investment Consultancy. Reproduced with permission.

If I as a councillor, MP or government minister see something wrong in society, I have ways available to try to put it right. If local residents see something wrong, they can take it to their representatives or a local campaign group or set up their own campaign in a real or virtual community. The group might even address the problem – litter picking, fundraising and Neighbourhood Watch spring to mind. When a company perceives something to be wrong in its community, why shouldn't it act as a concerned citizen would, with the added muscle and voice it has at its disposal?

Remembering the prerequisite for the business case, the company might engage with local school pupils to help ensure that enough qualified young workers are available for future recruitment; it might offer to pay for a road to be improved so that its lorries cause less disturbance to neighbours (and reduce vehicle maintenance costs through fewer potholes); it might provide free building materials for local allotment holders (who just happen to include some of its employees). I previously described a case from South Africa where Nestlé commissioned partners to work on a comprehensive programme to increase life expectancy within a community – prompted by the cost of AIDS and tuberculosis devastating its factory's skilled workforce (Levitt, 2012).

'Fusing assets and needs', says TSIC. I say: 'discharging their responsibilities as a corporate citizen through partnerships to create a better community'. I hope and expect more businesses to engage in this way, on an appropriate scale, not least because of the pressures that exist on service delivery now and for the foreseeable future discussed in Chapter 2. There's no doubt, for example, that Unilever's handwashing campaign in developing countries will sell more soap, but this is the price of an effective initiative to combat a suite of contagious, crippling and deadly diseases.

The business world is scared of change. It fears what it can't measure, and many sustainability metrics are by necessity complex or long-term. It doesn't like to be told it's wrong, and too much of it is wedded to the philosophies that saw it succeed throughout the twentieth century, according to twentieth-century criteria. It lacks clear leadership, and following the era of globalisation it has places it can hide. Its sheer size means the level of natural inertia is immense. It boasts that it already has a 'licence to operate' as it is currently regulated by the public collectively, through public institutions, and that shows little sign of being about to change – however much multi-trillion-dollar taxpayer bailouts of banks are resented and climate change is tut-tutted about.

The benefits of long-termism are there for all to see, and not just for the obvious candidates in business, pension funds, family concerns and those who are confronted with the consequences of resource depletion. Sustainability enhances reputations, trust and market position, while it's less than universal; when it becomes the norm there will be different drivers. It improves efficiency, saves costs, enhances employee loyalty and productivity, stimulates innovation and aids compliance; it's an outlook which enables the better management of risk and reduces volatility in the marketplace.

Of course, there's a role for government:

> A sustainable society needs local and central government to lead the way by consuming differently, and by planning effectively and efficiently in order to integrate sustainable practices in the services it provides to citizens, and throughout its estates and workforce.
> Local councils are uniquely placed to help deliver this change as they interact with their communities to develop local sustainability policies.[6]

Instead of cleaning up after each crisis, government needs to plan for stability, which means matching demand for resources to supply over the long term, reducing both the costs of and demand for energy (difficult in the short term, but essential in the long term), creating sustainable employment and, above all, leading by example and shouting about it. Building on the UK Companies Act 2006, the road to mandatory triple bottom line reporting is open and should be pursued; if there's a competitive advantage for companies to behave sustainably, then there's a competitive advantage for countries to do likewise.

Civil society won't take this cause forward by shouting from the sidelines. Partnerships based on sustainable principles are the way forward – such as the Worldwide Fund for Nature has forged with Coca-Cola, to the extent that Oxfam now regards the soft drinks merchant as the world's third most sustainable global food company.[7] Praising big businesses when they get it right really pays off (they are such vain creatures), and will produce opportunities for sharing resources and joint action which will in turn enhance the impact of civil society campaigns on both public and government.

---

6   'Public Sector Sustainability under the Spotlight' (April 2009): http://www.government sustainability.co.uk. Unfortunately the magazine *Government Sustainability* appears to have lasted only a few months.

7   http://www.behindthebrands.org/en/company-scorecard.

The goal of sustainability is not a green one, nor one aimed at simply getting the sums right. It's a goal of a changed society, one where every citizen is more aware of his or her actual and potential impact on the planet for good or ill, deliberate or accidental. It has to be of a society which cares more about itself collectively and as a cohort of individuals, one where business is a real partner to the people, and not an inhabitant of a parallel and virtual universe all of its own.

I leave the last word to Generation, Al Gore's investment management firm, because it 'gets it' in its approach to the world:

> Incremental change will prove insufficient to mainstream Sustainable Capitalism by 2020. So, like an artist at the easel, our goal is not to make superficial touch-ups that conceal deep structural flaws beneath. We are calling for a fresh canvas on which, together, we can paint a new picture of our future.

Appendix:

The New Ten Commandments for Business in a Better World

Here are ten urgent demands for a better world that leaders of businesses can and should deliver within their roles as corporate citizens *(with examples)*:

1. **Select and create leaders who value sustainability** – Appoint people committed to the long-term triple bottom line, engaged understanding and action, and the business case to support these.

2. **Redefine wealth, growth and assets** – Companies and nations should be valued according to overall environmental, social and economic impact, accounting for positive and negative externalities *(replacing GDP, as a measure of national and global development, with the Social Progress Index)*.[1]

3. **Invest for the long term, for your grandchildren's generation** – Behave in every respect as though you really want your company to exist in fifty years' time, as family-owned firms traditionally do *(abandoning quarterly reporting)*.

4. **Share skills, capacity and surplus with communities** – Work locally with voluntary organisations, the community's own agents of change, to deliver socially valuable outcomes *(sponsoring a manager to grow a community organisation's capacity/skills-related employee volunteering, delivering public health messages and incentives through the workplace)*.

---

1   The Social Progress Index was launched by Michael Porter, Michael Green and others in April 2014. In measuring it, countries are assessed according to a blend of 54 established social criteria. See www.socialprogressimperative.org.

5.   **Use legislation to facilitate rather than enforce progress** – persuasion and leading by example is more effective than compliance with legislation *(a UK Community Reinvestment Act, extending the Social Value Act to private sector procurement)*.

6.   **Be environmentally and resource-friendly in all that you do** – Commit zero waste to landfill, design waste out of the system, promote the use of renewable resources *(sharing vehicle capacity to reduce fuel consumption)*.

7.   **Commit to open and continuous comprehensive reporting** – Reduce commercial confidentiality to a minimum, and adopt standard and meaningful reporting procedures on an appropriate timescale *(adopting GRI standards)*.

8.   **Understand the value the five-pointed star of stakeholders** – Recognise that people – employees, suppliers, producers, customers, shareholders – are the most important resource of any business *(holding meaningful consultations on key issues)*.

9.   **Reward all employees on a rational basis** – All pay scales should be open and transparent, including any bonuses, which should be structured around the creation of long-term benefit *(ensuring employee representation on remuneration committees)*.

10.   **Reduce the influence of the middle-man between asset owners and assets** – Address the fact that good practice in fund management exists and is intended to be helpful to all, but agreed principles are not observed *(applying local authority pension fund management standards to private schemes)*.

Bibliography

Note: All Web references in the footnotes were accessed in February 2014.

Aldridge, H. et al., *Monitoring Poverty and Social Exclusion 2012*, Joseph Rowntree Foundation, 2012.

Bazalgette, L., Grist, M. and Cheetham, P., *Ageing Sociably*, Demos, 2012.

Bishop, M. and Green, M., *Philanthrocapitalism*, A. & C. Black, 2008.

Bishop, M. and Green, M., *The Road from Ruin*, A. & C. Black, 2011.

Bowles, D. and Cooper, C., *Employee Morale: Driving Performance in Challenging Times*, Palgrave Macmillan, 2009.

Bowles, D. and Cooper, C., *The High Engagement Work Culture: Balancing Me and We*, Palgrave Macmillan, 2012.

Bridges Ventures, *Ten Year Report*, Bridges Ventures, 2013.

Cohen, B. and Warwick, M., *Values-driven Business*, Berret-Koehler, 2006.

Cohen, E., *CSR for HR*, Greenleaf, 2010.

Cox, G., *Overcoming Short-termism within British Business: The Key to Sustained Economic Growth*, The Labour Party, 2013.

Crutchfield, L. and McLeod Grant, H., *Forces for Good: The Six practices of High Impact Non-profits*, Wiley, 2012.

Davis, S., Lukomnik, J. and Pitt-Watson, D., *The New Capitalists*, Harvard Business School Press, 2006.

Edgar, J. (ed.), *From Smoke to Grass*, Derbyshire County Council, 2004.

Featherby, J., *Of Markets and Men: Reshaping Finance for a New Season*, Tomorrow's Company, 2012.

Featherby, J., *The White Swan Formula*, London Institute for Contemporary Christianity, 2009.

Gitsham, M. and Wackrill, J., *Leadership in a Rapidly Changing World*, International Business Leaders Forum/Ashridge Business School, 2012.

Gore, A., *The Future*, W.H. Allen, 2013.

Goyder, M., *Living Tomorrow's Company*, Knowledge Partners, 2013.

Hackett, P., MacDougall, A. and McInroy, N., *Local Authority Pension Funds: Investing for Growth*, Smith Institute, 2012.

Handy, C., *The Hungry Spirit: New Thinking for a New World*, Arrow, 1998.

Hill, K., *A Brief Handbook on Social Investment*, City of London Corporation, 2013.

Hutton, W., *Liberal Social Democracy, Fairness and Good Capitalism*, Progressive Governance (Oslo), 2011.

Kay, J., *The Kay Review of UK Equity Markets and Long-term Decision Making: Final Report*, UK Department for Business, Innovation and Skills, 2012.

Keynes, J.M., *The End of Laissez-faire: The Economic Consequences of the Peace*, Macmillan, 1926.

Kiser, C. and Leipziger, D., *Creating Social Value: A Guide for Leaders and Change Makers*, Greenleaf, 2014.

Lager, F., *Ben & Jerry's: The Inside Scoop*, Crown, 1994.

Leadbeater, C., *It's Co-operation, Stupid*, Institute for Public Policy Research/Co-operatives UK, 2012.

Levitt, T., *Partners for Good: Business, Government and the Third Sector*, Gower Publishing, 2012.

Lillya, D., *The Guide to UK Company Giving 2013–14*, Directory of Social Change, 2013.

Mayer, C., *Firm Commitment: Why the Corporation Is Failing Us and How to Restore Trust in It*, Oxford University Press, 2013.

Miller, J. and Parker, L., *Everybody's Business: The Unlikely Story of How Big Business can Save the World*, Biteback Publishing, 2013.

Phillipson, N., *Adam Smith: An Enlightened Life*, Allen Lane, 2010.

Reed, S. and Ussher, K. (eds), *Towards Co-operative Councils: Empowering People to Change Their Lives*, The Co-operative Party, 2013.

Rotheroe, A., Joy, I. and Lomax, P., *Allia's Future for Children Bond: Lessons Learned*, New Philanthropy Capital, 2013.

Sainsbury, D., *Progressive Capitalism*, Biteback Publishing, 2013.

Sandel, M., *What Money Can't Buy*, Farrar, Strauss and Giroux, 2012.

Saltuk, Y. et al., *Perspectives on Progress: The Impact Investor Survey*, J.P. Morgan/Global Impact Investing Network, 2012.

Smith, A., *An Inquiry into the Nature and Causes of the Wealth of Nations*, 1776.

Smith, A., *The Theory of Moral Sentiments*, 1759.

Social Investment Consultancy, *The Future of Business*, The Social Investment Consultancy, 2012.

Social Investment Task Force, *Enterprising Communities: Wealth Beyond Welfare*, HM Treasury, 2000.

Social Investment Task Force, *Social Investment Ten Years On*, HM Treasury, 2010.

Tawney, R.H., *Religion and the Rise of Capitalism*, Harcourt, 1926.

Tease, S. and Berry, C., *Ethically Engaged? A Survey of UK Ethical Funds*, Fair Pensions, 2012.

Tomorrow's Company and Institute for Family Business, *Family Business Stewardship*, Tomorrow's Company, 2011.

von Drehle, D., *Triangle: The Fire that Changed America*, Grove Press, 2003.

Walker, C., *The Corporate Giving Almanac 2013*, Directory of Social Change, 2013.

Yunus, M., *Building Social Business: The New Kind of Capitalism that Serves Humanity's Most Pressing Needs*, Public Affairs, 2011.

Yunus, M., *Creating a World Without Poverty: Social Business and the Future of Capitalism*, Public Affairs, 2009.

Index

If you have found this book useful you may be interested in other titles from Gower

Partners for Good
Business, Government and the Third Sector
Tom Levitt
Hardback: 978-1-4094-3437-5
e-book PDF: 978-1-4094-3438-2
e-book ePUB: 978-1-4094-5942-2

Corporate Community Involvement
A Visible Face of CSR in Practice
Bilge Uyan-Atay
Hardback: 978-1-4724-1244-7
e-book PDF: 978-1-4724-1245-4
e-book ePUB: 978-1-4724-1246-1

Integral Community
Political Economy to Social Commons
Ronnie Lessem, Paul Chidara Muchineripi and Steve Kada
Hardback: 978-1-4094-4679-8
e-book PDF: 978-1-4094-4680-4
e-book ePUB: 978-1-4094-7236-0

New Normal, Radical Shift
Changing Business and Politics for a Sustainable Future
Neela Bettridge and Philip Whiteley
Hardback: 978-1-4094-5574-5
e-book PDF: 978-1-4094-5575-2
e-book ePUB: 978-1-4724-0819-8

GOWER

Organizations
A Systems Approach
Stefan Kühl
Paperback: 978-1-4724-1341-3
e-book PDF: 978-1-4724-1342-0
e-book ePUB: 978-1-4724-1343-7

People, Planet and Profit
Socio-Economic Perspectives of CSR
Edited by Samuel O. Idowu, Abubakar S. Kasum and
Asli Yüksel Mermod
Hardback: 978-1-4094-6649-9
e-book PDF: 978-1-4094-6650-5
e-book ePUB: 978-1-4094-6651-2

The Balanced Company
Organizing for the 21st Century
Edited by Inger Jensen, John Damm Scheuer and
Jacob Dahl Rendtorff
Hardback: 978-1-4094-4559-3
e-book PDF: 978-1-4094-4560-9
e-book ePUB: 978-1-4094-7471-5

Visit **www.gowerpublishing.com** and

- search the entire catalogue of Gower books in print
- order titles online at 10% discount
- take advantage of special offers
- sign up for our monthly e-mail update service
- download free sample chapters from all recent titles
- download or order our catalogue